Peregrine Pathways

S0-ARN-433

LEADING ORGANIZATIONS

Innovating for Performance Excellence

Olin O. Oedekoven, Ph.D.

Krishnamurthy B. Venkateshiah, Ph.D.

Douglas J. Gilbert, DBA, JD

Deborah K. Robbins, MPA

LEADING ORGANIZATIONS:
Innovating for Performance Excellence
by
Olin O. Oedekoven, Ph.D., Krishnamurthy B. Venkateshiah, Ph.D.,
Douglas J. Gilbert, DBA, JD, Deborah K. Robbins, MPA.

Copyright © 2019
by the Peregrine Leadership Institute, LLC.

ISBN: 978-1-946377-03-6 (hardcover)
ISBN: 978-1-946377-04-3 (paperback)
ISBN: 978-1-946377-05-0 (eBook)

Printed in the United States of America

OTHER BOOKS BY PEREGRINE PATHWAYS

Oedekoven, O. O., D. K. Robbins, B. Bishop, M. Thomas, & R. Mansheim. (2018). *Hiring: A Practical Guide for Selecting the Right People.* Gillette, Wyoming: Peregrine Leadership Institute.

The hiring you do today will determine the kind of culture, service standards, and reputation you have tomorrow. It will determine your future success, and that of your customers and business partners. In Hiring, we take you through the needed steps to identify, recruit, and select the RIGHT people for your organization.

Oedekoven, O. O., D. K. Robbins, J. Lavrenz, H. A. Dillon, Jr., & R. Warne. (2018, 2015). *Leadership Foundations: A Conversation Regarding the Character, Skills, and Actions for Leaders.* Gillette, Wyoming: Peregrine Leadership Institute.

Written by leaders for leaders, Leadership Foundations is an extensive dialogue on leadership designed to promote values-based leaders at all organizational levels, from first-line supervisor through senior executive. As the name implies, the book establishes the foundation for successful leadership, people who know their skills, exemplify their values, and do leadership that inspires others to achieve their potential.

Oedekoven, O.O., Lavrenz, J., & Robbins, D.K. (2018, 2014). *Leadership Essentials: Practical and Proven Approaches in Leadership and Supervision.* Gillette, Wyoming: Peregrine Leadership Institute.

Successful leaders understand that leadership is all about walking the talk. Leaders must fight through the chaos of the moment to see and understand the perspective of the situation. Leadership Essentials provides relevant, practical, and substantive tips and techniques to walk the talk of leadership by knowing the values of the leader, the skills of the leader, and the actions of leadership.

We would like to dedicate this book to the mentors who helped develop our strategic leadership capacities. Throughout our leadership journeys, key individuals took the time to teach, coach, and mentor us to become more enlightened strategic thinkers able to lead organizations. Perhaps most importantly, these individuals helped us through the challenging transition from senior manager to organizational leader.

We would also like to dedicate this book to our teams, without whom we would clearly not be successful. Our teams included highly dedicated, knowledgeable, and values-based employees willing to rise to any challenge and opportunity. Our teams helped define our roles as senior organizational leaders.

Contents

List of Figures

Section 5: The Workforce

Section 6: Performance Management

Section 7: Ethics

Section 8: Continuous Quality Improvement

List of Case Studies and Industry Examples

Chapter 8: How to Build Better Boards

Chapter 10: Corporate Governance Summary

Chapter 11: Planning as a Process

Chapter 12: Deliberate and Emergent Strategies

Chapter 13: Strategic Decision Making

Chapter 14: Strategic Leadership in Planning

Chapter 15: Organizational Structure

Chapter 26: Understanding Performance Management

Chapter 27: Performance Management Tools

Chapter 28: Performance Management Challenges

Chapter 30: Performance Management Summary

Chapter 31: Business Ethics

Chapter 32: Ethics in Practice

Chapter 33: Current Trends in Ethical Practice

Chapter 35: Quality and continuous Improvement

Chapter 37: Continuous Quality Improvement Summary

Acknowledgments

As with any strategic undertaking, it truly does take a team to make things happen. We would like to acknowledge the great work of our team in making Leading Organizations a reality, including Judith Briles our editor; Kim Rankin our project manager; Beth Folkerts our graphic designer; Nick Zelinger and Rebecca Finkel our layout and cover designers; and P.J. Burns our Director of Leadership Services. Thank you for your focus on excellence and quality in all that you do— you all are truly the stars that help make us shine more brightly.

Foreword

All of us are very much aware of the essential leadership transition from individual contributor to supervisor or manager with team-level responsibilities. Each of us made that transition and learned to grow as a leader. We learned the importance of setting the right example for our teams, leading in complex organizations, and leadership communications. We grew with each promotion and advancement during our careers.

There is a second major leadership transition that we do not talk about very often – the transition from senior manager to organizational leader, sometimes referred to as executive level leader. As organizational leaders, we find ourselves responsible for all aspects of the organization including those that we may not be very familiar with based on our experience and development within the organization. Our time horizons shift from months to years. Our responsibilities grow from single departments and functions to multiple departments and numerous functional areas.

The purpose of this book is to help you complete this transition; to further develop you as an organizational leader that include responsibilities for strategic leadership, organizational planning, governance, the workforce, customers, performance, quality, and culture.

As one of our seminar participants said, *leadership is about fighting through the chaos of the moment to see and understand the perspective of the situation.* It is our intention with this book that we help you with your strategic perspective so that you can be an effective organizational leader.

Preface
New Realities

Plus ça change, plus c'est la même chose
(The more things change, the more they stay the same).
Maybe not this time!

The oft-quoted statement of Jean Baptiste Alphonse Karr about change, reflects a cynicism about any new ideas on organizations or leadership as being the same bad ideas presented differently. When we look at the whole quote from his journal in 1849, the level of cynicism can grow even more.

> After so many upheavals, changes, it was time to notice something, it is like the cabaret: – green stamp, red stamp, etc. Sometimes the price is changed, sometimes the cork, but it is always the same bad wine that we are made to drink. – The more things change, the more they stay the same.
> —Jean Baptiste Alphonse Karr,
> *Les guêpes. Sixième serie* (1849)

So much of leadership literature is full of the recycled and repackaged ideas that perhaps Karr would consider those the same bad wine served on another day. It is time to move beyond the leadership flavor of the month. New and very different realities are facing organizations today. In this book we attempt to provide guidance on how to address the very different world that is evolving and unfolding.

As we look at the dramatic changes unfolding in the current organizational climate, four categories of changes can be used to help define what is happening. The changes can be summarized in the acronym **P3T** for People, Place, Process, and Tools.

On the people side, the early 21st Century is a time of both a major generational change in organizational leadership along and a dramatic shift in the center of gravity for economic activity. Population centers have shifted to Asia and will shift to Africa, educational standards are rising, and connectivity is dramatically changing how we work and think.

As education levels have increased in the developed and developing world, expectations for performance have risen not only for the workforce but also for leaders. The capability of workforce participants has increased, which translates into high levels of potential performance. Without capable leadership, the added capability of the workforce will be largely wasted.

The emergence of major centers of gravity in Asia and soon Africa means that the culturally implicit ways of working based in North American and European traditions will be called into question. This creates new demands on leaders to possess and exercise a portfolio of skills. In Section 1 we identify those key skills as *Anticipate, Challenge, Interpret, Decide, Align,* and *Learn.* In a globally connected world where missteps can be quickly amplified by social media, simply reacting is not enough.

In Sections 5 and 6 we address the people side of the near realities head-on. Workforce engagement and performance management must be front and center. The challenges extend beyond optimizing human resources. A higher skilled workforce has higher expectations of leadership. If those expectations are not met with meaningful work and an inviting climate, workforce members can much more easily decamp to another employer.

The place for modern organizations is also undergoing a radical shift. Organizations centered on knowledge do not need to bring everyone together in a knowledge factory building. The *where* we work is being replaced by *what* we do, *who* is involved and *how* work is structured. Distance may not be dead, but it is challenged as employees increasingly can work from anywhere.

We deal with these issues in several places. The workforce and performance management sections mentioned above shed light on engagement of a workforce that may be scattered and remote. Where the new realities of place are very evident is in the organizational structure that can be chosen. In Section 3 we address emerging new organizational structures such as holacracy and the teal organization that have the fluidity to develop in a modern placeless organization. In Section 4 the merger of organizational structure with customer value chains is examined through the technique of dynamic governance and customer-centric clusters.

The book has a variety of methods and processes, which are described as tools. As technology evolves it may change and often displace the tools described. The tools we have chosen are ones that have lasting value even if changed to fit new technologies. The extraordinary advances in computational power, the massive waves of data generated by the internet of things, and the moves to products centered on data place new demands on leaders. We address these challenges through the descriptions of continuous quality improvement in Section 8. Without a foundation of disciplined improvement, the deficiencies of the last generation of leadership will be magnified and amplified by technological advances.

A significant part of every section of the book focuses on process or, quite simply, how to get things done from a strategic perspective. Throughout the book and especially in the case studies we have sought to address some fundamental changes developing in leadership and management processes. Leadership has increasingly become a collaborative endeavor rather than using a hierarchy for command and control. Management, the necessary companion of leadership, is undergoing a shift where self-management of teams and groups has become the norm in advanced agile organizations. Finally, there is a needed and welcome shift underway of leadership mindset from a fixed mindset to a recognition of the need for dynamic, life-long just-in-time learning agility.

The following chapters carry one key theme throughout. The key drivers of performance are people: not ideas, processes, technologies, or tools. The effective engagement and collaboration with people is the ultimate driver of organizational success and the test of leadership and especially strategic leadership.

Section 1
Organizational Leadership

This section examines the current thinking on organizational, which may also be known as strategic leadership. After reading and understanding this part, you should be able to:

1. Understand the concept of organizational leadership.

2. Appreciate why organizational leadership is critical to business success.

3. Apply the concepts to your work, becoming a better organizational leader.

The terms strategic leadership and organizational leadership are often used interchangeably throughout this section unless otherwise indicated.

Chapter 1

Understanding Organizational Leadership

Companies or products don't fail; leadership fails.

It is fashionable to highlight success stories. After all, they make us feel good—but statistics tell a different story.

Open any business page of a leading newspaper, and you will discover it's filled with stories of leadership mishaps— mishaps that could have been easily averted.

Typically, leadership errors lie at the heart of failure.

Consider this:

#1: Financial Fraud

A leading bank opened thousands of fictitious accounts.

Why would they make this decision?

It turned out they were trying to artificially meet certain targets.

When the issue became public, a scandal erupted. Elected representatives generalized the phenomenon and ruthlessly roasted the CEO in public hearings. The responsible parties were forced to quit, and the brand image—built over a century—lay in tatters.

Who was responsible?

The leadership!

#2: Discrimination

A perfect company on the outside isn't so perfect on the inside.

Analysts valued an emerging company at unprecedented levels. Employees and potential investors eagerly awaited the initial public offering.

Then a disturbing email surfaced. It appeared a deep malaise concerning discrimination and sexual harassment plagued the company.

As in the bank's case, though for a different reason, a scandal erupted. The humiliation forced the founder CEO—a poster-boy for instant success—to step down. The board underwent significant changes, and a key city canceled ties with the company.

A fairytale became a nightmare.

Who was responsible?

The leadership!

#3: Security Breach

A massive data breach at a major company released hundreds of thousands of sensitive records into the wrong hands.

The event compromised bank records, social security numbers, and credit cards. An investigation revealed that the company did not upgrade its technology to meet changing security needs. Nobody in the organization had a clue how to fix the disaster.

Who was responsible?

The leadership!

> *As much as we want to think otherwise, failure is a function of leadership.*

A Deloitte study shows that:

- Nine out of ten companies fail.
- Nine out of ten new products fail.

The above statements should be modified.

Companies or products don't fail; leadership fails.

As much as we might want to think otherwise, failure is a function of leadership. There is not a single corporate history instance where the action of someone at the operational, or even the tactical, level caused such catastrophes.

Strategic leadership causes success as much as it helps us avoid disasters.

What is Organizational Leadership?

Organizational leadership, more commonly called strategic leadership, is a rare resource.

We define organizational leadership as the ability to think, act, and influence others in ways that ensure the enduring success of an organization. Studies suggest fewer than 10% of leaders possess these essential skills.

Company leaders often pressure their subordinate managers to show short-term results, so operational leadership replaces strategic leadership in such situations. Consequently, leaders feel paralyzed when complex problems arise—and these problems often have long-term implications.

The key drivers of organizational performance are people.

Strategic Organizational Leadership

Strategic leadership is the ability to think, act and influence others in ways that ensure the enduring success of an organization.

In *The Five Forces that Drive Strategy*, author Michael Porter states,

> "In essence, the job of the strategist is to understand and cope with competition. Often, however, managers define competition too narrowly."

In essence, Porter's view is through the lens of economics. He believes strategic leaders should be able to analyze and manage market forces. The concept of competitive advantage hinges upon a company's ability to stay ahead of competition—either by having costs lower than that of competition or by offering a differentiated product and charging a premium price.

In practice, the economic view misses a central point. Today's competitive landscape is full of rapid change, complexity, and ambiguity. More importantly, companies do not have an existence of their own (other than from a legal perspective). *The key drivers of organizational performance are people.*

Not only do strategic leaders function as practicing psychologists who can analyze and manage their thought processes; they need to be able to analyze and manage the thought processes of their people.

The competitive environment requires strategic leaders to seek opportunities to create value—all along the value chain. These unique, different, and dynamic strategies continuously challenge the status quo. It sounds counterintuitive, but the best opportunities are the hardest to spot and execute.

Consider a multiple-player industry with intense competition, and assume great leaders control all entities. The leaders can easily spot opportunities and exploit them to their advantage.

What happens in these scenarios?

In theory, the industry should reach an impasse because no opportunities exist.

*Managing conflicting expectations of stakeholders
is just as relevant as spotting prospects.*

In practice, omniscient leaders are rare. Therefore, superior opportunities remain available. The challenge lies in a lack of visibility, and most managers fail to spot these *hidden* gems.

The challenge of identifying and using hidden opportunities is difficult due to many reasons:

1. They require mental leaps few leaders can generate.

2. They generally require changes in the firm's identity, and employees resist such change.

3. Investors may not respond well to the shifts, leading to negative consequences.

So managing conflicting expectations of stakeholders is just as relevant as spotting prospects.

For example, in the late 1930s, Charlie Merrill transformed the banking industry by turning Merrill Lynch into a financial supermarket that offered a range of services. In the process, he created a new market—middle-class customers. From an economic perspective, it appears that Merrill merely noted a new segment of customers and utilized the opportunity.

From a psychological perspective, other bankers didn't see what Merrill saw, to their own detriment. Even more critically, Merrill obtained buy-in from employees, customers, and capital lenders by convincing them of the idea's potential.

Successful strategic leadership combines economic opportunities and an understanding of the context. The shift in perspective is radical—away from markets and competition to minds and clashing beliefs. Sustainability for any organization requires an economic framework to support the innovation.

A consideration of the psychological impact enhances the quality of strategic decisions.

Why is it difficult to spot these opportunities?

Strategic leaders identify trends similar to their current operations.

For example, Walmart shifted from predominantly rural areas to suburban areas. It was an intentional move that changed its cost structure as well as the organizational configuration. Why? Because preferences differ between urban and rural customers.

Despite these challenges, Walmart successfully retained its business model. The everyday low prices worked as well in a suburban setting as it did in a rural environment. The strategy shifted incrementally and not radically.

Consider the motorcycle industry.

The Japanese manufacturers—Honda, Kawasaki, and Yamaha—compete on efficiency and costs. In contrast, Harley-Davidson and Ducati compete on an entirely different set of characteristics—entertainment, adventure, and fun. The price is irrelevant.

One of the CEOs of Ducati stated, "Ducati is not only a motorcycle company. We sell a dream, a passion, a piece of history."

Consider the U.S. airline industry.

The major carriers—United, Delta, and American—compete for the same market. Despite massive consolidation, sustained performance hasn't materialized. In contrast, Southwest Airlines has remained profitable for 45 years by focusing on short routes, specific destinations, one type of aircraft, and low costs.

Consider the personal computer industry.

IBM pioneered the personal computer.

Their formidable reputation as the leader in mainframe computing gave them deep pockets. Marketing theory suggests that IBM had a clear winner. However, IBM ignored the potential of the PC. Its mainframe division didn't buy in. IBM's rejection of a great opportunity opened the doors for DELL, COMPAQ, and HP to enter the market. The irony is that ultimately IBM sold its PC business to a Chinese company, Lenovo.

In contrast, consider the case of INTEL.

The manufacturer of dynamic random-access memories was not involved in the microprocessor industry. Intel's team spotted the hidden potential of the microprocessor—and quickly made the radical move. Over the last four decades, the company deliberately cannibalized its products to take the lead over the competition. The impact on the PC industry has been so significant that the *Intel Inside* concept is synonymous with PCs and laptops.

The mental leap from DRAMs to microprocessors was radical. The shift has altered the way we look at microprocessors. By aggressively pushing Moore's Law—the observation that the number of transistors in a dense integrated circuit doubles approximately every three years—Intel increased processing speeds while reducing unit costs, an example of technology driving markets, as opposed to the traditional notion of markets driving technology.

This stands in contrast to AMD's approach. AMD's processors are not inferior to Intel's microprocessors. It constructs comparable processors to Intel, but AMD didn't benefit from the mental shift. The fact remains that AMD's revenues do not match Intel's profits. Intel not only spotted the microprocessor opportunity very early but also executed the transition in a manner that excited stakeholders rather than causing concerns.

Intel's success in spotting and executing a new opportunity is attributable to a concept identified as associative thinking. This associative thinking model, a requisite for strategic leadership, assists intelligent reasoning about novel and ambiguous contexts. It requires both deductive and inductive reasoning. Recognizing patterns, making unique associations between them, and developing refreshing frameworks drives business innovation.

Associative thinking helps leaders to deal with the cognitively distant opportunities and develop mechanisms for redefining a business. They inspire, motivate, and induce others to make similar associations and to understand how and why redefining an industry is critical for success. With a psychological understanding of strategic leadership, ambiguous ideas will be achievable.

Summing Up

Strategic leadership is the ability to think, act and influence others in ways that ensure the enduring success of an organization. Studies suggest fewer than 10% of leaders possess these essential skills. Leadership errors lie at the heart of failure. Strategic leadership causes success as much as it helps us avoid disasters.

The challenge of identifying and using hidden opportunities is difficult. It requires mental leaps that few leaders can generate. It generally requires changes in the firm's identity, and investors may not respond well to the shifts. Managing conflicting expectations of stakeholders is just as relevant as spotting prospects.

Recognizing patterns, making unique associations between them, and developing refreshing frameworks drives business innovation. It requires both deductive and inductive reasoning.

Strategic leaders identify trends similar to their current operations. Successful strategic leadership combines economic opportunities and an understanding of the context. Sustainability for any organization requires an economic framework to support the innovation.

Today's competitive landscape is full of rapid change, complexity, and ambiguity. The key drivers of organizational performance are people. Strategic leaders need to be able to analyze and manage the thought processes of their people.

Strategic leaders inspire, motivate, and induce others to make similar associations and to understand how and why redefining an industry is critical for success.

Chapter 2

Skills of
Strategic Leadership

Strategic leaders are open-minded and accept divergent
views without bias. Above all, they listen.

Components: Anticipate, Challenge, Interpret, Decide, Align, Learn

Strategic leaders need six skills to successfully grow their businesses. Research incorporating 20,000+ executives cites these six skills as distinct components: *anticipate, challenge, interpret, decide, align,* and *learn.*

Managers usually consider one or two of these skills in any given situation. Because the six skills are interdependent and complementary, isolated decision-making provides bad results.

Adaptive strategic leaders combine resoluteness with persistence and flexibility. They view errors (apart from cat-astrophic failures) as learning opportunities while anticipating and embracing change before their competitors.

Anticipate: Successful strategic leaders anticipate change. This anticipation requires an in-depth understanding of economic (market) factors and psychological (people) factors.

Anticipation is the skill that most leaders find difficult to master.

Strategic leadership is the ability to think, act, and influence others in ways that ensure the enduring success of an organization.

Digital Equipment Corporation (DEC) was a minicomputer pioneer, with its VAX series of minicomputers synonymous with efficiency and reliability. At its peak, DEC was revered.

PCs began gobbling market share. DEC leader Olsen and his team completely missed this change. They continued focusing on engineering precision for minicomputers. Soon, they had great products nobody wanted to buy. Failure to anticipate the impact of PCs on the market was a fatal mistake.

Failure to respond to the change added to DEC's misery. Eventually DEC collapsed—an unthinkable event even five years earlier. Compaq acquired DEC. Later, HP acquired Compaq.

Improve your ability to anticipate:

1. Listen to customers, suppliers, and other value chain partners.

2. Use scenario planning to figure out impending industry changes.

3. Use simulation to understand the consequences of different scenarios.

4. Study a rapidly growing competitor for insight on their focus.

5. Determine why former customers left.

6. Stay attentive 24/7 to catch signals affecting your business.

Challenge: Strategic leaders challenge the status quo and are not afraid to question assumptions—theirs as well as others. Strategic leaders don't make decisions in a hurry. They are open-minded and accept divergent views without bias. Above all, they listen.

Steve Jobs epitomized the quality of challenging the status quo. He created markets no one else anticipated. In the process, he created products with aesthetic appeal, great performance, and unique features.

He deliberately chose the path of differentiation and premium pricing. Even though technology has driven prices down, Apple priced its latest iPhone at over $1,000.

Jobs' fascination for perfection can be expressed by the following anecdote: During his final moments, as doctors prepared him for surgery, Jobs argued with them about the crude oxygen mask! Even on his deathbed, he wasn't willing to settle for mediocre products.

Improve your ability to challenge:

1. Focus on the cause, not the symptom. Don't give up; find out the cause and come up with a solution.

2. Evaluate long-standing assumptions about your organization, your processes, and your people. Modify or give up any invalid assumptions you find.

3. Provide for psychological safety—create opportunities where people can express their views openly without fear of ridicule.

4. Examine the creation of a rotating position specifically charged with challenging the status quo.

5. Ensure teams represent diversity in thought; like-minded people are a sure recipe for mediocrity.

6. Seek inputs from non-stakeholders to receive an objective perspective.

Interpret: When you challenge the status quo, expect conflicting information. Combining conflicting viewpoints and interpreting the outcome while restraining emotion is a key step in strategic leadership.

For over three decades, Ratan Tata headed the $100 billion conglomerate Tata Group. Tata observed thousands of people driving motorcycles and scooters in India. Often, he found a family on the two-wheeler (the rider, the spouse, and one or two children).

Out of this observation, he visualized the Tata Nano, launched in 2008, a small car with a two-stroke engine. It seated two adults in front and two children in the rear. Despite great initial enthusiasm, the car has not done well, suffering low capacity utilization.

Tata's observation was spot-on. His solution was not.

First, the launch of the car was delayed. Second, the initial price of $2,500 quickly rose to $4,000 due to a raw material price increase. The entry-level car of India's leading manufacturer Maruti-Suzuki also cost $4,000, in addition to offering more room, a Japanese fuel-efficient engine, and unmatched country-wide service facilities. The Maruti 800 has been on the market for over 30 years. Some Marutis purchased in 1984 are still in use. Millions of middle-class customers in India aspire to own Marutis.

Transitioning from two-wheelers to the Nano does not fulfill their aspirations. Hence, the Nano has failed to live up to expectations.

Ratan Tata had the right observation, the right data, and ended up with the wrong interpretation.

Improve your ability to interpret:

1. Look for at least three explanations when analyzing data. Involve different stakeholders in this process.

2. Start with small details, then enlarge out to a big picture view (most leaders do the opposite).

3. Search for missing information and evidence challenging your assumptions.

4. Combine qualitative information with quantitative analysis.

5. Focus on other projects for a short time; then re-visit the idea with an open mind.

Organizations suffer when decisions focus on personalities and not on issues.

Decide: Decision-making is tricky. Without complete information, or when under time-constraints, the process becomes even more difficult. Leaders often miss an important aspect of decision-making; never make decisions a binary choice: yes/no, go/no-go. Instead, look at the trade-offs, and understand long- and short-term implications. Try to combine the best of two conflicting solutions and come up with a creative new solution.

HP's acquisition of Compaq is a classic example of how not to make decisions. At its peak, the acquisition was a clash of egos—between the then-CEO and a descendant of one of HP's founders. Both parties took out full-page ads to explain their respective positions.

Organizations suffer when decisions focus on personalities and not on issues. The wise approach required the parties to sit down and have an honest conversation. Scholars caution against hubris—the illusion of control—during mergers and acquisitions because decisions not made on merit are usually poor decisions.

Improve your ability to decide:

1. Reframe binary decisions by examining alternatives.

2. Break down complex decisions into components. Look for unintended consequences at each stage.

3. Have one set of criteria for shorter-term decisions; another set for longer-term decisions.

4. Listen to others when about to make a decision— they could still be looking for information.

5. Be clear about who is part of the decision process; who can influence the outcome.

6. Try pilot runs before project roll-outs or any major commitment.

Align: Stakeholders have widely differing expectations. Strategic leaders consciously balance expectations and find common ground. Success is a function of proactive communication, trust, and engagement.

Toyota operates worldwide, with a reputation for exemplary service to customers, enduring relationships with suppliers, and frequent engagement with key stakeholders. The result is a network model very difficult to replicate.

When a supplier's plant suffered extensive fire damage, competitors predicted Toyota's production would suffer for months. Instead, Toyota re-started operations within 48 hours. The secret? Their cooperative network of suppliers—if one fails, others can readily take the extra load.

Through relentless pursuit of continuous improvement, embracing new technologies of the future, and focusing on quality and reliability, Toyota is an example of extreme alignment across the value system.

Improve your ability to align:

1. Communicate early and combat the two most common complaints in organizations: "No one asked me" and "No one told me."

2. Identify key stakeholders and understand their expectations. Search for lack of alignment, hidden agendas, and coalitions.

3. Use constructive dialogue to expose misunderstanding and resistance.

4. Reach out directly to those opposing change and address their concerns.

5. Monitor stakeholders' positions during implementation. Anticipate approaching trouble.

6. Recognize and reward colleagues actively working toward alignment.

Learn: Strategic leaders lead organizational learning. They also promote a culture of constructive inquiry, a fearless analysis of failures, and celebrate success.

Google is an example of organizational learning. Every day they bring in experts to interact with groups of executives, while also encouraging experimentation—without any strings attached. They go for moonshots—projects that may have great potential—and they will abandon the project if difficult problems arise or if results differ widely from expectations.

Here is an example of Google's open culture: When Malcolm Gladwell addressed Google executives, he discussed how perceived advantages may, in fact, be disadvantages and vice-versa. During Q&A, an executive asked him whether Google might fail and what they might do to avoid failure.

Never one to mince words, Gladwell said: "Sure, Google may fail one day. Just as Larry Page and Sergei Brin came up with a great idea and executed the idea, someone may come up with a better idea and dwarf Google. That is life. The old must give way to the new. But you don't have to fail. Many of you can become entrepreneurs. Create your version of your dreams." Thunderous applause reinforced the openness of both speaker and audience.

Improve your ability to learn:

1. Institute after-action reviews, document lessons learned, and communicate insights. Create opportunities for everyone to learn.

2. Recognize—and possibly reward—honest failure.

3. Conduct annual learning audits; as important as financial audits.

4. Identify initiatives not producing intended results. Determine the cause without bias.

5. Create a culture where inquiry is valued and respected, and mistakes are learning opportunities.

Remember, the most successful strategic leaders synthesize all six skills. Research shows that strength in one cannot easily make up for a deficit in another skill.

Summing Up

Strategic leadership is a rare resource. Studies suggest fewer than 10% of leaders have the necessary strategic skills to lead their organizations.

Leaders are often under pressure to show short-term results. In these situations, operational leadership replaces strategic leadership. One consequence of short-term focus is leaders feel paralyzed when facing complex problems with long-term implications.

Strategic leadership is the ability to think, act, and influence others in ways that ensure the enduring success of an organization.

Chapter 3

Approaches
To Strategy

*We need to change our mental models to deconstruct
the complexity of the 21st Century.*

Most leaders can probably explain their current strategy. Some leaders may be able to explain how their strategy has changed over time.

How do you make decisions about changing your strategy? Less than 10% of strategic leaders have a coherent answer to this question.

Michael Porter has espoused two approaches—cost leadership and differentiation. Either approach permits addressing a large market or focusing on a niche market. Thus, you have four classical approaches: broad cost leadership, focused cost leadership, broad differentiation, and focused differentiation.

Other scholars have argued that the two approaches—cost leadership and differentiation—are not mutually exclusive. The two approaches can be combined into an integrated strategy.

Michael Treacy and Fred Wiersema have espoused three approaches to achieve competitive advantage—operational excellence, product leadership, and customer intimacy. Customer intimacy emphasizes the importance of the customer experience in business success.

W. Chan Kim and Renee Mauborgne of INSEAD, France, have argued that traditional approaches are fights in red oceans. They urge companies to look for blue oceans—uncontested market space—to be ahead of the competition. Whichever approach you choose, how you make changes to your strategy has significant implications.

This section explores the available approaches and their relative merits.

Four Approaches to Set Strategy

Jan Rivkin and others have proposed four typologies for setting strategy. Consider two dimensions: processes and employee engagement.

The *process* dimension (from a low to a high) reflects the extent the firm uses recurring routines and embedded processes to trigger strategic changes.

The *engagement* dimension (do employees simply attend meetings and nod their heads or do they provide inputs that lead to the strategic change) considers the level of input from employees (from a low to a high).

With two dimensions and two extremes, we get four distinct approaches. See Figure 3.1.

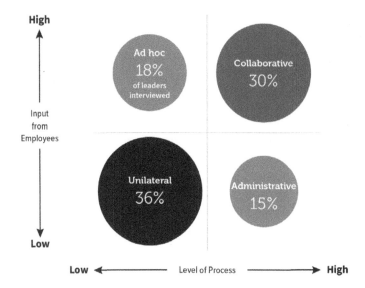

Figure 3.1. Four Approaches to Strategic Decision-Making, adapted from Teti, Yang, Bloom, Rivkin, & Sadun (2017).

Unilateral Approach: As the name suggests, the unilateral approach is a top-down approach with little or no process and no employee engagement. The strategic leader decides and announces to the employees.

Benefit: Leaders can make decisions quickly … leaders avoid the complexities of debate, discussion, and divergent views.

Limitation: The unilateral approach often leads to bad decisions… if the leader procrastinates, no one else can speed up the decision.

GE under Jack Welch is a classic example of the unilateral approach. If every organization ceased operations because they weren't number one or number two in their industry, the result would be chaos and confusion. The principle is wholly arbitrary and without logic. It is one thing to have key performance indicators to drive strategy, but it is entirely different to rely on ranking to decide the fate of business units.

Approaches to strategy: unilateral, ad hoc, administrative, and collaborative.

Ad Hoc Approach: The *ad hoc* approach is low in process and high on inputs. The firm doesn't have a well-defined, recurring process for making strategic changes. When a change is needed, the leader assembles a group, discusses the issue, and then decides. The people and the process can change, depending on each decision.

Benefit: Since there are no rigid rules, the leader can adapt to each situation by changing the length and type of discussion, number and type of people, and other factors.

Limitation: In the absence of a process, the firm learns nothing and does not improve strategic decision-making over time.

The leader can play favorites and exclude people with diverse perspectives. When the leader includes people who agree with the leader's views, there is no debate. As a result, the *ad hoc* approach is a glorified form of the unilateral approach.

Oracle is known for the *ad hoc* approach. Larry Ellison makes the most critical decisions. Ex-employees report that Ellison does not like dissent. Thus, even when he calls others into a discussion, he makes sure that only those who agree with him are present.

Administrative Approach: The administrative approach has rigorous processes, but little employee engagement. While extensive data is collected, there is hardly any debate.

Benefit: The extensive documentation provides an opportunity to improve decision making.

Limitation: Since the leader cannot consider all the data and information, and with no consultation, the approach potentially leads to bad decisions. The administrative approach is theatrical with very little substance. The sheer volume of data precludes fixing accountability which can prove disastrous.

The big pharmaceutical firms and the national regulator (FDA) both exemplify the administrative approach. In pharmaceutical research, new projects typically require approval from five or six committees. When the FDA approves a new drug, the accompanying documentation can exceed ten thousand pages. The fine print masks potential risks and dangers. What a sad situation in an industry that deals with the lives of people.

Collaborative Approach: The collaborative approach has rigorous processes and high employee engagement. The collaborative approach shows consistency across many strategic decisions because the leader and the employees consider everything as a unit.

Benefit: Leaders don't miss any steps. The probability of success of the strategic decision increases when compared with the other three approaches.

Limitation: The extensive process and consultation can slow down the decision.

Time-sensitive issues/projects do not lend themselves to the collaborative approach.

Adobe has made a dramatic shift to the collaborative approach. Since the firm focuses on software as a service, agile teams ensure time-sensitive projects are completed on or ahead of schedule. Zappos with its complete elimination of hierarchy is another powerful example of collaboration and cross-fertilization of ideas.

Analysis: Each approach has benefits and limitations. Which approach should you adopt? Let us first examine the five attributes of good strategic decisions:

1. *Alternatives:* Does your firm consider alternatives before making strategic decisions?

2. *Information:* How much information do you use to initiate a discussion?

3. *Implementation:* Do you draw a detailed blueprint before implementation?

4. *Learning:* How much do you learn from your successes and your failures?

5. *Communication:* How do you communicate strategic changes through the organization?

Figure 3.2 shows the executives' survey responses based on a quantitative rubric. A score of 100 represents perfection. Results are based on a 2017 survey of 92 current CEOs, founders, and senior executives.

PERCENTAGE OF MAXIUMUM POSSIBLE SCORE

	Unilateral	Ad hoc	Administrative	Collaborative
Alternatives	43%	43%	45%	70%
Information	51	53	71	76
Implementation	20	35	31	32
Learning	31	50	50	55
Communication	25	46	54	50

Figure 3.2. How Different Strategic Approaches Compare, adapted from Teti, Yang, Bloom, Rivkin, & Sadun (2017).

Unilateral firms score lower levels of statistical significance on all five criteria than collaborative firms; on four of the five than administrative firms; and on three of the five than *ad hoc* firms.

The low scores of the unilateral approach raise serious questions about the approach. If using the unilateral approach, pressure-test it to find out whether it is the best option for your firm.

The other three approaches don't show statistically significant differences. Keep in mind the benefits and limitations while trying out the approaches in your decision making.

Blue Ocean Strategy

W. Chan Kim and Renee Mauborgne of INSEAD argue that traditional competition results in nothing but a bloody red ocean of rivals fighting over a shrinking profit pool. Lasting success doesn't come from battling competitors but from creating *blue oceans*—untapped new market spaces ripe for growth.

Canon's strategic move—creating the personal desktop copier industry—is a classic example of blue ocean strategy. Traditional copier manufacturers targeted offices who wanted large, durable, and fast machines that didn't require extensive maintenance. Defying industry logic, Canon created a blue ocean of new market space by shifting their target customers from corporate purchasers to end users. With their small, easy-to-use desktop copiers and printers, Canon created new market space by focusing on the key competitive factors that the mass of noncustomers—the staff who used copiers—wanted.

By questioning conventional definitions of who can/who should be the target buyer, companies can find fundamentally new ways to unlock value. By shifting focus to a previously overlooked set of buyers, companies can unlock new value and create uncontested market space.

How do you avoid the red ocean traps? Most companies don't understand market complexity and customer expectations. It is not surprising that most companies fail to spot noncustomers—the starting point for creating blue oceans.

Trap 1: Making Existing Customers Happier

Generating new demand is the heart of any market-creating strategy. Organizations in general—and marketing managers in particular, obsessed with making customers happier—continue on the path of incremental improvements.

Happy customers don't create new markets. Creating new markets requires organizations to identify noncustomers. How many earth-shattering ideas have you received by asking your existing customers how to make them happier?

Reliance Communications is part of India's Reliance group. The group chairman, Mukesh Ambani, is the richest man in India and one of the richest in the world. A short time ago, Mukesh upended the red ocean of mobile communication with a stunning offer—for about $23, you could have a mobile handset, and three years of voice communication.

At the end of three years, your $23 would be refunded. In other words, he created a blue ocean for the millions who do not want fancy features on a mobile phone. All they want is a means to communicate with their loved ones, friends, and the authorities to receive early warnings of an impending storm or cyclone. In three months, Reliance Jio garnered 136 million customers.

In the first year of operations, the company has a decent profit after interest and before taxes. All the other players, with their fancy data and app offerings, are forced to slash prices. The result is a long-overdue consolidation of the nearly 700 million strong Indian mobile market.

Generating new demand is the heart
of any market-creating strategy.

Trap 2: Treating Market-Creating Strategies as Niche Strategies

Marketing places great emphasis on increasingly sophisticated methods of segmentation and it treats niche markets as the holy grail. Niche markets can sometimes be very effective but identifying a niche in an existing market is different than creating a new market.

MTR Foods is an Indian vegetarian food manufacturer. The firm started as a stand-alone restaurant nearly 80 years ago and is still a flourishing business. In the last decade, MTR has opened branches, and the restaurants have a typical wait-time of an hour.

MTR Foods specializes in ready-to-eat, easy-to-prepare foods for India's ever-growing segment of middle-class families. World-class hygienic conditions, machinery made in Germany and France, a relentless pursuit of quality, and an attractive price have all combined to make MTR Foods a success story.

Identifying the large Indian population concentrated in NJ, Seattle, the Bay Area, and Houston, MTR Foods has introduced ready-to-eat frozen vegetarian food into this attractive new market. After microwaving for a minute, the product retains its freshness, and its quality is so good it is difficult to believe it is made 10,000 miles away. MTR Foods has created a blue ocean in the ready-to-eat vegetarian food industry. The products are available in Europe, the Middle East, and Southeast Asia as well. Other players have tried to enter but without success— you cannot replicate the capability built over 80 years and a culture where all employees received full salary and benefits when the firm decided to close for 18 months in 1975 due to an internal emergency.

Trap 3: Confusing Technology Innovation with Market Creating Strategies

Innovation is important in any business. But market creation is not always about technological innovation.

Consider the passenger transportation industry.

The success of Uber and Lyft is not about technological innovation. It is about creating a new value proposition—one that is easy to use, fun, and seamless with available technology.

Airbnb is another example. The company started with the founder's two air beds in a small room, hardly an innovation. The business model and the new market they created is a mental leap, not a technological innovation. Airbnb has completely changed the hospitality industry. Even before an IPO, the company has a valuation of over $70 billion.

The elements of value discussed in the course of Customer Service provides insights into value creation.

Trap 4: Equating Creative Destruction with Market Creation

Joseph Schumpeter's theory suggests that innovation inherently displaces an earlier technology, product, or service. Market creation does not always involve destruction.

The Nobel Laureate, Mohammed Yunus, created Grameen Bank in Bangladesh to provide microfinance to women in rural areas. The typical loan is $75, and the loan recovery rate is over 98%. Grameen Bank didn't destroy traditional banks. It destroyed money-lenders charging the highest rate (over 120%) to the poorest people in Bangladesh.

Cost leadership focuses on operations and procurement. Differentiation focuses on innovation and marketing.

Trap 5: Equating Market-Creation with Differentiation

The default position in strategic choice is cost leadership or differentiation. The either-or choice arises out of the economic concept of the productivity frontier—an implicit tradeoff exists between value and cost. Scholars have questioned this assumption.

Cost leadership focuses on operations and procurement. Differentiation focuses on innovation and marketing.

Why can't firms do both at the same time?

IKEA is an example in the furniture industry. The company keeps costs low by using modern production systems characterized by negligible waste and maintaining enduring relationships with suppliers. IKEA provides differentiation through its modular design—using one set of components to make different types of furniture. TOYOTA in automobiles, INTEL in microprocessors, and SOUTHWEST in aviation are examples of companies that have successfully combined cost leadership and differentiation.

Trap 6: Equating Market-Creation with Cost Leadership

Equating market-creation with cost leadership is the other side of Trap 5—companies attempting to achieve a competitive advantage solely by driving down costs. Merely driving down costs and failing to consider efficiency and service is a recipe for disaster.

Captain Gopinath founded Deccan Airlines as a low-cost airline. His vision was to bring flying within everyone's reach. He offered certain seats on some sectors at less than $1. While the promotion caught the eyes of some customers, the airline was a disaster. The airline industry has some fixed costs: lease amount for the aircraft, airport charges, aviation turbine fuel, maintenance, crew salary, and baggage handling, to name a few. Operational costs can't be reduced below a certain level. When you price some tickets at $1, you are inviting trouble. All the aircraft were 48-seat turboprops, with a limited range. The ridiculously low price for a few seats attracted new customers, but the business model was not sustainable. Gopinath ended up applying a low-cost model to a market that could not support the model, and the company collapsed.

Customer focus can improve products and services.

It is important to remember that the six traps are not bad or wrong. When used judiciously, they can produce great results. Customer focus can improve products and services. Low cost or differentiation are effective strategies.

However, when organizations invest heavily without understanding whether they are creating new markets or new customers, stand-alone approaches often lead to failure. We need to change our mental models to deconstruct the business complexity of the 21st century.

Summing Up

Most leaders can probably explain their current strategy. Most leaders may also be able to explain how the strategy has changed over time. How do you make decisions about changing your strategy? Less than 10% of strategic leaders have a coherent answer to this question.

Michael Porter has espoused two approaches—cost leadership and differentiation. With either approach, you can address a large market or a niche market (focus). Thus, there are four classical approaches: broad cost leadership, focused cost leadership, broad differentiation, and focused differentiation.

Scholars have argued that the two approaches—cost leadership and differentiation—are not mutually exclusive. You can combine the two and have an integrated strategy.

Michael Treacy and Fred Wiersema have espoused three approaches to achieve competitive advantage: operational excellence, product leadership, and customer intimacy. The concept of customer intimacy emphasizes the importance of the customer experience in business success.

Chan Kim and Renee Mauborgne of INSEAD, France, have argued that traditional approaches are fights in red oceans.

They urge companies to look for blue oceans—uncontested market space—to be ahead of the competition.

Whatever approach you choose, how you make changes to your strategy has significant implications.

Chapter **4**

21st Century Strategic Leadership

*In the long-term, new ideas generate more sales,
and more sales generate the resources to support other
new ideas. In the short term, though, sales and innovation
have competing priorities.*

Leaders face contradictory challenges almost daily. Do we improve existing offerings, or do we create new offerings? Do we cater to a global network or do we focus on one region? Do we centralize or decentralize processes and decisions? Do we manage for the short-term or the long-term? Do we cater primarily to our shareholders or our customers?

While addressing the challenges, leaders make a fundamental mistake. They believe, perhaps passionately, that optimization is possible in any situation. They believe that balance is possible between conflicting expectations. Unfortunately, these beliefs have no basis in the real world.

As Herbert Simon demonstrated over fifty years ago, optimization is impossible in the real world. He coined the term "satisficing" to explain the process of decision-making.

Professor Roger Martin of the Rotman School of Management has refined the concept. He views decision-making in organizations as the *least-worst* solution to a problem.

When confronted with dilemmas, people usually take an either-or approach, rather than thinking of integrative approaches to decision making.

The Paradoxes of Leadership

Leaders often face what appear to be either-or choices. We can identify three types of paradoxes leaders face.

Paradox 1: Short Term vs. Long Term. One of the fundamental premises in management is the going concern concept. Organizations are assumed to be perpetual entities. Long-term survival depends on our willingness to experiment, take risks, and learn from failure as we pursue new products, services, and processes. Short-term success depends on consistency, discipline, and attention to our current products, services, and processes. Thus we have the innovation paradox between today and tomorrow, current offerings and new ones, stability, and change.

Paradox 2: Do we adhere to our core or cross boundaries? In articulating the paradox, we are struggling with several boundaries—geographic, functional, cultural, industrial, and process-related. A global supply chain can be incredibly efficient yet it may lack agility and flexibility. A dispersed model of innovation may generate multiple ideas but sacrifice the benefit of having the brightest minds working together in one place. Thus we have the globalization paradox between global standardization and local customization, breadth and depth, competition and collaboration.

Paradox 3: Shareholders or Stakeholders? Milton Friedman famously said that the only business of business is to maximize profits. Shareholder wealth maximization became finance's driving principle. Over time, value creation became the new slogan. Finance focuses on wealth maximization and value creation. Marketing focuses on customer satisfaction and customer experience. Human Resources focuses on employee engagement and retention. Society expects responsible corporate citizenship. The world expects a clean environment and sustainable growth.

The result is the **obligation paradox:** an over-emphasis on customers depriving value for shareholders, an over-emphasis on wealth harming the environment, and an over-emphasis on people driving up costs.

The either-or questions do not have definite answers. They are not black and white choices. They are as much interdependent as they are contradictory. Innovation may conflict with operational efficiency. Innovation involves experimentation. Experimentation involves trial and error. Operational efficiency demands consistency, agility, and reliability. Innovation is impossible without efficiency—what is process innovation?

Organizations won't be around to innovate unless they learn to be efficient. Therefore, instead of looking at the paradoxes as either-or choices, we should look at them as both/and experiments. How can we accomplish both A and B?

It is by no means easy to accomplish both A and B. Let's focus on the short-term and ignore innovation. We are likely to miss opportunities to increase profits. The risk of missed opportunities increases with time. If we focus on the long-term, profits in the short-term may suffer due to heavy investments in market-creating innovation. Shareholders could drive down stock prices leading to a panic situation.

Moreover, tensions exist, not only among functions and divisions but also at different levels of the organization. Researchers are often rooted in academic disciplines and communities. They have a long-term view and seek rewards for ideas. Marketers are close to customers, seek rewards for sales, and have a short-term view.

In the long-term, new ideas generate more sales, and more sales generate the resources to support other new ideas. In the short term, though, sales and innovation have competing priorities.

Organizations do not have an actual existence, except in a legal sense. Their people are the critical resource. Employees tend to associate with one side of the paradox, which causes conflict. Top management usually have stock options and are vulnerable to pressures from financial markets seeking instant returns. If marketing believes in long-term relationships, there is potential for a rift.

Investments in building goodwill are invariably the first to get the axe in any cost-cutting exercise. Product designers like new designs requiring new tooling and new processes; they may resent pressures for standardization.

The strategic leader's challenge is not to choose between alternatives, but to be able to address both of the alternatives. Leaders must execute purposeful mind-shifts that enable both growth and sustainability.

The Paradoxical Mindset: First, let's reexamine some basic assumptions about leadership.

Assumption 1: Consistency is often considered a virtue in strategic leaders. Consistency has its roots in the Aristotelian logic of a unified truth: if one idea is right, its opposite must be wrong. Cognitive dissonance is seen whenever values conflict. Studies show that employees understand dual missions—for example, Unilever's mission of profit and environmental goals. When they have to state the mission, most employees mention only one—profit or sustainability. Consistency can be a hazard for strategic leaders; it prevents leaders from dealing with paradoxes. Successful strategic leaders can manage the contradictions effectively—for example, Unilever has better results than its competitors over a five-year time horizon.

Assumption 2: Resources are scarce. Traditional leadership approaches suggest that time, money, people, and other resources are scarce. Hierarchical structures bind operational level employees into a fixed mindset where all resources are viewed as scarce.

As people move up the hierarchy, they find it difficult to move away from the position of resource constraints. When leaders view resources as scarce, they try to *optimize* a zero-sum game. If we allocate resources toward one goal, the resources are not available for another goal. The assumption that resources are scarce leads to either-or situations. Strategic leaders need to view resources as abundant and generative. Instead of cutting the pie into smaller slices, strategic leaders grow the pie—through collaborative partnerships, alternative technologies, and flexible time-frames. Pursuing multiple strategies can enable more resources for each. Ikea's modular design and production offer excellent examples of turning *scarce* resources into *abundant* resources.

Assumption 3: Organizational design requires stability and simplicity. Traditional management emphasizes a common culture, with everyone heading in the same direction, speaking the same language, and sharing *best* practices. In rapidly changing environments, embracing stability results in defensive and detrimental decisions.

Polaroid once boasted of 33 patents for its instant photography. However, they lost the battle in the digital space due to its adherence to an irrelevant business model—people no longer want to print all their pictures.

Paradoxical leadership embraces dynamism and change. Strategic leaders need to be humble and accept that the future is uncertain. They must be willing to change course whenever necessary.

Lego is an example of successfully merging the traditional notion of building blocks into the new world of virtual blocks.

Managing Dynamic Equilibrium

When leaders make the transition from a single truth to multiple truths, from scarce resources to abundant resources, from stability to dynamism, they can help their organizations reach a state of dynamic equilibrium. This transition is the heart of paradoxical leadership. Shifting mindsets is time-consuming and challenging. Leaders need to develop organizational competencies to separate and connect opposing forces.

Separate opposing forces: Create business units by functions, geographies, products, or any other criteria. Allow each division to have its leader, mission, metrics, and culture, as long as these align with the organization's core values. A strong sales and marketing division focuses on serving its primary stakeholders—customers. A strong finance division ensures organizational image is consistent with expectations of financial stakeholders.

In many cases, divisions can lead into sub-divisions. For example, innovation is comprised of multiple elements— one focuses on market-creating or market-changing innovation, a second one focuses on sustaining innovations, and a third one focuses on efficiency innovations.

Build an overarching organizational identity and unite people in a higher purpose.

Connect opposing forces: Connecting involves finding linkages and synergies across goals.

Build an overarching organizational identity and unite people in a higher purpose. That helps leaders and followers alike recognize the interdependence of opposing strategies.

NASA's scientists worked in silos, because they did not like collaboration. Jeff Davis overcame the scientists' resistance by re-defining NASA's top goal: *We aspire to keep astronauts safe in space.* In the pursuit of safety, scientists could support the value of open innovation.

LEGO overcame the resistance to move into the virtual world by reaffirming the company's mission: *Building the builders of tomorrow.*

Digital Data Divide (DDD) melds its business goals and its social goals by declaring its commitment to *stop the cycle of poverty.*

Leaders can also integrate processes by creating new roles for talented people; for example, a business integrator to link innovation with existing products.

Dynamic Equilibrium: Organizational success depends on both separating and connecting. A mission of creating shared value (Porter) can seamlessly integrate functions and processes with conflict built into them. The mere creation of autonomous units without integrating them can increase conflict.

Similarly, connecting without separating can be equally problematic. If leaders focus too much on organizational identity, functional heads and stakeholder groups feel marginalized.

Strategic leaders must design metrics and reward systems at two or even three levels—individual, team or division, and organization. Organizations are reluctant to identify star performers and divisions, which outperform others, for fear of creating disengagement. The challenge for strategic leaders is creating a dynamic entity where individuals and teams are focal points, while simultaneously fostering a culture of collaboration and learning. Embracing paradoxes is an ongoing challenge. It also requires humility.

To quote the Nobel Prize–winning physicist Niels Bohr: "How wonderful that we have met with a paradox. Now we have some hope of making progress."

Summing Up

Leaders face contradictory challenges almost on a daily basis. Do we improve existing offerings, or do we create new offerings? Do we cater to a global network or do we focus on one region? Do we centralize or decentralize processes and decisions? Do we manage for the short-term or the long-term? Do we care primarily for our shareholders or our customers?

While addressing the challenges, leaders make a fundamental mistake. They believe, perhaps passionately, that optimization is possible in any situation. They believe balance is possible between conflicting expectations. Unfortunately, these beliefs have no basis in the real world.

As Herbert Simon demonstrated over fifty years ago, optimization is impossible in the real world. He coined the term "satisficing" to explain the process of decision-making. Professor Roger Martin of the Rotman School of management has refined the concept. He views decision-making in organizations as the *least-worst* solution to a problem.

When confronted with dilemmas, we take an either-or approach. We rarely think of integrative approaches to decision making.

Chapter 5

Leadership Training That Works

Leadership skills are not innate.
They can be acquired and honed.

Corporations across the world invested $356 billion in 2016 on employee training and education. U.S. Companies invested $160 billion in 2016 on employee education and training.

Consider this fact—a leading manufacturer invested $20 million in state-of-the-art safety training. In the year following the training, the company had more fatalities than in the previous five years. How can this anomaly be explained?

CEB (a subsidiary of Gartner) reports that only one in four senior managers perceive training as critical to business outcomes. Studies indicate over 75% of training programs don't facilitate organizational change. In a classic industry study, all the companies that invested hundreds of millions of dollars on training thousands of employees lagged on all key performance indicators—behind the only company which invested nothing at all!

The lessons learned are simple. Training programs don't work because systems are difficult to change. Individuals have much less control over systems than systems have on individuals.

Why do training programs fail?

Professor Amy Edmondson of Harvard and Professor Anita Woolley of Carnegie Mellon have argued that organizations need *fertile soil* in place before the *seeds* of training interventions can grow.

Organizational training, development, and change initiatives succeed when leaders support the initiatives. Leaders should create conditions for employees to apply what they learn, foster immediate improvements in individual and organizational effectiveness, and put systems in place which sustain learning.

If the system doesn't change, people are set up to fail. For any initiative to work, leaders must change. Arranging training and development programs doesn't achieve anything.

Training programs don't work because systems are difficult to change.

Why don't leaders understand this?

There are two reasons.

First, leaders tend to view organizations as an aggregation of individuals. Starting with this understanding, HR defines the requisite individual competencies and sells top management on programs designed to develop those competencies, believing that organizational change will follow.

Organizations are systems of interacting elements. Organizational structure, processes, and leadership style define roles, responsibilities, and relationships of employees. Individuals' backgrounds, education, experience, and culture interact with the system to drive organizational behavior and performance. If the system doesn't change, it can not and will not support individual behavior and change.

Second, HR managers and others find it difficult to confront senior leaders with an uncomfortable truth. Senior leaders craft policies and practices. The policies and practices are at the center of success or failure. Individual performance or deficiency can contribute but isn't the cause of failure. Leaders must first fix policies and practices. Training should follow.

HR managers find it much easier to blame problems on individual competencies. Therefore, training is the solution. Senior leaders are much more receptive to this (wrong) diagnosis than to the fact that they (leaders) need to change first.

Overcoming Barriers: Researchers have identified six common barriers to change.

1. Unclear strategy and values.

2. Senior executives who do not work as a team and have personal agendas.

3. A top-down style of management.

4. Poor organizational design, leading to lack of coordination and collaboration.

5. Inadequate time and attention given to talent issues.

6. Employees' fear of being open about the obstacles they face.

As a corollary, overcoming the barriers involves six steps.

1. The leader defines values and sets an inspiring strategic direction.

2. Employees at all levels provide anonymous inputs on the barriers. Based on their input, the leader redesigns roles, responsibilities, and relationships.

3. Day-to-day coaching increases peoples' effectiveness in the new design.

4. The leader adds training whenever and wherever necessary.

5. The leader measures success using new metrics in changing behavior.

6. To sustain organizational change, the leader adjusts systems for hiring, evaluating, developing, promoting, and retaining people.

Note that the suggested process is a bottom-up phenomenon. By addressing management practices and leadership behavior shaping the system before training individual employees, leaders create a favorable environment for applying learning.

Organizational redesign must precede individual development.

A new capability development approach: Organizations should ask and answer six questions:

1. Is leadership clear about a strategy and a set of values?

2. Has leadership collected unvarnished employee feedback on barriers to effectiveness and performance?

3. Has leadership redesigned the organization, systems, and practices to address employee concerns?

4. Does HR offer employee coaching to help them practice new attitudes and behaviors?

5. Do corporate training programs support the change agenda?

6. Does each unit/division/function represent a fertile ground for improvement?

If your answer to any of the questions is no, your company probably (with good intentions) is overinvesting on training and education, while failing to place talent development in its proper strategic context.

Thought Leaders on Leadership

Daniel Goleman gave the concept of emotional intelligence. What distinguishes great leaders from merely good ones? It is emotional intelligence—a group of five skills enabling leaders to maximize their own and their followers' performance.

Empirical evidence suggests that if the senior leaders of an organization have emotional intelligence, organizational/ divisional goals go up by 20%.

The five skills are:

1. *Self-awareness* – knowing one's strengths, weaknesses, drives, values, and impact on others.

2. *Self-regulation* – controlling or redirecting disruptive impulses and moods.

3. *Motivation* – relishing achievement for its own sake.

4. *Empathy* – understanding other people's emotional makeup.

5. *Social skill* – building rapport with others to exert influence on their actions and behavior.

We are each born with certain levels of emotional intelligence. We can strengthen these abilities through persistence, practice, and feedback from colleagues or coaches.

Peter Drucker espoused the best leaders have certain characteristics in common, although their personalities may vary wildly. The best leaders get the right things done, in the right ways, by following eight simple rules:

1. Ask what needs to be done.

2. Ask what is right for the enterprise.

3. Develop action plans.

4. Take responsibility for decisions.

5. Take responsibility for communicating.

6. Focus on opportunities, not problems.

7. Run productive meetings.

8. Think and say *We*, not *I*.

> *We are each born with certain levels of emotional intelligence. We can strengthen these abilities through persistence, practice, and feedback from colleagues or coaches.*

Using discipline to apply these rules, you gain the knowledge you need to make smart decisions, convert that knowledge into effective action, while ensuring accountability throughout the organization.

John Kotter argues that leadership skills are not innate. They can be acquired and honed.

First, you have to understand how leadership differs from management skills.

Management is about coping with complexity. Management brings order and predictability to a situation. These days, that isn't enough. Organizations must be able to adapt to change if they want to succeed. Leadership is about learning how to cope with rapid change.

How does this distinction play out?

1. Management involves planning and budgeting. Leadership involves setting direction.

2. Management involves organizing and staffing. Leadership involves aligning people.

3. Management provides control and solves problems. Leadership provides motivation.

Warren Bennis coined the term *crucibles*. What enables one leader to inspire confidence, loyalty, and hard work, while others, with equal vision and intelligence, stumble? How individuals deal with adversity provides a clue.

Extraordinary leaders find meaning in—and learn from—the most negative events. Like phoenixes rising from the ashes, they emerge from adversity stronger, more confident in themselves and their purpose, and more committed to their work.

Such transformative events are called crucibles—a severe test or trial. Crucibles are intense, often traumatic—and always unplanned.

Jim Collins studied 1,435 Fortune 500 companies. He found that only 11 achieved and sustained greatness. Collins outlines five levels of leadership:

Level 5. Exceptional Leader: Builds enduring greatness through a paradoxical combination of personal humility and professional will.

Level 4. Effective Leader: Catalyzes commitment to and vigorous pursuit of a clear and compelling vision; stimulates the group to high-performance standards.

Level 3. Competent manager: Organizes people and resources toward the effective, efficient pursuit of predetermined objectives.

Level 2. Contributing team member: Contributes to the achievement of group objectives; works effectively with others in a group setting.

Level 1. Highly capable individual: Makes productive contributions through talent, knowledge, skills, and good work habits.

Level 5 leaders blend the paradoxical combination of deep personal humility with intense professional will. This rare combination also defies our assumptions about what makes a great leader.

Darwin Smith, CEO of paper-products maker Kimberley Clark from 1971 to 1991, epitomizes Level 5 leadership. Shy, awkward, shunning attention, he also showed an iron will, redefining the firm's core business despite Wall Street's skepticism. The formerly lackluster company became the worldwide leader in its industry, generating stock returns 4.1 times greater than the market, significantly outperforming others within this market. In other words, he outperformed the competition – an essential component of competitive advantage.

In recent times, the idea of the authentic leader has gained considerable attention. In its simplest form, authenticity is being yourself.

Being an authentic leader is a journey, not a destination. Along the journey, it is useful to ask the following questions:

1. Which people and experiences in your early life had the greatest impact on you?

2. What tools do you use to become self-aware?

3. What are your most deeply held values?

4. What motivates you extrinsically? How do you balance your intrinsic and extrinsic motivations?

5. What kind of support team do you have?

6. Is your life integrated? Are you able to be the same person in all aspects of your life—personal, work, family, and community?

7. What does being authentic mean to you personally?

8. What steps can you take today, tomorrow, and over the next year to develop your authentic leadership?

Peter Senge argues that the notion of the complete leader is a myth; the notion that anyone has all the answers has to be a myth. Senge suggests a better way to lead is to accept that you are human, with strengths and weaknesses.

Understand the four leadership capabilities all organizations need:

1. Sensemaking – interpreting developments in the business environment.

2. Relating – building trusting relationships.

3. Visioning – communicating a compelling image of the future.

4. Inventing – coming up with new ways of doing things.

Find and work with others who will provide the capabilities you are missing. Take this approach, and promote leadership throughout your organization, unleashing the expertise, vision, and new ideas your organization needs to excel.

Summing Up

Corporations across the world invested $356 billion in 2016 on employee training and education. U.S. companies invested $160 billion in 2016 on employee education and training. A leading manufacturer invested $20 million in state-of-the-art safety training. In the year following the training, the company had more fatalities than in the previous five years.

CEB (a subsidiary of Gartner) reports only one in four senior managers perceive training as critical to business outcomes. Studies indicate over 75% of training programs don't facilitate organizational change. In a classic industry study, all the companies that invested hundreds of millions of dollars on training thousands of employees lagged on all key performance indicators—behind the only company which invested nothing at all!

The lessons learned are simple. Training programs don't work because systems are difficult to change. Individuals have much less control over systems than systems have on individuals.

Chapter 6

Organizational Leadership Summary

Achieving and sustaining performance excellence by embracing a model such as the Baldrige Excellence Framework is a substantial internally-driven change process that touches every part of an organization.

Leadership is at the heart of business success. The reality is, failure is a function of leadership. There is not a single instance in corporate history where the actions of someone at the operational or tactical level have caused failure. Strategic leadership is the cause of failure just as it is the cause of success.

Now that you have read and understood this section, you should be able to:

1. **Understand** and explain the concept of strategic leadership.

2. **Appreciate** why strategic leadership is critical to business success.

3. **Apply** the concepts to your work and be on the path to be a strategic leader.

Reflective Questions

Reflection Question #1: Ask yourself the following questions and discuss the answers with someone you trust:

1. Am I growing?
2. Am I taking care of my people?
3. What decisions in the past year would I take back?
4. Am I leading or managing?
5. Am I making a difference?

Reflection Question #2: Think of your organization. Identify at least one person who exemplifies Level 1, Level 2, Level 3, and Level 4 leadership proposed by Jim Collins. You don't have to name the person. You may identify the position that the person currently holds. Explain the reasoning behind your selection. What steps have you initiated to inspire them to reach higher levels?

If you have not initiated any steps as described yet, what steps do you propose to take in the next year? In the next three years? Explain the reasoning behind your answer.

Short Case Study: Where Will Apple Be?

Calculated by market capitalization, Apple is the most valuable company in the world. On August 6, 2018, Apple became the first company to reach a trillion dollars in market capitalization. Founded by Steve Jobs and Steve Wozniak, the company has had its ups and downs. At one time, Steve Jobs lost his position as CEO. He returned later and led the company to unprecedented success. He had his share of critics – particularly about his overbearing style and his obsession with perfection.

Despite the criticisms, Jobs steered the company to heights that few people envision.

Following Jobs' untimely death, Tim Cook became the CEO. While the company has continued to grow, the innovations that marked Jobs' leadership seem to be missing. Apple is not included in Fortune's Future 50, a list of companies likely to dominate global markets in the next two decades.

What do you think has gone wrong? Compare the leadership styles of Steve Jobs and Tim Cook. Suppose you were the CEO of Apple, what changes would you make and why? How would you ensure that Apple became the world's first trillion-dollar company?

Case Study: District 49 Schools—Leading Beyond Leadership

Introduction

Peter Hilts, the Chief Education Officer, had just learned that Falcon District 49 (D49) will be a recipient of the Peak award offered by Rocky Mountain Performance Excellence (RMPEx), a regional organization administering local awards patterned after the Malcolm Baldrige National Quality Award. The Peak award was the crowning step of an effort spanning several years to move D49 through a performance excellence journey. The award qualified D49 to seek the coveted Malcolm Baldrige National Quality Award, the U.S. Presidential quality award.

The senior leaders and Board of Education of D49 recognized that achieving awards such as the RMPEx Peak or Baldrige alone was a significant achievement. Concerns existed behind the scenes that such a level of excellence might not be sustainable over time.

Hilts knew many organizations make great strides in performance excellence, only to find that the change of a top leader results in the dismantling of the efforts. To address the challenge of sustaining excellence, D49 had already put in place a unique top management structure termed APEx, which parsed the traditional superintendent role into three positions: chief operations officer (COO), chief business officer (CBO), and chief education officer (CEO).

APEx Origins

APEx is an acronym for Aligned-Partner Experts. The first APEx leadership team emerged from senior leadership in 2011. Following a decision by the D49 Board of Education to organize the district into innovation zones, the conventional structure of a solo superintendent was replaced with the APEx team of three chief officers—responsible for business, education, and operations.

The model modeled professional services firms where teams at the top often represented different areas of expertise. Instead of a solitary generalist with expert assistants, the D49 board employed three senior leader experts who each reported directly to the board. Because each officer was an expert in one domain of district leadership, decision-making in the Chief Officer APEx team was consensus-based with appropriate deference to individual expertise.

The APEx team topped an organizational structure comprised of a 24-person senior leadership team that managed through a matrix of four geographic innovation zones. The innovation zones were not identically structured geographic components, due to Colorado's open choice school system. This system allowed for different types of schools—such as building-centric charter schools and open enrollment—under which students can select their choice of schools on an annual basis.

Hilts has been known to say that "if there is any type of special school in Colorado, D49 has one." D49 has a total of 28 different school accreditations, including charter schools, innovation schools, alternative education campuses, and a vocational school, in addition to typical district schools. D49 serves over 21,000 students, despite being smaller than some neighboring districts. All districts compete against each other for students under open enrollment.

Meeting the Challenge of Sustaining Excellence

In addition to an approach for managing complexity, the APEx structure addresses a key challenge of sustaining momentum faced by organizations on a multiple-year journey to excellence. Organizations often begin an excellence journey, only to have progress halted or delayed by a leadership change. Achieving and sustaining performance excellence by embracing a model such as the Baldrige Excellence Framework is a substantial internally-driven change process that touches every part of an organization.

The loss of a top manager or CEO—which in the case of a typical school district would be the solo superintendent—often stops change process. The passion for performance excellence and knowledge of change is often lost with the departure of a solo leader. The model embraced by D49 seeks to avoid that risk by nesting the change effort in a team at the top, with the understanding some—but not all—of the team members in the APEx team could change at any given time.

Beyond the basic APEx team structure, D49 anchors its top leadership approach in several aspects of the Baldrige Framework. The team is explicitly responsive to three sets of performance principles: a cultural compass, key strategic priorities, and guiding principles from the Baldrige Educational Framework.

The cultural compass (Figure 6.1) provides the guiding vision for how to lead and manage the district. The outer circle represents the key directions focusing the organization's efforts for serving students. The inner circle of the compass key shows actions supportive of the vision.

Figure 6.1. The District 49 Cultural Compass.

In addition to the cultural compass, D49 has adopted a version of the core values of the Baldrige Educational Framework as its values. Those values include:

- Systems perspective
- Visionary leadership
- Student-centered excellence
- Valuing people
- Organizational learning and agility
- Focus on success
- Managing for innovation
- Management by fact
- Societal responsibility
- Ethics and transparency
- Delivering value and results

Finally, strategic priorities are displayed as big rocks, shown in Figure 6.2. The priorities round out the mission, vision, and value by providing key waypoints which guide the APEx team and the organization.

Figure 6.2. District 49 Strategic Priorities.

What Will the Future Hold?

As D49 continues its journey of excellence, a question has arisen. Are the APEx structure and processes strong enough, despite being supported by the strategic elements of a cultural compass, Baldrige-based core values, and key priorities, to withstand the natural erosion which occurs with organization and top management change.

Case Discussion Questions

Consider the following when discussing this critical incident case:

1. What are the key challenges in leading an organization through the change process of attaining performance excellence?

2. What are the barriers to sustaining change toward performance excellence over time?

3. How could the leadership structure adopted by D49 help or hinder sustaining change on a journey toward performance excellence?

Section 2
Corporate Governance

Corporate governance is a legal and regulatory compliance issue. In the 21st century landscape, a purely legal and regulatory framework is counterproductive. Respecting the law of the country is important. However, it is not sufficient for the sustained success of the business. Being legal and complying with regulation is not the same as being ethical or even socially responsible. Evidence suggests that organizations that follow the Triple Bottom Line concept (TBL) – of profit, people, and planet – outperform their peers. Profit with purpose and shared value are alternative constructs used to define the scope of corporate governance today.

The roots of corporate governance go back to the 1930s and the seminal work of Adolf Berle and Gardiner Means. Corporate governance as we know it today began in the 1970s.

First, corporate efforts shifted from profit maximization to shareholder wealth maximization. Second, there was a distinct shift from producers to customers. Third, regulation created new boundaries for organizations. Over time, the term *stakeholder* replaced the word *shareholder*. Today's organizations need to satisfy competing stakeholders. Shareholders expect good returns on their investment and they value appreciation.

Customers expect quality products and exemplary services. Employees expect a fair compensation, benefits, a safe work environment, and a culture that fosters creativity and excellence. Suppliers expect stable and mutually beneficial relationships. Regulators expect compliance with the laws of the country. Society expects organizations to be good corporate citizens, espouse community interests, and improve the quality of life for everyone. Activists expect organizations to follow practices that do not harm the environment.

This section explores how organizations can address the conflicting expectations. After reading and understanding this section, you will be able to:

1. **Understand** the concept of governance and its importance.

2. **Recognize** the best practices in corporate governance.

3. **Appreciate** the role of the board and the role of shareholders and stakeholders.

4. **Develop** a template for successful board management.

Chapter 7

What Is Corporate Governance?

*Good corporate governance comprises a system
of structuring, operating, and controlling a company,
with a goal of achieving measurable success for
all stakeholders while upholding ethical principles
and respecting the rule of law and regulation.*

Corporate governance is one of the most hotly debated topics in boardrooms today.

While the roots of governance date back to the work of scholars during the 1930s, the field assumed importance in the 1970s. Governance has taken center-stage on the heels of the financial meltdown of 2007–2008.

Governance is primarily a responsibility of the board of directors. What happens when the board is comprised of members who think and act alike? What happens when independent directors fail to ask relevant, even if uncomfortable, questions? A frequent debate is about the role of the board relative to the composition of the board. Most boards lack the diversity and depth of expertise to ensure good governance practices.

Challenges of Governance

Consider the following two requisites related to the independence of the board of directors and decision-making:

1. Every board should meet regularly without the CEO being present and engage directly with executives below the CEO level to ensure the independence of the board.

2. Boards need to recruit directors with complementary and diverse skills, backgrounds, and experiences. The board should strive to balance experience and tenure against the fresh thinking and perspective of newer board members. A diverse board would lead to better decisions.

Do these happen in your organization? If the answer is yes, you are probably doing very well in your industry. If the answer is no, you are not alone. You belong to the vast majority (over 98%) of listed companies that should do a lot more in addressing the expectations of various stakeholders.

The two action plans are among the most significant made in the Commonsense Corporate Governance Principles, adopted in July 2016 by a group comprising major asset managers, publicly listed corporations, a pension fund, and an activist investment firm. The group includes JPMorgan Chase, Berkshire Hathaway, Blackrock, and T Rowe Price.

Here is the irony. As late as in 2012 (four years post-meltdown), JPMorgan Chase had no directors with risk expertise on the board's risk committee. JPMorgan Chase corrected the deficiency after Bruno Iskil, the *London Whale*, caused

$6 billion in trading losses through what JPMorgan Chase's CEO, Jamie Dimon, called a *Risk 101 Mistake.*

Just look at the chasm between precept and practice. The corporate governance watchdog Institutional Shareholder Services (ISS) issues a *QuickScore* for every major U.S. public company. Unfortunately, it won't tell you how your company's score is calculated or how to improve it – unless you pay for this *advice.*

The problem starts at a fundamental level—the definition of corporate governance. The most widely used definition is "the system which directs and controls companies" (Cadbury Committee, 1992).

The IFC defines governance as "the relationships among the management, board of directors, controlling shareholders, minority shareholders, and other stakeholders."

The OECD Principles of Corporate Governance states that "Corporate governance involves a set of relationships between a company's management, its board, its shareholders, and other stakeholders. Corporate governance also provides the structure through which the company sets its objectives and the means of attaining those objectives and monitoring performance."

According to the Director's Monthly, "Effective corporate governance ensures the establishment of long-term strategic objectives and plans. Governance ensures that proper management structure is in place to achieve those objectives. At the same time, governance makes sure that the structure functions to maintain the corporation's integrity, reputation, and accountability to its relevant constituencies."

The issue of governance emanates from the separation of ownership and control, so one can argue governance is common sense. As long as managers (agents) act in the best interests of shareholders (owners) while also addressing the concerns of the communities they serve, following the rule of law, treating employees fairly, and preserving the environment, everything should be fine.

The problem arises due to the inherent friction in meeting these disparate goals. Organizations invariably view corporate governance as being cost ineffective, bringing little or no benefits (thus explaining the emphasis on the short-term), and at best, an unnecessary burden.

As long as managers (agents) act in the best interests of shareholders (owners) while also addressing the concerns of the communities they serve, following the rule of law, treating employees fairly, and preserving the environment, everything should be fine.

Empirical evidence demonstrates that companies with pro-social goals as their driving force do much better than companies focusing only on hedonistic goals or gain goals. However, there is also pronounced reluctance on the part of companies to practice corporate governance in precept and practice.

On one hand, "We live in a time of unprecedented prosperity" as evidenced by the IMF's World Economic Outlook 2016, the Human Development Report of the United Nations 2015, and the World Bank policy paper 7432 of 2015. "We also live in a time of growing economic inequality and uncertainty" as reflected in the deep mistrust of political and corporate elites.

Further, recent advances in artificial intelligence, machine learning, robotics, and distributed ledger technology have compounded inequality, dislocation, and discontent.

The writing on the wall is large and clear. Unless leaders change their ways and address real problems with sustainable solutions, the benefits of globalization and technological breakthroughs may soon evaporate—at enormous cost and consequences to humanity.

Good corporate governance comprises a system of structuring, operating, and controlling a company, with a goal of achieving measurable success along five dimensions:

1. An organizational culture rooted in sound business ethics.

2. Fulfill the long-term expectations of the shareholders (owners) while addressing all key stakeholders' expectations.

3. In particular, to meet or exceed the expectations of employees, customers, suppliers, and all constituents of the organizational ecosystem.

4. Meet or exceed the needs of the environment, and the communities in which the organizations operate.

5. Compliance with all applicable legal and regulatory requirements of countries and geographies in which the organizations operate.

Best Practices in Corporate Governance

The best management practices include the best corporate governance practices. After all, what constitutes success in business?

- A clear and attainable goal
- An appropriate and feasible strategy to attain the goal
- An organizational structure designed to align with the strategy
- A transparent and accurate reporting mechanism to monitor progress

The best governance practices support the achievement of all the constituents of business success. At the same time, they address the expectations of all key stakeholders while ethically managing the organization.

Thus, the best corporate governance practices include:

- A clear, ethical foundation for the business
- Business goal alignment—addressing the expectations of shareholders, customers, employees, suppliers, value chain constituents, and the community

- Effective strategies to achieve *shared value* among stakeholders

- An organizational structure that complements the chosen strategy—functional, divisional, cooperative, SBU, competitive, matrix, web, holacracy, Teal

- A reporting system that embraces transparency and accountability

A New Paradigm—Combining Purpose with Profits

CASE STUDY: The Tata Group (India)

Ratan Tata headed the Tata Group in India for nearly three decades. During this period, the group saw sustained growth, enhanced value for shareholders, satisfied employees, value chain partners proud to be associated with the group, and a grateful community. The latter resulted from the excellent facilities built by the group in education, healthcare, and recreation (sports). The group has consistently found a place in Fortune's list of the Most Admired Companies and Best Places to Work. How was all this achieved?

A sense of purpose. Ratan Tata describes purpose as "a spiritual and moral call to action; it is what a person or company stands for." The Tata Group, one of India's largest conglomerates, had revenues of over $95 billion in 2015. Founded in 1868 by Jamsetji Tata, today a family-founded trust manages the conglomerate. The trust holds 66% of the equity capital in the holding company, Tata Sons.

Tata's pro-social goal is "to improve the quality of life for the communities we serve." The corporate website declares:

"The community is not just another stakeholder in business, but is, in fact, the very purpose of its existence."

The holding company spends its profits on doing good to the community in the sectors mentioned—education, health care, and recreation. In 2015, the total social expenditure across the group was more than $200 million.

It is common to find employees starting their career with one of the group companies and staying with them until retirement. All the CEOs of the subsidiary companies have come from within. The group was among the first to have independent directors, long before the practice became a regulatory requirement. The group has been in the news more than once for rejecting projects involving some form of quid-pro-quo.

Thus, due to an environment of honesty, trust, and transparency, the group successfully managed to grow consistently —first when the country was still under British rule, then under a highly regulated system during the first four decades of independent India, and in a highly competitive market during the last 25 years.

Thus, a clear sense of purpose and an emphasis on pro-social goals is a strong foundation for long-term success.

CASE STUDY: Handelsbanken (Sweden)

The banking industry is known for experiencing crises at regular intervals. Svenska Handelsbanken, established in 1871, stands out as an extraordinarily resilient and successful operation.

Unlike its competitors, the bank successfully steered through the Swedish financial crisis in the early 1990s with no government help. During the last eight years of a turbulent business environment, the bank has grown in earnings per share even while garnering top customer satisfaction ratings.

How was this possible?

The bank's pro-social goal is very simple: To be customer-focused.

Operationalizing this goal has been through:

- **Decentralization** based on customer requirements—thus, all decisions regarding individual customer's relationship with the bank are made close to the customer.

- A **management model** that **supports the goal**—individual branches have more discretion than similar banks on customer relations and also on employee benefits and working conditions.

- Pioneering the *beyond-budgeting* concept, turning the budget-making process from a top-down to a bottom-up model.

- **De-emphasizing** the concept of **maximizing shareholder returns**; the goal is simply to be above the industry-weighted average on both customer satisfaction and profitability.

- **Goals linked** to a **profit-sharing** and **employee stock option** plan called Oktogonen. Profits are shared equally across the organization (not on an individual basis), and shares are issued to all employees when the after-tax return on equity is higher than the industry average. Today, **employees own nearly half the total equity**, and many long-term employees have become millionaires.

The Purpose of Corporate Governance

To understand corporate governance, we must first understand the concept of legitimacy. Organizations are legitimate to the extent that their activities are congruent with the goals and values of the social system within which they function.

From this perspective, we see legitimacy will prevail when there is agreement between the corporation's activities and society's expectations. While legitimacy is a condition, legitimation is a dynamic process by which business seeks to perpetuate its existence.

The dynamic nature of the process has to be clearly understood because society's values and norms change, and businesses have to adapt if their legitimacy is to continue. Also, legitimacy can be considered both at the *micro* level—the extent to which individual firms meet society's expectations—and at the *macro* level—the extent to which the corporate system, as a whole, meets society's expectations.

The purpose of corporate governance is a direct outgrowth of the question of legitimacy. For a business to be considered legitimate in the eyes of ordinary people, and for the business to maintain its legitimacy, it must be managed to correspond to people's expectations. Thus, corporate governance focuses on the relative roles, responsibilities, privileges, and accountability of various stakeholder groups: owners, directors, the board, managers, employees, government, society, and others who may have a stake in the organization.

The role of four stakeholder groups is particularly important while considering corporate governance issues.

Under corporate law, *shareholders* are the owners of a corporation. Since a corporation can have hundreds of thousands of shareholders, it isn't practical for the shareholders (owners) to manage the corporation. They select and appoint the board of directors. The extent of each shareholder's right to select a director is proportional to the shares owned by the shareholder.

The *board of directors* is responsible for ensuring managers put the interests of shareholders above their own. *Management* refers to the group of individuals appointed by the board to run the corporation on a daily basis. *Employees* are people hired by a company to perform operational work—be it in marketing, finance, manufacturing, services, information technology, research, maintenance, human resources, or any other function.

Thus, *shareholders, the board of directors, management,* and *employees* represent the four stakeholder groups directly responsible for corporate governance. Employees represent nonmanagerial personnel.

In corporate governance, the principal issue involved is the separation of *ownership* and *control.* Before the corporation became the norm for business entities, owners typically *managed* their business. Thus, the owners also *controlled* the business.

Shareholders, the board of directors, management, and employees *represent the four stakeholder groups directly responsible for corporate governance.*

As corporations have grown and stock ownership has become widespread, the owners (shareholders) no longer *manage* and *control* the business. It is unlikely that any shareholder will have sufficient shares to influence policies or decisions.

Thus, *management* and *control* are the responsibilities of the board of directors, management, and employees.

There is no way to ensure that managers and employees will always act in a manner that best serves the interests of shareholders. Since ownership is wide, shareholders no longer consider themselves owners. They prefer to be called *investors.*

If you hold 1000 shares in a corporation with 100 million shares outstanding, you cannot claim to be an owner. Your theoretical *ownership* can be lost by a mere phone call if you decide to sell your shares.

Another factor that has added to management's power is the proxy process – the method by which shareholders elect directors.

Over time, the process has resulted in boards having like-minded people who will collect their fees and endorse management's decisions. Instead of acting in the interests of shareholders, managers have been pursuing their own interests.

We thus have the classic Agency Problem. This occurs when the interests of the owners (shareholders) and their agents (directors and managers) are not aligned.

The Need for Board Independence

A critical factor in good governance is the need to maintain the board of directors, independence from management. The distinction between *inside* directors and *outside* or *independent* directors becomes more important.

Inside directors may be executives of the company or relatives of the founder and invariably have some interest in the firm.

Independent directors, on the other hand, are top executives at other firms, academics, or eminent persons. They have no substantive relationship with the firm. *Independent* directors can ensure that the interests of shareholders and other stakeholders are given due consideration while making decisions. Ideally, *independent* directors should make up fifty percent of a corporate board.

Even so, management can try to influence the board through other ways. CEOs often control such matters as director compensation and representation on various committees. Directors who go against management's line may find themselves in the cold by not being part of any committee that matters. While some progress has occurred after the debacle of once-mighty corporations like Enron, a lot more needs to happen. As one board member has observed, CEOs don't want independent directors.

Compensation Issues

Consider this: Compensation of the bottom 5% of Fortune 500 CEOs in 2016 was greater than the top 5%. Over the last decade, CEO compensation of the Fortune 500 companies increased about 40% each year compared with the average increase in executive compensation of just about 10%. Two important issues emerge: the extent which organizations should tie CEO compensation to performance and the size of CEO compensation itself.

The debate about tying CEO compensation to performance has been going on for over two decades. One of the most widely used methods is via stock options that allow executives to purchase stock in the future at today's price. Stock options are supposed to motivate executives to act in a manner that will enhance company performance, resulting in a higher value of the stock.

Unfortunately, the system is routinely abused in several ways. For example, through backdating—where the beneficiary can buy the stock at yesterday's price.

Spring-loading also occurs; granting a stock option at today's price, but with the inside knowledge that something positive is about to happen that would push the price upward.

Or through bullet-dodging, when the stock option occurs only after some bad news. Along with other practices, these measures have invariably led to situations of rewarding even poor performers.

Marissa Mayer of Yahoo is expected to receive $186 million in severance when her services are terminated pursuant to the acquisition of Yahoo's internet businesses by Verizon. In fact, for what is by any standards a dismal performance, Mayer received $218 million over the four years that she was CEO of Yahoo.

Adam Lashinsky of Fortune has questioned whether the benefits of stock options are worth the problems they create. He adds: "So here's a radical proposal. Scrap the whole system. Pay employees a competitive and living wage. Pay them more when the company does well but only after rewarding shareholders. Do that in the form of transparent bonuses and profit-sharing plans. Reserve outsized riches for the company founders, not the hired help, which, let's face it, is what most executives are."

Excessive CEO Pay: CEO pay today is in the news for all the wrong reasons. An analysis of the Fortune 500 companies shows that the bottom performing 5% had higher CEO compensation than the top performing 5%. Such anomalies indicate the much-publicized concept of pay-for-performance is a myth.

The ratio of CEO pay to the average worker compensation is currently 331:1; compared to 42:1 thirty years back. Real wages have hardly increased during the same period. The resulting inequality naturally causes anxiety, fear, and anger in the minds of large demographics of people. If the minimum wage had increased at the same rate as CEO pay between 1990 and 2015, the federal minimum wage would have been $27 per hour.

Suppose high executive compensation is found out to be the result of dubious practices—such as window-dressing of accounts, for example. Shareholders should then have the right to recover the excessive amounts paid. Until recently, adequate mechanisms were not available for this purpose. The increasing adoption of clawback provisions—compensation recovery mechanisms that enable a company to recoup funds paid to top executives if the payment was due to financial juggling or executive misbehavior—is growing, although specific instances of amounts recovered are rare in the corporate world.

Executive Retirement Plans: Retirement plans do not garner the same attention that excessive compensation does, but they represent another reason for the growing frustration of the *middle class.*

The former Chairman and CEO of the New York Stock Exchange, Richard Grasso, is reported to have received a retirement package of $139.5 million amid slumping stocks and cost pressures.

Part of the frustration arises from the fact that these figures bear no resemblance to the wages of an ordinary employee. A majority of employees have to be content with the defined contribution approach rather than the defined benefit plans reserved for the top executives.

Outside Director Compensation: A hundred years ago, it was illegal to pay non-executive board members. With increasing emphasis on independent board members, the need to attract talented people to serve as board members, and enhanced oversight requirements resulting from the failure of large corporations, it is now recognized that non-executive board members need to be compensated adequately for their efforts. The catalyst for change includes regulatory requirements, such as Sarbanes-Oxley and Dodd-Frank, enhanced proxy disclosure rules, and increased shareholder activism.

Within the ranks of non-executive directors, audit committee members receive the highest compensation, followed by remuneration committee members, and independent directors.

Impact of the Market for Corporate Control

Mergers and acquisitions are another form of corporate governance, one that comes from outside the corporation. The expectation is that the threat of a possible takeover will motivate managers to pursue shareholder interests, rather than self-interest.

The economic prosperity of the 1980s induced many small firms and individuals to try to take control of larger firms. During this period, CEOs were focused more on self-preservation than on doing what was best for shareholders.

Two of the key top management practices emerged during this period—*poison pills* and *golden parachutes*. A poison pill is intended to discourage or prevent a hostile takeover. A golden parachute is a contract stating a corporation agrees to make payments to key officers in the event of a change in the control of the corporation.

Summing Up

Corporate governance is one of the most hotly debated topics in boardroom today. Governance has taken center-stage consequent upon the financial meltdown of 2007 – 2008.

The role of the board is frequently debated. Most boards lack diversity and depth of expertise to ensure good governance practices. Critics blame the composition of boards—the predominance of CEOs, lack of representation for women and minority groups, and lack of transparency in operations.

This section examined a few critical issues—the importance of corporate governance, best practices in governance, and the purpose of governance.

Chapter 8

How to Build Better Boards

*The biggest failure of corporate governance
is the emphasis on short-term performance.*

Building a better board involves several steps:

1. Defining the role of the board and explicitly stating financial goals.

2. Widening the talent pool for directors, and finding the best candidates to serve the firm now and in the future.

3. Aim for 50% independent directors, and encourage constructive dissent.

4. Divide and delegate work. This will promote greater involvement, more thorough analysis, and decisions based on reasoning.

5. Aim for the diversity of the board without compromising quality.

Building a better board is the responsibility of each board member:

1. Be willing to challenge the status quo. Offer constructive criticism.

2. Be willing to learn about the firm, the competition, and the industry environment.

3. Be willing to research important issues before meetings.

4. Control the flow of information—ensure that board discussions remain with the board.

5. Meet other board members and executives to better understand the firm.

6. Don't sacrifice performance for collegiality.

Board Diversity: Despite improvements that have come about in the last 50 years, board diversity is still a distant goal. A recent study has shown that women represent just 15% of all directors, and almost 5% of publicly listed companies do not have women directors. Minorities represent 14% of all directors, with 9% African-American, 4% Hispanic, and 1% Asian directors.

In many countries, the situation is worse. For example, in the UK, only 10% of all directors are women. Some countries, such as Norway, have a quota for female representation.

Does diversity matter? Several studies indicate that diverse boards are better able to hear concerns of stakeholders and respond to their needs. It is also quite likely that diverse boards are better insulated against group-think because the board members represent different perspectives. This might prevent a pre-determined course of action by those responsible for day-to-day management.

Also, it's been shown that board diversity leads to better financial performance. Due to the complex nature of the business and the factors that might influence a firm's performance, a causal relationship between any two variables is difficult to establish.

Along with diversity, having outside directors is important. Institutional investors appear to value board independence and are willing to pay a premium for a firm with adequate representation for outside directors. Researchers have found that outside directors positively influence corporate social responsibility.

Board Committees: The *audit* committee is responsible for assessing the adequacy of internal control systems and the integrity of financial statements. The *nominating* committee is responsible for ensuring that competent, objective board members are selected. The *compensation* committee evaluates executive performance and recommends the terms and conditions of employment for senior executives. The *public policy* committee provides guidelines for responding to major public/social issues.

Board Member Liability: Until the year 2000, the business judgment rule prevailed in the corporate world. The rule holds that courts shouldn't challenge board members who act in good faith, making informed decisions reflecting the company's best interests instead of their own self-interest. Proponents of the business judgment rule believe board members need to be free to take risks without fear of liability. The issue of good faith is key here because the rule was never intended to absolve board members from personal liability.

In cases where boards do not uphold the good faith doctrine, board members have to pay a hefty price, as demonstrated in cases such as Enron, WorldCom, TransUnion Corporation, Cincinnati Gas and Electric, and Caremark.

Directors can only be held liable if the director utterly fails to implement any reporting or information systems or controls; or having implemented such a system of controls, consciously fails to monitor/oversee its operations, disabling their ability to be informed of risks or problems requiring their attention.

The Role of Shareholders

Shareholders are the owners of the corporation. They have a right to have their voices heard. Translating this right into practice brings several challenges.

Although many countries take pride in their democratic traditions and institutions, the privileges do not extend to shareholders in corporate matters. In the U.S., votes against board members are often not counted, and corporations have been free to ignore shareholder resolutions.

Many European firms don't have one vote per stock share issued. The ability of shareholders to elect board members is important because the elected board members will govern the corporation. If shareholders aren't able to select their representatives, the board can become a self-perpetuating oligarchy.

Shareholder democracy begins with board elections. Three key issues have arisen as a result of the activism of shareholder groups in general, and institutional investors in particular: *majority vote*, *classified boards*, and *shareholder ballot access*.

Majority vote requires that board members get a majority of votes cast. The natural desire to let the majority rule through a fair one-person/one-vote system is subject to criticism by those who view majoritarianism as an anathema to the protection of fundamental minority rights.

The inherent conflict between protecting the rights of the minority while allowing the democratic majority to rule has been used to justify implementation of voting decision rules, such as the supermajority or unanimity. However, pressure from institutional investors and activist investors has brought about the adoption of the majority rule concept by a growing number of corporations. In due course, majority rule will likely become the standard.

Classified boards are boards which elect their members to staggered terms. Many shareholder activists oppose classified boards because of the time required to replace the board. Proponents of classified boards argue that board members need a longer term to get to know the firm and to make long-term-oriented decisions.

The push for declassification has gathered momentum. Almost 90% of S&P 500 companies have annually elected boards. Vote-no campaigns also seem to be increasing. Vote-no campaigns, particularly by large pension fund investors, led to certain board members resigning in companies such as HP and JPMorgan Chase.

Shareholder ballot access provides shareholders with the opportunity to propose nominees for the board of directors. The Securities and Exchange Commission (SEC) approved changes which make it easier for shareholders to nominate directors of public companies. These changes allow groups owning at least 3% of a company's stock to list their nominees for board seats on the annual proxy ballot sent to all shareholders.

Shareholder activism refers to the increasing trend of minority shareholder groups coming together to fight for issues they consider important. Shareholder activism isn't a new phenomenon. It has a history of over eighty years.

Boards should give shareholders an orderly voice.

The movement we see today emanated in the 1960s and early 1970s out of a period of political and social upheaval—civil rights, the Vietnam War, pollution, and consumerism. Shareholder activism's first big success was with GM; it resulted in the constitution of a public policy committee on the board and the appointment of the first African-American director. A direct consequence of the success of the campaign at GM was the growth of church activism. The Interfaith Center on Corporate Responsibility (ICCR) was instrumental in convincing Kimberly-Clark to divest the cigarette paper business and pressurizing PepsiCo to move out of then-Burma (now Myanmar). Shareholder activism started out with laudable goals; however, in recent times, the emphasis has turned to profits. In fact, money managers and hedge funds are now advertising their activist orientation, in the belief that being seen as aggressive gives them an edge.

Case Study: Monitoring the Monitors

Board members are typically disciplined by not being reelected by a shareholder vote. While shareholder vote can sometimes address firm performance issues, it isn't as effective in addressing less public issues promptly. The Hewlett-Packard board found itself dealing with this type of problem when the details of confidential board discussions found their way to the press. Details of the firm's strategies and its CEO hiring deliberations were made public, but it was unclear which board member was supplying the information.

After interviews with board members failed to elicit the source of the leaks, then-board chairperson Patricia Dunn engaged an outside licensed investigative firm to determine who had provided the confidential information to the media. The firm used *pretexting* (conscious misrepresentation to obtain information) as one of the techniques for collecting the information. Investigators pretended to be the board members. The investigators found the source of the leaks. However, the episode caused an uproar.

- Who should be responsible for taking action when a board member engages in problematic behavior?

- One complaint was that HP provided the board members' home phone numbers to investigators. Does this action breach the privacy of board members? Why or why not?

- An innocent board member chose to resign in protest, stating the investigation invaded his privacy. Was he right?

- The law against pretexting is unclear. While it is illegal to obtain financial records, the use of pretexting in other situations is not necessarily illegal. Should it be?

- What could have happened if the ethicality rather than the legality of the practice had been the issue? Are the two synonymous or is there a difference?

Principles of Good Governance

Boards should have the right to manage the company for the long-term. The biggest failure of corporate governance is the emphasis on short-term performance. Ironically, companies have to go private to focus on the longer term. Michael Dell took Dell private in 2013 because he claimed the company could not achieve the changes needed in the glare of public markets.

End earnings guidance. With holding periods of stock markets today averaging less than six months, it is difficult to avoid short-termism. Dispensing with earnings guidance would lessen the obsession with short-term profitability.

Bring back a variation of the staggered board. When a board is staggered, one-third of its directors are elected each year to three-year terms. This structure promotes continuity and stability in the board, but shareholder activists dislike it. With an increase in shareholder activists, the number of staggered boards fell from 60% in 2002 to 12% in 2014. The result is that most corporate directors are elected every year to one-year terms (creating so-called unitary boards).

It goes without saying that directors elected to one-year terms will have a shorter-term perspective than those elected to three-year terms. Shareholder activists argue a staggered board may discourage an unsolicited offer that a majority of stakeholders would like to accept. Firms can avoid this drawback if they dismantle the stagger by removing all the directors or by adding new ones. Dismantling a staggered board in this way would combine the longer-term perspective of three-year terms with the responsiveness to the takeover marketplace that shareholders want. A tri-annual check would allow longer-term investments to play out. It would be better aligned to wealth creation than an annual check on all directors.

Boards should have mechanisms to ensure the best possible people hold seats on the board.

Install exclusive forum provisions. In litigation-prone societies (such as the U.S.), there is a tendency for plaintiffs' attorneys (representing shareholders who typically hold only a few shares) to look for any hiccup in stock price or litigation against the corporation and its board. Attorneys are especially attracted to major transactions, such as mergers and acquisitions.

At present, any public company announcing a major transaction is likely to be sued—sometimes within hours—regardless of how much care the board places in its decision.

A U.S. corporation is subject to jurisdiction wherever it has contacts—its headquarters state, state of incorporation, and states where it does business.

Plaintiffs' attorneys take advantage of this provision to bring suit in multiple states—particularly those that permit jury trial for corporate law cases. The prospect of inexperienced jurors deciding on a complex corporate case leads many companies to settle in a hurry.

This provision is bad for corporate governance and society overall.

Exclusive forum provisions permit litigation against a company solely in its state of incorporation. A large majority of U.S. companies are incorporated in Delaware. The implication of such incorporation means an experienced judge on the Delaware Chancery Court can hear the case.

Despite the clear benefits, shareholder activists express a knee-jerk reaction to exclusive forum provisions.

Exclusive forum provisions give plaintiffs' attorneys a fair fight in a state where the rules of the game are clear. In exchange for such a provision, boards might consider renouncing draconian measures, such as a fee-shifting bylaw forcing plaintiffs to pay the company's expenses if their litigation is unsuccessful.

Directors would be accountable for their actions, but only as judged by a corporate law expert. The result would be a greater willingness among directors to make longer-term decisions, without fear of a jury's 20/20 hindsight.

Boards should have mechanisms to ensure the best possible people hold seats on the board. In exchange for their right to run the company for the long term, boards must ensure a proper mix of skills and perspectives in the boardroom. Activists have proposed some measures—principally age limits and term limits—but also gender and other diversity requirements. Approximately 50% of U.S. companies have age limits, and only 8% have term limits.

Boards often don't take a hard look at their composition and whether the director's skill set reflects the needs of the company. This lack can provide motivation for activists and rating agencies.

Too often directors are allowed to continue because it is difficult to ask them to step down. Age and term limits are a blunt instrument for achieving optimal board composition.

As for age limits, directors who have retired from full-time employment can devote themselves to their work on the board. As for term limits, directors will often need a decade to shape strategy and evaluate the success of its execution. Directors who have been on the board longer than the current CEO are more likely to be able to challenge her or him when necessary. These are precisely the directors who would be forced out by age limits or term limits.

Corporate governance should approach the issue of board composition in a tailored manner, focusing more on making sure that boards engage in meaningful selection and evaluation processes rather than ticking boxes.

In particular, corporate governance should:

Require meaningful director evaluations. For effective functioning of the board, an independent third party should design a process and conduct reviews. The process should include grading directors on various company-specific attributes in order to evaluate their contributions relevantly. It is important to share evaluations with the individual director, with comments reported verbatim when necessary, to clarify any opportunities for improvement. Evaluations should also go to the chairperson or lead director, to provide objective evidence in order to have difficult conversations with underperforming directors. Such actions would have subtle effects on board composition and boardroom dynamics. Foreseeing a rigorous and independent review process, underperforming directors would voluntarily not stand for reelection. Even more important, directors would work hard to make sure the perception that they are underperforming does not occur.

Consider shareholder proxy access. Shareholders with a significant ownership stake in the company should have the right to put director candidates on the company's ballot. For example, a company proxy could have ten candidates for eight seats on the board.

HP and Western Union, among others, have implemented shareholder proxy access. After the D.C. Circuit Court of Appeals invalidated the move to impose proxy access on all companies, the SEC now allows companies to implement it on a voluntary basis. Implementing a proxy access would help ensure the right mix of skills in the boardroom. For example, if JPMorgan Chase had a proxy access rule, it seems likely it would not have lacked directors with risk expertise on the risk committee at the time of the London Whale incident. In fact, more than a year before the event, CtW Investment Group, an adviser to union pension funds, highlighted the point: "The current three-person risk policy committee, without a single expert in banking or financial regulation, is simply not up to the task of overseeing risk management at one of the world's largest and most complex financial institutions."

With a proxy access regime, either the board would have nominated someone with risk expertise on the risk committee, or a significant shareholder could have nominated such a person. The shareholders collectively would have decided whether the gap was worth filling.

We are not suggesting that if JPMorgan Chase's risk committee had included directors with risk expertise, the directors would have prevented the London Whale incident. The odds of identifying the problem would have been higher in a proxy access regime. It is worth noting that the JPMorgan Chase board added a director with risk expertise after the firm took a multibillion-dollar hit. Shareholder proxy access regime should be considered as a supplement to meaningful board evaluations, to ensure the right composition of directors in the boardroom.

Boards should give shareholders an orderly voice. When an activist investor threatens a proxy contest, or a strategic buyer makes a hostile tender offer, boards tend to see their role as *defender of the corporate bastion*, which often leads to a no-holds-barred, scorched-earth campaign against the party seeking to wrest control.

Commonwealth REIT, one of the largest real estate investment trusts in the U.S. had properties worth $7.8 billion against $4.3 billion in debt in December 2012. Its market capitalization stood at only $1.3 billion. Corvex Management and Related Companies saw an investment opportunity. In February 2013, they announced a 9.8% stake in Commonwealth and proposed acquiring the rest of the company for $25 a share, which represented a 58% premium over Commonwealth's unaffected market price.

The Corvex-Related strategy was simple. Commonwealth had no employees. It paid an external management company to manage the real estate assets. This company, REIT Management & Research, was run by Barry and Adam Portnoy, a father-and-son duo who also constituted two-fifths of the Commonwealth board. Corvex and Related's investment thesis boiled down to three words: Fire the Portnoys.

The board, in a war mode, made the acquisition difficult by imposing onerous information requirements, lobbying (unsuccessfully) with the Maryland legislature to amend its takeover laws to protect the company, and amending the bylaws to insist that arbitration alone could resolve any dispute, not a Maryland court. After 18 months of arbitration hearings and sharply worded press releases, Corvex and Related finally replaced the Commonwealth Board with their nominees in June 2014. Today, Commonwealth (renamed Equity Commonwealth) trades at over $30 a share, compared with $16 before the offer.

Commonwealth's board took the typical scorched-earth approach, which was not necessary. The principle of *orderly shareholder voice* involves a different conceptualization of the board's role—to guarantee a reasonable process whereby shareholders get to decide (rather than defend) the corporate bastion at all costs. Even when a board genuinely believes that the competing vision is flawed, its fiduciary duty—contrary to popular belief—does not require preventing shareholders from deciding. The directors can campaign hard for their point of view but the decision must be left to the shareholders.

Orderly is a critical qualifier because some shareholders are undeniably disorderly. With the steep decline in poison pills, hedge funds and other activist investors can buy substantial stakes in a target company before they have to disclose their positions.

J. C. Penney did not have a poison pill in 2010. Roth and Ackman secretly bought a 27% stake. The company put them on the board. Apple executive Ron Johnson replaced Mike Ullman as CEO. Johnson planned to give Penney a younger look. The strategy was a disaster. The stock price dropped from $30 to $7.50 over two years. Johnson was forced out in 2013—and replaced by none other than Mike Ullman. Ullman steadied the sinking ship, but the results were not as expected. In 2015, he handed over the reins to Marvin Ellison. Ellison is trying to re-invent the company. Currently, J. C. Penny shares are trading at $10 (with a 12-month high of $12 and a low of $6). Roth and Ackman have reportedly lost over $800 million due to their fiasco at J. C. Penney.

In theory, companies have protection against such lightning-strike raids by the SEC rule that shareholders must disclose their ownership position after crossing the 5% threshold. But they have ten days in which to do so, and nothing stops them from buying more shares in the meantime.

That is what happened in the J. C. Penney case. By the time Roth and Ackman had to make the disclosure, they had bought more than a quarter of the company's shares. The rule dates back to the 1960s when ten days was a reasonable amount of time. Today, ten days in the securities markets is an eternity; no one designing a disclosure regime from scratch would dream of giving shareholders such a long window. Shareholder groups have resisted change on the rather questionable grounds that the Roths and Ackmans of the world need sufficient incentive to keep looking for underperforming targets.

Under an enlightened corporate governance system, boards would get early warning of lightning-strike attacks. One way to do this would be a *notice* poison pill—a pill with a 5% threshold but also an exemption; any shareholders that disclosed their positions within two days of crossing the threshold would avoid triggering the pill and could continue buying shares without being diluted.

An alternative is the *window closing* poison pill. Either kind of pill would give directors fair warning that their company was *in play* before the bidder could build up an unassailable position.

Evidence suggests that a change in corporate governance usually occurs when shareholders threaten a withhold vote against the board unless the board implements certain reforms. An enlightened corporate governance would take a proactive approach that achieves the same (desirable) goals in a holistic, better way. Managers actively engage with shareholders from a functional perspective (What are we all trying to achieve?)

rather than an issue-by-issue reactionary perspective (Should we surrender, or do we fight?).

A board wanting to adopt an enlightened corporate governance perspective could do so unilaterally in many jurisdictions (including, for the most part, Delaware), though it would be better advised to adopt enlightened corporate governance through a shareholder vote. This shift is critical in the U.S. because the power of shareholders has increased in the last decade and the natural instinct of boards is simply to cave into activist demands.

An enlightened approach to corporate governance is vital outside the U.S. as well, particularly in emerging economies where companies are trying to achieve the right balance of authority between boards and shareholders to gain access to global capital markets.

Over the long term, an enlightened approach to corporate governance would transform governance from a never-ending conflict between boards and shareholders to a source of competitive advantage in the marketplace.

Summing Up

Building a better board involves several steps:

1. Defining the role of the board and explicitly stating financial goals.

2. Widening the talent pool for directors, and looking for the best candidates to serve the firm now and in the future.

3. Aim for 50% independent directors and encourage constructive dissent.

4. Divide and delegate work to promote greater involvement, more thorough analysis, and decisions based on reasoning.

5. Aim for the diversity of the board without compromising quality.

6. Building a better board is the responsibility of each board member:

7. Be willing to challenge the status quo and offer constructive criticism.

8. Be willing to learn about the firm, the competition, and the industry environment.

9. Be willing to research important issues before meetings.

10. Control the flow of information—ensure that board discussions remain with the board.

11. Meet other board members and executives to understand the firm.

12. Don't sacrifice performance for collegiality.

Chapter 9

Perspectives on the Role of the Board of Directors

*It is the responsibility of management to operate
the corporation effectively and ethically in order
to produce value to the shareholders.*

The Board of Directors can bring a shining light to the
direction of a company—supporting, guiding, and at
times, challenging the CEO. All are a good thing. What's not is
when it becomes a *rubber stamp*, allowing for a once thriving company to slip into mediocrity and possible demise.

Role of the Board in Governance: A legal perspective

The Duty of Care: The duty of care is the most important duty
owed by a director to a corporation. A typical (state) corporation statute defining a director's duty of care provides
that a director's duties must be performed *with such care,
including reasonable inquiry, as an ordinarily prudent person
in a like position would use under similar circumstances.* The
duty of care is very broad and requires directors to perform
their obligations diligently.

Business Judgment Rule: The Business Judgment rule works
in conjunction with the director's duty of care. Under this

rule, a firm cannot hold a director responsible for mere negligence if exercising her or his duty of care. The rule is *a director who exercises reasonable diligence and who, in good faith, makes an honest, unbiased decision will not be held liable for mere mistakes and errors in business judgment.* The rule protects directors from decisions that turn out badly for their corporation, even when directors acted diligently and in good faith in authorizing the decision.

The Duty of Loyalty: The duty of loyalty exists as a result of the fiduciary relationship between directors and the corporation. A fiduciary relationship is a relationship of trust and confidence, such as between a doctor and patient, or attorney and client. The nature of the relationship includes the concept that neither party may take selfish advantage of the other's trust and may not deal with the subject of the relationship in a way that benefits one party to the disadvantage of the other. A director must perform her or his duties in good faith and in a manner in which the director believes are in the best interests of the corporation and its shareholders.

Essentially, this duty means that while serving a corporation, the director must give the corporation the first opportunity to take advantage of any business opportunities that she or he becomes aware of and that are within the scope of the corporation's business. If the board of directors chooses not to take advantage of a business opportunity brought to its attention by a director, the director may then go forward without violating her or his duty. Liability can exist for officers and directors when they cause financial harm to the corporation, act solely on their behalf and to the detriment of the corporation, or commit a crime or wrongful act. Certain acts may subject an officer or director to personal liability, and other acts, although they would otherwise subject them to liability, may be either indemnified by or insured against by the corporation.

Role of the Board: A Governance Perspective

The paramount duty of the board of directors of a public corporation is to select the Chief Executive Officer (CEO) and to oversee the CEO and senior management in the competent and ethical operation of the corporation.

> **Liability can exist for officers and directors when they cause financial harm to the corporation, act solely on their behalf and to the detriment of the corporation, or commit a crime or wrongful act.**

It is the *responsibility of management* to operate the corporation effectively and ethically in order to produce value to the shareholders. Senior management is expected to know how the corporation earns its income and what risks the corporation is undertaking in the course of carrying out its business. The CEO and board of directors should set a *tone at the top* that establishes a culture of integrity and legal compliance. Management and directors should never put personal interests ahead of or in conflict with the interests of the corporation.

It is the *responsibility of management,* under the oversight of the *audit committee and the board,* to produce financial statements that fairly present the financial condition and results of operations of the corporation and to make the timely disclosures investors need to assess the financial and business soundness and risks of the corporation.

It is the *responsibility of the board*, through its *audit committee*, to engage an independent accounting firm to audit the financial statements prepared by management, issue an opinion that those statements are fairly prepared by Generally Accepted Accounting Principles (GAAP) and oversee the corporation's relationship with the outside auditor.

It is the *responsibility of the board*, through its *corporate governance committee*, to play a leadership role in shaping the corporate governance of the corporation. The corporate governance committee also should select and recommend to the board qualified director candidates for election by the corporation's shareholders.

It is the *responsibility of the board*, through its *compensation committee*, to adopt and oversee the implementation of compensation policies, establish goals for performance-based compensation, and determine the compensation of the CEO and senior management.

It is the *responsibility of the board* to respond appropriately to shareholders' concerns.

It is the *responsibility of the corporation* to deal with all stakeholders—customers, employees, suppliers, government, society, and other constituents—in a fair and equitable manner.

Role of the Board: An Alternate Perspective

The board needs to take charge of its focus, agenda, and information flow. Such an approach enables a board to provide management with meaningful guidance and support.

The board must ensure that management not only performs but performs with integrity. Selecting, monitoring, and compensating—and, when necessary, replacing—management, is at the heart of board activity.

The board must set expectations about the values and culture of the organization. The standards of ethics and business conduct that the board follows, or may not, throughout a company impact the bottom line and reputation in many ways. Setting the right examples at the top should be a priority and not viewed simply as a compliance matter.

The board should work with management to formulate a corporate strategy. After agreeing to a strategic course with management through a prescribed process, the board should determine the benchmarks evidencing success or failure in achieving strategic objectives. The board should then regularly monitor performance against those objectives.

The board must ensure that the corporate culture, the agreed strategy, management incentive compensation, and the company's approach to audit and accounting, internal controls, and disclosure are consistent and aligned.

The board must help management understand the expectations of shareholders, regulators, and the community. Boards should help management recognize that shareholders have a legitimate interest in meaningful input into the board selection process regarding both nominating procedures and voting methods. Similarly, boards can help management recognize and address the concerns that excessive compensation raises among shareholders, regulators, and rating agencies.

Enlightened Value Maximization

Enlightened value maximization recognizes that communication with and motivation of an organization's managers, employees, and partners is extremely difficult. If we simply tell all participants of an organization that its sole purpose is to maximize value, we will not get maximum value for the organization.

Value maximization is not a vision or a strategy or even a purpose. It is the scorecard for the organization. We must give people enough structure and context to understand what maximizing value means so that it can guide them. Therefore, they have a chance to actually achieve it. They must be enthusiastic about the vision or strategy in the sense that it taps into some human desire or passion of their own – for example, to design and build the world's best phone or to create a film or play that will touch peoples' emotions for decades. All this can be not only consistent with value-seeking but a major contributor to it.

Indeed, it is a basic principle of enlightened value maximization that we can't maximize the long-term market value of an organization if we ignore or ill-treat any important constituent. We cannot create value without good relations with customers, employees, suppliers, shareholders, institutions, regulators, and communities. We can use the value criterion for choosing among the competing interests. No constituent can be denied satisfaction if the firm is to survive and flourish. Moreover, we can be sure – apart from the possibility of externalities and monopoly power – that using this value criterion will result in making society as well off as possible.

Enlightened value theorists can see, even though shareholders are not some special constituency that ranks above all others, the long-term stock value is an important determinant (along with the value of debt and other instruments) of total long-term firm value. Value creation gives management a way to assess the tradeoffs among competing constituencies. It allows for principled decision-making, independent of the personal preferences of managers and directors.

Even though shareholder value maximization is increasingly under scrutiny on practical as well as moral grounds, its roots in private property law—a profound element in the American ethos—guarantee that it will continue to dominate the U.S. approach to corporate governance in the foreseeable future.

Summing Up

Corporate governance is a legal and regulatory compliance issue. In the 21st century landscape, a purely legal and regulatory framework is counterproductive. Respecting the law of the country is important. However, it is not sufficient for the sustained success of the business. Being legal and complying with regulation is not the same as being ethical or even socially responsible. Evidence suggests that organizations that follow the Triple Bottom Line concept (TBL) – of profit, people, and planet – outperform their peers. Profit with purpose and shared value are alternative constructs used to define the scope of corporate governance today.

Chapter 10

Corporate Governance Summary

The roots of corporate governance go back to the 1930s and the seminal work of Adolf Berle and Gardiner Means. Corporate governance as we know it today emanated in the 1970s. First, there was a shift from profit maximization to shareholder wealth maximization. Second, there was a distinct shift from producers to customers. Third, regulation created new boundaries for organizations. Over time, the term *stakeholder* replaced the word *shareholder*.

Today's organizations need to satisfy competing stakeholders. Shareholders expect good returns on their investment and value appreciation. Customers expect quality products and exemplary services. Employees expect fair compensation, benefits, a safe work environment, and a culture that fosters creativity and excellence. Suppliers expect stable and mutually beneficial relationships. Regulators expect compliance with the laws of the country. Society expects organizations to be good corporate citizens, espouse community interests, and improve the quality of life for everyone. Activists expect organizations to follow practices that do not harm the environment.

This section has explored how organizations can navigate through the conflicting expectations. Now that you have read it, the following learning outcomes should be apparent:

1. What is governance and why is it important?

2. What are the best practices in corporate governance?

3. What is the role of the board of directors?

4. What is the role of shareholders?

5. What constitutes successful board management?

Reflective Questions

Reflection Question #1: Billionaire Nelson Peltz heads Trian Fund Management, one of Proctor & Gamble's largest shareholders, with a $3.3 billion stake. Peltz does not like the direction that P&G has taken in recent years. He has pointed to disappointing shareholders returns, deteriorating market share, and excessive cost and bureaucracy. He argues that the company is highly resistant to change. Peltz wants to be on the board of P&G. The current board does not want him. The shadow fight has been going on for months. After a shareholder vote, the company claims that shareholders have rejected Nelson Pletz's candidature. Peltz disputes the claim and says the votes are too close and should be scrutinized by a third party.

Research the publicly available information on the fight for a place on P&G's board. Analyze the issue from a governance perspective. Would P&G be better off or worse off with Nelson Peltz as a director? Justify your answer.

Reflection Question #2: Germany-based Volkswagen is an 80-year old company. In 2012, Volkswagen was the second-largest automobile producer in the world. In 2013, Volkswagen had a rank of No. 9 in Fortune's Global 500 List. In 2014, Volkswagen produced over ten million vehicles. Volkswagen's troubles started when regulators discovered a software device designed to fool emission tests.

Volkswagen's vehicles did not meet the emission standards. The company installed software to show acceptable results whenever regulators conducted emission tests. The scandal is one of the largest in the history of automobiles. Volkswagen has agreed to pay fines totaling $20 billion. The company has agreed to modify millions of cars to meet emission standards. The CEO has stepped down.

Analyze the effects of the emission scandal from a governance perspective. Who is responsible for the blunder? Should the entire board be held accountable? Why or why not? Can you develop a case for criminal liability? Why or why not? What lessons can you learn from the scandal?

Section 3
Strategic Planning

Management planning has been defined as the process of setting and assessing an organization's goals and then determining a detailed course of action for achieving the goals. In other words, planning is asking and answering the following questions:

What do we want to achieve? A majority of organizations answer: to create profits. A generic answer such as profits raises further questions—how much profit? Even assuming that achieving profit is a worthy goal, you need to relate that to another variable—investment, assets, or equity.

A more important question to ask is: *Why do we want to achieve X?* Most try to find a rational justification for the goal. Without such a justification, one may be tempted to adopt questionable means to achieve said goal. Next, we need to set a time frame for achieving the goals. Do we wish to achieve our goals in five years? Ten years?

Once you are clear about the goals and the time frame, the critical question arises: *How do we achieve the goals?* You need to consider various alternatives; for example, whether to offer the best possible product or service and charge a premium price, or whether to keep costs down and charge a low price. Should we address a local, state, regional, national, or global market? Where do we locate our facilities? How do we put together a great team?

This section tries to provide you with answers. Specifically, by reading and understanding this section, you should be able to:

1. **Understand** the concept of planning in general, and strategic planning in particular.

2. **Appreciate** the idea of strategy as an emergent process.

3. **Comprehend** strategic decision making, challenges, and techniques for improvement.

4. **Recognize** the role of strategic leadership in achieving goals.

5. **Design** suitable organizational structures for achieving your stated goals.

6. **Realize** the role of strategic control systems in achieving your stated goals.

Chapter 11

Planning as a Process

Organizing involves developing an organizational structure and allocating human resources to ensure the accomplishment of objectives.

Planning involves the setting of goals and a detailed blue-print or course of action to achieve the goals. Planning has different time horizons – daily, weekly, monthly, quarterly, yearly, multi-yearly, and longer time horizons.

Planning is carried out at all levels—at the operational level, at the level of supervisors and middle managers, and at the top management level. The emphasis at each level is different.

Inevitably, planning involves choices. You can achieve a given goal by following different alternatives. Which particular alternative to choose in a given situation is at the heart of decision-making.

The Planning Process

Planning is a three-step process. The first step is to research the issue at hand. For example, if one is trying to establish a promotional plan, research should focus on the target market. This step is known as environmental scanning. The second step is to establish SMART (Specific, Measurable, Achievable, Relevant, and Timely) goals based on the research. Finally, you need to detail action steps for achieving each of the goals. Thus, planning involves the setting of objectives and determining a course of action for achieving them. Planning requires that managers be aware of environmental conditions facing their organization and have the ability to forecast future conditions. Planning also requires managers to be good decision makers.

Organizing is the process of arranging tasks or resources for optimal performance.

Planning is done at different levels:

1. **Strategic** – usually carried out by top management; analyzes strengths, weaknesses, opportunities, and threats; determines competitive positioning for competing effectively; has a long-term focus; based on organization's mission and vision.

   In 1990, when Walmart had revenues of just $46 billion, Sam Walton declared his vision to achieve $125 billion in revenue by the year 2000. Even his close friends thought the plan was unrealistic. By constantly initiating steps to achieve the over-arching objective, Walmart achieved $125 billion in 1996 – four years ahead of schedule. The EDLP (Every Day Low Pricing) model of Walmart has succeeded beyond expectations. The company remains No. 1 on the Fortune 500 list with revenues of nearly $500 billion.

2. **Tactical** – usually carried out by mid-level managers; designed to align with the strategic plan; details activities at the business unit level for achieving objectives; has a time horizon of one to three years.

   In the technology sector, customers constantly look for improvements and innovations. Companies such as Apple and Samsung routinely introduce 4–6 new variants of their products every year. The entire consumer durables industry uses incremental improvements to attract customers.

3. **Operational** – carried out across the organization; aligns with strategic and tactical plans; outlines day-to-day activities; time horizon can be daily, weekly, bi-monthly or monthly.

   Fast-food chains such as McDonald's and D omino's track sales across their chains every day. Software companies track project progress on an hourly basis. Airlines monitor flight performance in real time to ensure on-time departures and arrivals.

Organizing is the process of arranging tasks or resources for optimal performance. Organizing facilitates an efficient work environment and increases the probability of employees achieving their goals at work.

Organizing involves developing an organizational structure and allocating human resources to ensure the accomplishment of objectives. The structure is the framework within which you coordinate the effort. The structure provides a representation of the chain of command within an organization. Decisions related to the structure are known as organizational design decisions.

Organizing also involves the design of individual jobs. You have to decide the roles, duties, and responsibilities of individuals, and the manner in which the duties should be carried out. Decisions made about individual jobs are known as job design decisions. Organizing is a mechanism for clustering jobs to coordinate the effort effectively.

Methods for clustering include:

1. Functional (marketing, finance, human resources, and operations)

2. Geographical (Americas, Europe, South Asia, Asia-Pacific, Middle East)

3. Product-based (computers, phones, TV, on-demand services)

4. Divisional (business units)

5. Matrix (used in project management where an individual may report to two persons)

6. Flat (with minimal hierarchy), Cooperative, and Competitive. Current trends in organizational design focus on empowering employees and creating synergy instead of charts, which may not mean much.

Planning	Organizing	Leading	Controlling
1. Vision & Mission	1. Organization Design	1. Leadership	1. Systems/Processes
2. Strategizing	2. Culture	2. Decision Making	2. Strategic Human Resources
3. Goals & Objectives	3. Social Networks	3. Communications	
		4. Groups/Teams	
		5. Motivation	

Figure 11.1. Specific Activities within the Four Heads of Planning, Organizing, Leading, and Controlling.

Strategic Planning

Strategic planning is an organizational management activity that is used to set priorities, focus energy on resources, strengthen operations, ensure that employees and other stakeholders are working toward common goals, establish agreement around intended outcomes/results, and assess and adjust the organization's direction in response to a changing environment.

Strategic planning is a disciplined effort that produces fundamental decisions and actions shaping and guiding what an organization is, whom it serves, what it does, and why it does it, with a focus on the future. Effective strategic planning articulates not only where an organization is going and the actions needed to make progress, but also how it will know if it is successful.

The Association of Strategic Planning (ASP), has developed a Lead – Think – Plan – Act rubric to capture and disseminate best practices in the field of strategic planning and management. The criteria developed by the non-profit ASP are:

- Use a Systems Approach that starts with the end in mind.

- Incorporate Change Management and Leadership Development to transform an organization to high performance effectively.

- Provide Actionable Performance Information leading to better decisions.

- Incorporate Assessment-Based Inputs of the external and internal environment, and an understanding of customers and stakeholder needs and expectations.

- Include Strategic Initiatives to focus attention on the most important performance improvement projects.

- Offer a Supporting Toolkit, including terminology, concepts, steps, tools, and techniques that are flexible and scalable.

- Align Strategy and Culture, with a focus on results and the drivers of results.

- Integrate existing Organization Systems and align the organization around Strategy.

- Be simple to administer, clear to understand and direct, and deliver practical benefits over the long-term.

- Incorporate Learning and Feedback, to promote Continuous Long-Term Improvement.

Decision making is the process of making choices by setting goals, gathering information, and assessing alternative options. The process usually has seven steps:

1. Identify the decision to be made

2. Gather relevant information

3. Identify alternatives

4. Weigh evidence

5. Choose among alternatives

6. Take action

7. Review decision and consequences

Decision-making requires patience, objectivity, and intelligence. Patience is needed to overcome the desire to get the decision-making over with and eliminate uncertainty. Patience allows us to sit with uncertainty and accept it. Patience implies using the time available as effectively as possible, avoiding analysis paralysis, avoiding the panic and the rush.

Planning occurs at different levels –
strategic, tactical, and operational.

Objectivity is needed to clear one's mind of the emotional attachment to an idea because one owns it. Objectivity requires questioning everything. Objectivity implies that greed, ignorance, and anger do not drive your decisions. Objectivity also implies the kind of pragmatism that enables decision-makers to accept less than perfect outcomes.

Intelligence has two meanings. One is about the information required to make an effective decision. The other is the ability to acquire and use knowledge and experience. Without the right information, even the most intelligent people are likely to make poor decisions. Without the ability to acquire and synthesize the information at hand, the decision will be poor, even with huge amounts of the right information.

When we combine patience, objectivity, and intelligence, we have the factors that make for effective decisions. Effective decisions are a critical factor for successful projects.

A project is a temporary endeavor undertaken to create a unique product, service, or result. A project is temporary in that it has a defined beginning and end in time, and therefore, a defined scope and resources. A project is unique in that it is not a routine operation, but a specific set of operations to accomplish a singular goal. Thus, a project may include people who normally do not work together and sometimes may have people from different organizations and geographies.

The development of a product or service, improvement of a business process, construction of a public transport system, the relief effort after a natural disaster – these are all projects. They have resource and time constraints, and quality requirements. Project teams must learn from the processes and methods they deploy, and the learning needs to be codified and stored for possible use in the future.

Project Management is the application of knowledge, skills, tools, and techniques to project initiatives to meet the project requirements.

Summing Up

Planning occurs at different levels – strategic, tactical, and operational. The scope and time horizon shrink as we move from strategic to operational levels.

Organizing is the process of arranging tasks or resources for optimal performance. Organizing involves structure and culture.

Strategic planning focuses on the future—usually a time horizon of three to five years. The Lead – Think – Plan – Act rubric is a useful tool for strategic planning and management.

Decision-making is the process of making choices by setting goals, gathering information, and assessing alternative options. Decision-making requires patience, objectivity, and intelligence.

A project is a temporary endeavor undertaken to create a unique product, service, or result. Project management is the application of knowledge, skills, tools, and techniques to project initiatives to meet the project requirements.

Chapter **12**

Deliberate and Emergent Strategies

Despite the many criticisms, research suggests that formal planning systems do help managers make better strategic decisions than random approaches.

The traditional notion of strategic planning states it is a deliberate and rational process. Such a view holds, to a certain extent, in mature and stable industries.

Today, the competitive environment has three critical components – uncertainty, complexity, and ambiguity. Under such an environment, holding onto a deliberate strategy regardless of the outcome is a recipe for disaster.

Adaptation is the key to success. Thus, new strategies can emerge out of failed strategies. Organizations need to rapidly change their approach in the face of new information.

A consequence of adaptation is scenario planning—being ready with different approaches to respond to changing situations or scenarios. The scenario planning process is a useful tool for planning under conditions of uncertainty, complexity, and ambiguity.

The basic assumption behind strategic planning is that planning can be a rational and structured process. Many scholars have criticized the formal planning model for three reasons:

1. Unpredictability of the real world

2. The role that lower-level managers play in the strategic management process

3. Many successful strategies are the result of serendipity, not rational strategizing

Strategy under Uncertainty

The business environment today is characterized by uncertainty, complexity, and ambiguity. The most carefully drawn strategic plans can be rendered useless in the light of relentless change.

The race for autonomously-driven automobiles is a classic example to illustrate the futility of formal planning systems. All the major companies have invested in this nascent field. Tesla, GM, Toyota, Ford, Honda, and Volvo have committed billions of dollars to be the first to exploit the technology commercially. There is a distinct possibility that new entrants such as drive.ai, a start-up founded by former lab mates of Stanford University's Artificial Intelligence Lab may outsmart the incumbents. The start-up is working on creating AI software based on *deep learning* for autonomous vehicles.

Google's *pay-per-click* business model disrupted the online advertising industry in wholly unpredictable ways. Players like Microsoft and Yahoo were forced to change their strategies.

Even so, the results have not been satisfactory. After a four-year struggle, Yahoo's internet business has been acquired by Verizon.

Rapid adaptations to changing environments run counter to the framework of traditional strategic planning models with their emphasis on the long-term and the inherent rigidity in modeling.

Autonomy and the Role of Lower-level Managers in Strategy

Conventional wisdom has glamorized the strategic planning process as a process driven by top management, particularly by the CEO. Research shows that the default position of CEOs is the status quo because of their emotional attachment to a particular strategic direction. To that extent, top management is often a conservative force that causes inertia.

Disruptive change, on the other hand, is likely to emanate at lower levels. Lower-level managers are not bound emotionally to a strategic direction and are willing to take chances. One can argue that in truly autonomous organizations, the operational level executives may be the ones to spot a change and to suggest ways of meeting the challenge.

Intel was a company that focused on DRAM memory chips (Dynamic Random Access Memory). As recounted by Andy Grove, the shift from memory chips to RISC-based microprocessors was a strategy shift driven by field personnel. Top management had no role in this strategy except embracing the change when R&D was able to develop the first microprocessor

– the 4004 chip developed in 1971. The processor had 2,300 transistors. The latest generation (2016) microprocessors have a transistor count of over 5 billion.

Starbucks is known for coffee. Its foray into music was not an initiative driven from the top. Rather, the manager of the company's Seattle University outlet, Tim Jones, used to bring his collection of tapes to play in the outlet. Soon, customers wanted copies of the music. Tim suggested to CEO Howard Schultz that Starbucks could sell its music. It took considerable lobbying by Tim for the skeptical CEO to approve.

Today, Starbucks has its own downloading app and recently launched a new digital music experience with leading streaming music service Spotify, allowing Starbucks Mobile App customers to immediately discover music playing overhead in Starbucks stores, save Starbucks-curated songs to a playlist on Spotify and listen to Starbucks music anywhere they go. This music experience, driven by an operational level manager, reaches customers at over 7,500 Starbucks company-operated stores in the U.S., 10 million My Starbucks Rewards loyalty members, and U.S. Spotify users.

Many planned strategies fail because of unpredicted changes in the environment.

Serendipity and Strategy

Many successful strategies are not the result of well-thought-out plans, but of serendipity; that is, stumbling across good things unintentionally.

When IBM developed the personal computer, it was looking for an operating system. Bill Gates learned about this and started visiting the many independent developers working on operating system software. One of these had a version that had many bugs in it and was called QDOS, for Quick and Dirty Operating System. Bill Gates negotiated with the developer, and using a loan from his father, bought the software for $50,000. He fixed the bugs, made some refinements, licensed it to IBM as PC-DOS, and a little later, started marketing the software as MS-DOS. The rest, as they say, is history. The paradox is that the QDOS developer was close to IBM's headquarters and yet no one in the company knew about the software. What is more, the leader in its category, instead of buying exclusive rights to the software, tried to save money by licensing, thus paving the way for Microsoft to emerge.

3M was producing fluorocarbons for sale as a coolant in air-conditioning equipment. A researcher working with fluorocarbons accidentally spilled some of the liquid on her shoes. Later, when she spilled some coffee on her shoes, she noticed that the coffee formed little beads and ran off, without leaving a stain.

Thus was born the idea to protect fabrics from liquid stains, along with Scotchgard, one of the most profitable products of 3M in a category that it had never planned to enter. Similar is the story of Post-It Notes, which was developed accidentally by an employee looking for a suitable bookmark for use during Sunday services at his church.

Intended and Emergent Strategies

Henry Mintzberg has argued that a company's realized strategy is the product of whatever planned strategies are put into action (the company's deliberate strategies) and of any unplanned or emergent strategies. Many planned strategies fail because of unpredicted changes in the environment (that is, they are unrealized).

Emergent strategies are the unplanned responses to unforeseen circumstances. They arise from autonomous action by individual managers deep within the organization, serendipitous discoveries or events, or an unplanned strategic shift by top-level managers in response to changed circumstances. They are not the product of top-down planning mechanisms.

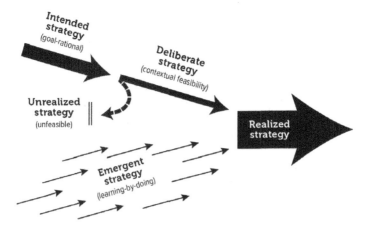

Figure 12.1. Understanding Realized Strategy from Intended and Emergent Strategies, adapted from Mintzberg (1985).

Mintzberg maintained that emergent strategies are often successful and may be a better fit for the organization than intended strategies.

Honda Motor Co. wanted to enter the U.S. motorcycle market with 250 CC and 350 CC motorcycles (intended strategy). The attempt was a disaster (unrealized strategy). Executives of Sears Roebuck and Co., who watched the Japanese executives driving around Los Angeles on 50 CC mopeds, were eager to sell the line through their retail outlets. Selling motorcycles through a general retailer rather than a specialty motorcycle retailer was an unexplored channel. So was the opportunity to sell 50 CC mopeds (emergent strategy). By 1964, one out of every two motorcycles sold in the United States was a Honda.

The critical point demonstrated by this example is that successful strategies can often emerge within an organization without prior planning and in response to unforeseen circumstances. Mintzberg has noted that strategies can take root wherever people have the capacity to learn and the resources to support that capacity.

Thus, while the emergent strategy took shape far away from Honda's headquarters, credit should be given to the Japanese management for recognizing the strength of the emergent strategy and for pursuing it with rigor.

In practice, the strategies of most organizations are probably a combination of the intended (planned) and the emergent.

Strategic Planning in Practice

Despite the many criticisms, research suggests that formal planning systems do help managers make better strategic decisions than random approaches. A study of strategic planning in over 600 companies found that both formal planning methodologies and emergent strategies form part of a good strategy formulation process, particularly in unstable and dynamic environments.

For strategic planning to work, it is important that top-level managers plan, not just in the context of the current competitive environment, but also in the context of the future competitive environment. It is also important that these managers involve operational managers in the planning process as they seek to shape the future competitive environment by emphasizing strategic intent.

Scenario Planning

One reason that strategic planning may fail over the long run is that strategic managers, in their initial enthusiasm for planning techniques, may forget that the future is inherently unpredictable. Even the best-laid plans can fall apart if unforeseen contingencies arise; that happens all the time in the real world.

Scenario Planning involves formulating plans involving what-if scenarios about the future. In the typical scenario-planning exercise, some scenarios are optimistic, and some scenarios are pessimistic. Teams of managers are asked to develop specific strategies for each scenario. A set of indicators is chosen as signposts to track trends and identify the probability that any particular scenario is coming to pass.

The idea is to encourage managers to understand the dynamic and complex nature of the environment, to think through problems in a strategic fashion, and to generate an alternate range of strategic options that the organization might pursue under different circumstances.

Scenario Planning at Royal Dutch Shell. Royal Dutch Shell can be said to have pioneered scenario planning. Pierre Wack, the *Father of Scenarios*, headed Shell's Global Planning Division in the 1970s. He successfully applied scenario planning to the oil crisis of the 1970s. Wack fostered the belief that a business which imagines multiple ways the future may unfold is better prepared to overcome challenges and seize opportunities.

Today, Shell's 40-year experience with scenarios encompasses three hard truths:

1. Global energy demand is surging

2. Supply will struggle to keep up

3. Climate change is a pressing reality

Consequently, Shell looks at two scenarios:

1. **Blueprints** – an energy future in which emerging coalitions of interests eventually accelerate regulatory developments and the implementation of lower-carbon energy and technology.

2. **Scramble** – a future based on governments focusing narrowly on their energy interests, neglecting demand-side management, and leaving them unprepared for broader supply stresses until it is too late.

Decentralized Planning

The most common error in strategic planning is to treat it as an exclusively top management responsibility. This ivory tower planning can result in strategic plans formulated in a vacuum by top managers who have little understanding or appreciation of current operating realities. As a result, top managers may formulate strategies that do more harm than good. The ivory tower concept of planning can also lead to tensions between corporate, business, and functional level managers.

When family sizes decreased to parents and their children, the top managers at GE concluded that the small families would require smaller appliances. The range of small appliances subsequently developed by GE was a disaster. The top managers did not consult home builders and retailers. They did not even consult their operating personnel.

The key to success is adaptation and agility.

Had they made the necessary inquiries, they would have realized that, even though family size had decreased, the size of kitchens and bathrooms had not. When couples both worked, there was a demand for larger refrigerators (due to less frequent visits to the grocery store) and larger washing machines (with capacities to take weekly or fortnightly laundry loads). Thus, centralized or ivory tower planning failed.

Again, GE had corporate level managers drawn from consulting companies or Ivy League business schools. As a result, functional and business-level managers felt alienated and deprived of opportunities for growth. Even when corporate managers were right, lower-level managers opposed their ideas.

For instance, top managers rightly diagnosed the emerging threat from Japanese companies as a consequence of the forces of globalization. On the contrary, lower-level managers looked at Sears Roebuck as their main competition and refused to take pro-active steps to meet the new competition. The result was GE lost out on the appliances market.

Successful strategic planning cuts across organizational levels. Functional and business-level managers should do the bulk of planning. The role of corporate-level managers should be to facilitate the plans drawn to be in alignment with broad strategic goals and then to provide the resources needed to ensure that the organization achieved its goals.

Summing Up

The traditional notion of strategic planning states it is a deliberate and rational process. Such a view holds, to a certain extent, in mature and stable industries.

Today, the competitive environment has three critical components—uncertainty, complexity, and ambiguity. Under such an environment, holding onto a deliberate strategy regardless of the outcome is a recipe for disaster.

Adaptation is the key to success. Thus, new strategies can emerge out of failed strategies. Organizations need to rapidly change their approach in the face of new information.

Emergent strategies are the result of adaptation in the face of failure. Of course, in stable and mature industries, a well-thought-out strategy might well succeed. Thus, we have a range of strategies from planned, to realized, to emergent.

Since the future is unpredictable, organizations should look at various scenarios—alternatives that might occur in the future—and plan for those scenarios.

The scenario planning process is a useful tool in considering alternatives in the face of uncertainty.

Chapter **13**

Strategic
Decision Making

*The success of strategic planning depends on
the extent to which accurate and timely information
is available to make decisions.*

You may claim that your decisions are rational and objective. Such rationality and objectivity have boundaries. You also have cognitive biases and limitations. The biases include confirmation bias, escalating commitment, reasoning by analogy, representativeness, and the illusion of control.

The biases and limitations lead many of your decisions to failure. Techniques to improve decision-making include Devil's Advocacy, Dialectic Inquiry, and Reference Class Decision Making.

The success of strategic planning depends on the extent to which accurate and timely information is available to make decisions. Even with the ready availability of information, decisions can fail due to cognitive biases inherent in the decision-making process. Thus, even good managers make bad decisions. The first step in avoiding this is to understand the various biases that can creep into decisions.

*The first step in overcoming biases
is to understand them.*

Cognitive Biases in Decision Making

Herbert Simon has argued the rationality of human decision makers is bounded by their cognitive capabilities and limitations. Since your capacity to process information is limited, you tend to follow certain rules of thumb—or heuristics—while making decisions. These rules lead to systematic errors in decision-making—that is, errors that occur again and again. Some cognitive biases have been proven to prevail repeatedly in laboratory settings. We all are prone to them. The first step in overcoming the biases is to understand them.

Prior Hypothesis Bias or Confirmation Bias – the tendency to interpret and search for information, and to make decisions thereof, that are consistent with one's prior beliefs. In the late 1960s and 1970s, the big three U.S. automobile makers believed customers were looking for luxury and styling because this was consistent with their experience of the previous decade. They completely overlooked the oil crisis and the need for fuel-efficient and safe cars. The Japanese automakers seized the opportunity and took away valuable market share. Today, over 40% of cars in America have a foreign label on them.

Escalating Commitment – the tendency to continue committing resources to projects, even when these projects show clear signs of failing. For example, the Long Island Lighting Company started a project to build a nuclear power plant on Long Island in 1966. The project was supposed to go operational by 1973, and the estimated cost was $75 million. The company abandoned the project in 1986 without producing any energy, after a colossal investment of over $6 billion.

Reasoning by Analogy – the tendency to make inappropriate decisions based on simple analogies. For example, many managers compare business competition to war. In this analogy, you can only win at someone's expense. Management is considered a zero-sum game. Such managers will inevitably fail when they are required to cooperate, as in the case of joint ventures.

Representativeness – the tendency to generalize from a single sample or even a single vivid anecdote. Many online retailers have tried to replicate the success of Amazon but without success. The enormous success of Google has spawned scores of companies that have just faded into oblivion. The rapid expansion of—and the equally rapid collapse of—dot-com companies is attributable to reasoning by analogy and representativeness.

The Illusion of Control – the tendency to overestimate one's ability to control events. Richard Roll argues that such overconfidence leads to what he has termed the *hubris hypothesis* of takeovers. Top managers typically are overconfident about their ability to create value by acquiring other companies. The overconfidence lets them pay much more than warranted for the acquisition. Servicing the debt taken on to finance the acquisition makes it all but impossible to make money from the transaction.

Microsoft's acquisitions are classic examples. The software giant took a combined $13.9 billion in write-downs on its acquisitions of online ad company aQuantive (2007) and phone maker Nokia (2014). The company has little to show for its $8.5 billion purchase of Skype (2011). In 2016, the company has acquired LinkedIn for $26.2 billion in cash, an amount not warranted either by LinkedIn's revenues or by its profits.

Availability Error – arises from our predisposition to estimate the probability of an outcome, based on how easy the outcome is to imagine. For example, more people seem to fear a plane crash than a car accident. Statistically, one is far more likely to be killed in a car on the way to the airport than in a plane crash. They overestimate the probability of a plane crash because the outcome is easier to imagine and because plane crashes are more vivid events than car crashes, which affect relatively small numbers of people at a time. As a result of the availability error, managers might allocate resources to a project whose outcome is easier to imagine than one that might have the highest return.

Techniques to Improve Decision Making

Devil's Advocacy – requires the generation of both a plan and a critical evaluation of the plan. One member of the decision-making group acts as the devil's advocate, bringing out all the reasons that might make the plan or proposal unacceptable. Decision makers can thus become aware of the possible perils of a recommended course of action. With open minds, the group can mitigate the perils or even jettison the plan.

Dialectic Inquiry – is a team-based approach that requires the development of a plan (a thesis) and a counterplan (an antithesis) that reflect plausible but conflicting courses of action. Strategic managers can debate with both teams as to which proposal might lead to higher performance. Quite often, such a process can lead to a new and more encompassing conceptualization of the problem, which can then form the basis for a final plan (or synthesis).

Outside View or Reference Class Decision Making – proposed by the Nobel Laureate Daniel Kahneman and associates, requires planners to identify a reference class of analogous past strategic initiatives, determine whether those initiatives succeeded or failed, and then evaluate the project on hand against the past initiatives. According to Kahneman, this technique is particularly useful in countering the illusion of control (hubris), reasoning by analogy, and representativeness. He provides this illuminating—if embarrassing—example:

The inside view (that is, an estimate of the members of a team) was that a book project could be completed in a mean time of two years (with an optimistic estimate of a year-and-a-half and a pessimistic estimate of two-and-a-half years).

The outside view (considering the time taken by others in similar situations, as noted by an expert) was a minimum of seven years and a maximum of ten years, with 40% of the sample failing to complete the project altogether.

Despite such stark evidence, the team decided to go ahead – and completed the book project in eight years! By then, the initial enthusiasm of the sponsors had reduced significantly, and there was no reason to use the book.

Summing Up

It is not possible to be rational and objective at all times. This is because we have limitations and biases in our thinking. These biases range from our propensity to generalize from one or a limited amount of information to illusions of control.

You can mitigate the effect of the biases and improve decisions by following methods such as Devil's Advocacy, Dialectic Inquiry, and Reference Class Decision Making.

Chapter 14

Strategic Leadership in Planning

A critical success factor for high-performance organizations is the need for both general and functional managers to use their knowledge, skills, energy, and enthusiasm to provide strategic leadership to their team members.

Strategic leadership in planning exhibits certain key characteristics:

- The ability to develop a compelling vision and articulate it consistently.

- A sound business model rooted in a strong foundation.

- Commitment—to the organization, to the colleagues, customers, and other stakeholders.

- Knowledge and the wisdom to appropriately use it.

- Willingness to delegate, empower, and coach.

- Astute use of power.

- Emotional and spiritual intelligence.

Skills of Strategic Leaders in Planning

A critical success factor for high-performance organizations is the need for both general and functional managers to use their knowledge, skills, energy, and enthusiasm to provide strategic leadership to their team members.

The key characteristics of good strategic leaders, as identified by scholars, are vision, articulation, and consistency; a sound business model that everyone can relate to; commitment; being well informed; willingness to delegate, empower, and coach; an astute use of power; emotional intelligence; and spiritual intelligence.

Vision, articulation, and consistency: A compelling vision is the starting point for a high-performance organization. Gary Hamel has argued that vision or strategic intent should lead to stretch goals—the envisioned future state must be worthy of pursuit; challenging but attainable.

Bill Gates envisioned a computer on every desk. Practically all that he envisioned has turned into reality. Jack Welch relentlessly pursued the goal of GE being the first or second player in every business portfolio. Neither his predecessor nor his successor matched Welch's performance. Sam Walton's theme of passing on the twin benefits of cost savings from suppliers and efficient operations to customers in the form of everyday low prices are all examples of audacious but attainable goals.

Sound Business Model – a business model is a manager's conception of how the strategies pursued by a company fit into a congruent whole. Dell's business model is rooted in direct sales and configured-to-order concepts. By doing away with intermediaries and providing customers with computers built according to the customer's specifications, the company was able to rapidly move ahead in the PC industry. Whether it can sustain the growth from the initial years, particularly after Michael Dell's decision to make it private in 2013, remains to be seen. Dell's acquisition of EMC closed in September 2016. The new company, known as Dell Technologies, is one of the largest high-tech mergers/acquisitions, valued at $63 billion.

Southwest Airlines' business model, crafted by the brilliant Herbert Kelleher, is centered around cost leadership. The airline uses just one type of aircraft; the fuel-efficient Boeing 737. Southwest eliminated intermediaries and offered limited destinations. The Federal Aviation Administration has consistently ranked Southwest number one on timely departures and arrivals, and efficient service. All these factors have allowed the airline to maintain a competitive edge, even during periods of economic downturn.

Commitment – leaders walk the talk and practice the precept. In other words, they lead by example. Ken Iverson, the legendary CEO of Nucor for many years, led the company in its relentless drive to minimize costs in the notoriously competitive steel industry. He drew the lowest salary among Fortune 500 CEOs, flew coach class, stayed in modest hotels, drove his own car, had only one secretary, and led a simple life. Iverson has retired, but his legacy lives on. Nucor takes pride in its ability to recycle scrap into quality steel.

IKEA's Ingvar Kamprad, at one time one of the richest people on the planet, drove an older Volvo car well into his eighties, and always flew economy class. The company's business model—with its sharp focus on sustainability and waste elimination—has few parallels.

Being well informed – great leaders develop formal and informal networks inside and outside their organizations to get a real sense of what is going on—within their organizations and in the industry.

Jack Welch was fond of visiting GE's manufacturing facilities unannounced. Records suggest that one of the first things he would do when visiting a plant was to observe the cleanliness and hygiene in the restrooms.

> *SAS, the Scandinavian Airline System,*
> *introduced an extreme form of*
> *delegation and empowerment.*

Very early in Hewlett Packard's history, the founders would frequently go to the shop floor, greeting employees and making polite inquiries about their families. This practice was so powerful in creating a bond between employees and management that it has morphed into a management concept–MBWA–Management by Walking (or Wandering) Around. Such interactions are key because traditional channels often have gatekeepers who filter out any discomforting information.

Willingness to delegate, empower, and coach – leaders understand the limits of their capabilities and over time, voluntarily spin off decision making to subordinates. The lower the level where a given decision is made, the higher the degree of empowerment. SAS, the Scandinavian Airline System, introduced an extreme form of delegation and empowerment by committing that:

The first employee that a customer met would be able to solve the customer's problem—be it booking a flight, or making a cancellation, getting a refund, obtaining information, or concern about service.

The precedent-setting innovation came after a yearlong interaction with customers in an experiment called *Moments of Truth*—the few minutes that a customer may interact with an employee. Professor Sidney Finkelstein of the Tuck School of Business, who introduced the term *Superbosses*, argues that great leaders typically coach and mentor their immediate reports to be great leaders as well. The late J.R.D. Tata of India was a phenomenal leader who coached a number of his protégés to become CEOs of group companies.

Astute use of power – for decades, scholars have argued that position power is among the least important sources of power in an organization. Edward Wrapp defines the astute use of power as the ability to build consensus. Jeffrey Pfeffer has articulated the notion of the *intelligent use of power* as the ability to harness the power of human resources similar to leveraging capital, information, and knowledge resources. Thus, one can be at any level in an organization and yet influence outcomes in a significant manner.

Emotional and Spiritual Intelligence – Daniel Goldman coined the term emotional intelligence to describe several attributes many leaders exhibit—self-awareness, self-regulation, motivation, empathy, and social skills—friendliness with a purpose. Leaders with these attributes tend to be more effective than those who lack the attributes.

Spiritual intelligence, according to Paul Tillich, is the domain of ultimate concern, defined in humanistic terms as living the full possibilities of being human authentically.

Summing Up

Strategic leadership exhibits certain key characteristics:

- The ability to develop a compelling vision and articulate it consistently.

- A sound business model rooted in a strong foundation.

- Commitment—to the organization, to the colleagues, customers, and other stakeholders.

- Knowledge and the wisdom to appropriately use it.

- Willingness to delegate, empower, and coach.

- Astute use of power.

- Emotional and spiritual intelligence.

Chapter 15

Organizational Structure

*Organizational structure assigns employees
to specific value creation activities and roles.*

Strategy drives organizational structure. Structures take different forms: Simple, Functional, Web, Matrix, and Divisional. Experimental structures currently under development are Holacracy, Sociocracy, and Teal.

As an organization grows, it moves from a simple to a functional to a divisional, matrix, or web structure. Unicorns that have risen quickly to the top of their industries are also trying new structures—rather, the absence of any specific structure.

Traditional Organizational Structures

Strategy implementation involves the use of organizational design, the process of deciding how a company should create, use, and combine organizational structure, control systems, and culture in order to pursue a business model successfully.

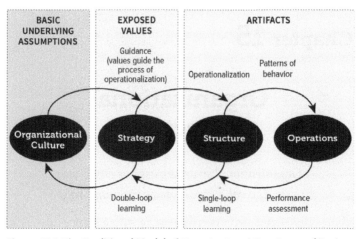

Figure 15.1. The Traditional Model of Organizational Structure and Design.

Organizational structure assigns employees to specific value creation activities and roles. The organization specifies how these activities and roles are to be linked together to achieve superior efficiency, quality, innovation, and customer responsiveness—the building blocks of competitive advantage. The objective of organizational structure is to coordinate and integrate the efforts of all employees to achieve synergy and fulfillment of the organization's strategies.

> *Organizational structure, control, and culture shape people's behaviors, values, and attitudes and determine how they will implement an organization's business model and strategies.*

Organizational structure by itself does not guarantee performance because the structure does not motivate on its own. Thus, there is a need for control systems. The purpose of a control system is to provide managers with a set of incentives to motivate employees toward increasing efficiency, quality, innovation, and customer responsiveness. The control system will also provide feedback on performance that can drive employees at all levels to embrace continuous improvement as a key driving force.

Organizational culture is the collection of values, norms, beliefs, and attitudes which are shared by people and groups in an organization. The organizational culture controls the way people and groups interact with each other and with stakeholders outside the organization.

Organizational structure, control, and culture shape people's behaviors, values, and attitudes and determine how they will implement an organization's business model and strategies. Effective organizational design allows a company to obtain a competitive advantage and achieve above-average profitability.

Managers must make three choices while designing an organizational structure:

1. How best to group activities into functions and to group functions into departments, divisions, or business units to create distinctive competencies and to pursue a particular strategy.

2. How to allocate authority and accountability to the functions, departments, divisions, or business units.

3. How to increase the level of coordination or integration between functions, departments, divisions, and business units as a structure evolves and becomes complex.

The business historian Alfred Chandler studied some U.S. corporations and concluded that organizational structure follows the range and variety of tasks that the organization chooses to pursue. The organizational structure changes in a predictable way as strategy changes over time.

A function is a collection of people who work together and perform similar tasks or hold similar positions in the organization. For example, the salespeople in a car dealership belong to the sales function. The sales function could be a part of a marketing department that includes market research, prospecting, pricing, promotion, distribution, and service functions.

As organizations grow, they can be organized into divisions or business units to reduce bureaucratic costs of information and knowledge transfer between functions and departments. For example, a large car dealership could have separate divisions for sedans, SUVs, and sports vehicles.

When an entity is autonomous regarding developing a strategy, renders itself for meaningful measurement of key performance indicators, and under certain circumstances, can compete on its steam, it is called a business unit or strategic business unit (SBU).

A small organization in the initial stages tends to follow a simple structure. The owner/entrepreneur makes all the key decisions, there are no departments or divisions, and everyone reports to the owner. The span of control is as wide as the number of employees. Authority is centralized and rests with the owner. There is little or no formal process for any activity or process, and the day-to-day operations are tuned to the requirements of the owner. In the initial stages of a small organization, the simple structure yields the desired result.

As the organization grows and becomes unwieldy for one person to manage, it typically morphs into a functional structure. A functional structure is made up of the key areas required for an organization to operate smoothly—marketing, finance, operations, human resources, information technology, and innovation/research and development. The functional structure lends itself to cost leadership and differentiation strategies.

When *cost leadership* is the chosen strategy, operations and procurement are the key drivers of value creation.

When *differentiation* is the chosen strategy, the focus is on innovation (research and development) and marketing. Apple's ability to command premium prices is due to its relentless emphasis on design (innovation) and marketing (Apple Stores, iTunes). Apple also follows the principle of flat organization, with minimal layers, and easy accessibility. Thus, it combines the functional and web structures.

While the hierarchy of authority and span of control are important concepts, top managers would do well to follow a basic organizing principle: the principle of the minimum chain of command. This principle states that a company should choose the hierarchy with the fewest levels of authority necessary to use organizational resources efficiently and effectively.

Within the context of a divisional structure, one can envisage:

- **Product-based structure** – a diversified company could thus have an industrial electronics division, a home appliances division, and a components division.

- **Market-based structure** – residential, commercial, and government.

- **Geography-based structure** – Americas, Europe, South Asia, Asia-Pacific, and the Middle East.

- **Process-based structure** – customer acquisition, order fulfillment, service, and research and development.

Matrix Organizational Structure

A matrix organizational structure does not follow the traditional, hierarchical model. Instead, employees typically have dual reporting relationships. For example, one relationship relies on functions such as marketing, sales, and service. Another relationship relies on products – industrial electronics, home appliances, and components.

A solid line in a matrix structure represents a strong, direct-reporting relationship. A dotted line in a matrix structure represents the secondary relationship, which is not as strong as the primary relationship. Matrix structures are popular in project-based organizations because these structures provide flexibility and balanced decision-making. The major pitfall of the matrix structure is that as organizations grow, the structure may become very complex; this may lead to confusion among employees.

Emerging Structures

Holacracy: Traditional hierarchies have reached their limits. Flat management alternatives lack the rigor needed to run a business effectively. Holacracy is a third way to bring structure and discipline to a peer-to-peer workplace. Holacracy is a complete, packaged system for self-management in organizations. Holacracy replaces the traditional management hierarchy with a new peer-to-peer operating system that increases transparency, accountability, and organizational agility. Through a transparent rule set and a tested collaborative process, holacracy allows businesses to distribute authority, empowering all employees to take a leadership role and make meaningful decisions. The concept of holacracy draws on an earlier tradition termed sociocracy, which originated in the Netherlands. The approaches are very similar with the exception that key leadership roles in sociocracy are elected while they are not in holacracy.

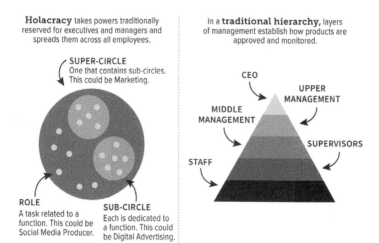

Figure 15.2. Holacracy vs. Hierarchy Organizational Design, adapted from Business Insider (Feb. 2, 2016).

In a holacracy, roles are defined around the work, not the people. Roles are regularly updated. People fill several roles. Authority is delegated to teams and roles. Decisions are made locally. The organizational structure is regularly revised through small iterations. Every team self-organizes. Everyone is bound by the same rules, the CEO included. Rules are visible to all.

Holacracy at Zappos: According to Tony Hsieh, founder and CEO of Zappos, when companies get bigger, innovation and productivity per employee go down. In contrast, every time a city doubles in size, innovation or productivity per resident increases by 15%. Therefore, Zappos is trying to figure out how to structure the company more like a city, and less like a corporation. Hsieh says:

In a city, people and businesses are self-organizing. We are trying to do the same thing by switching from a normal hierarchical structure to a system called holacracy, which enables employees to act more like entrepreneurs and self-direct their work instead of reporting to a manager who tells them what to do.

In a holacracy, roles are defined around the work, not the people.

Holacracy is not for everyone. It may not be suited to every organization. Context and culture matter.

Teal Organizations

The Teal paradigm refers to the next stage in the evolution of human consciousness. The Teal paradigm emphasizes the identity and purpose of the organization as a separate entity, and not merely as a vehicle for achieving management's objectives. Whereas Achievement-Orange speaks of organizations as machines and Pluralistic-Green uses the metaphor of families, Teal organizations refer to themselves as living organisms or living systems.

Teal organizations focus on their members' abilities to self-organize and self-manage to achieve the purpose of the organization. The hierarchical *plan-and-control* of Orange Organizations is replaced with a self-organizing structure consisting of small people-teams that assume all the traditional management functions. Positions and job descriptions are replaced with roles, where one person can fill multiple roles.

Unlike the fixed structures of Amber, Orange, and Green organizations, the organizational structure in Teal is fluid and dynamic, changing and adapting as circumstances demand to achieve the organization's purpose.

We can understand the Evolutionary-Teal paradigm by understanding the level of human consciousness. The previous organizational paradigms (Red, Amber, Orange, and even Green) operate from a human consciousness that revolves around the ego. Many scholars use the term *first-tier* consciousness for all stages up to Green and the term *second-tier* for the stages starting with Teal.

All *first-tier* stages believe that their worldview is the only valid one and that all other people are dangerously mistaken. People transiting to Teal can accept, for the first time, that there is an evolution of consciousness, that there is a momentum in the evolution toward ever more complex and refined ways of dealing with the world.

The transformation from Green to Teal represents a leap in human consciousness, rather than an incremental transformation. By looking at our ego from a distance, we can suddenly see how its fears, ambitions, and desires often run our lives. We can learn to minimize our need to control, to look good, to fit in. We need no longer be fused with our ego, and we don't let its fears reflexively control our lives. In the process, we make room to listen to the wisdom of deeper parts of ourselves.

What replaces fear? A capacity to trust the abundance of life. All wisdom traditions posit the profound truth that there are two fundamental ways to live life: from fear and scarcity, or trust and abundance. In Evolutionary-Teal, you cross the chasm and learn to decrease your need to control people and events.

You and others come to believe that even if something unexpected happens or if you or someone else makes mistakes, things will turn out all right; and when they don't, life will have given you an opportunity to learn and grow. Evolutionary – Teal turns the page from the rational-reductionist worldview of Orange and the post-modern worldview of Green to a holistic approach to knowing: wisdom beyond rationality.

The characteristics of Teal organizations are:

- **Self-management** (peer relationships, without the need for hierarchy or consensus)

- **Wholeness** (invites us to reclaim our wholeness and bring all of who we are to work—emotional, intuitive, and spiritual parts in addition to the rational part)

- **Evolutionary Purpose** (listen and understand, instead of trying to predict and control)

Summing Up

Strategy drives organizational structure. Structures take different forms including Simple, Functional, Web, Matrix, and Divisional.

Experimental structures currently under development are: Holacracy and Teal.

As an organization grows, it moves from a simple to a functional to a divisional, matrix, or web structure. Unicorns that have risen quickly to the top of their industries are trying new structures—rather, the absence of any specific structure.

Chapter 16

Strategic Control Systems

A control system contains the measures or yardsticks allowing managers to assess how efficiently they are producing goods and services.

Strategic control systems are tools to monitor and evaluate whether a chosen strategy and structure are working well. Control systems provide insights for improvement and change.

Strategic control systems are used along all the four dimensions of creating and sustaining competitive advantage: Efficiency, Quality, Innovation, and Customer Responsiveness.

Control systems exist at all levels of the organization: Corporate level, Strategic Business Unit or Divisional level, Functional level, and Individual level.

The Balanced Score Card is an excellent tool for strategic control. Strategic reward systems complement strategic control systems.

Types of Strategic Control Systems

Strategic Control Systems are tools to monitor and evaluate whether a chosen strategy and structure are working as intended, how they could be improved, and how they should be changed if they are not working. Beyond measurement, strategic control systems should aim to create the incentives which keep employees motivated. Once employees focus on the important problems that may confront an organization in the future they can work together to find solutions that help an organization perform better as time progresses.

Control and Efficiency – Managers must be able to measure how many units of inputs (capital, raw materials, human resources, time) are being used to produce a unit of output. Managers must also be able to measure the number of units of output (goods and services) they produce.

A control system contains the measures or yardsticks allowing managers to assess how efficiently they are producing goods and services. Further, if managers experiment while seeking a more efficient way to produce goods and services, the measures tell managers how successful they have been. Without a control system in place, managers would have no idea how well their organizations are performing, and how they can make it perform better, something that is critical to success in a competitive environment.

In high-performance organizations, innovation is considered to be everyone's business.

Control and Quality – Competition often requires increasing the quality of goods and services. Strategic control is important in determining the quality of goods and services. There is an increasing tendency toward such concepts as Six Sigma and Zero Defects. If managers consistently measure the number of customer complaints, customer retention, and customer desertion, they would have a good indication as to the extent they are delivering on their promise.

Control and Innovation – Successful innovation takes place when managers create an organizational culture that fosters creativity, risk-taking, and the ability to consistently come up with better solutions. Decentralization and empowerment are often the keys to innovation. In high-performance organizations, innovation is considered to be everyone's business. Some of the best-selling products at companies such as 3M have emanated from ordinary employees working in different departments or functions.

Control and Customer Responsiveness – Control Systems should measure how well employees with customer contact perform this critical function. Today attempts at improving customer responsiveness focus on satisfying customers about the value promise, and to create a customer experience that brings customers back again and again to an organization. As noted by many scholars, it is much more expensive to prospect and create a new customer than it is to retain an existing customer.

Strategic Control Systems are the formal target-setting, measurement, and feedback systems that allow managers to evaluate whether an organization is achieving superior efficiency, quality, innovation, and customer responsiveness. An effective control system should have three characteristics:

1. **Accuracy** – whatever is measured must convey a true picture of the organization.

2. **Timeliness** – every measurement should be timely. Decisions made based on outdated information is a recipe for failure.

3. **Flexibility** – the system should be capable of being changed depending on the circumstances and the competitive environment.

Levels of Strategic Control: Strategic control systems are developed to measure performance at four levels of an organization:

1. **Corporate** level

2. **Strategic Business Unit** or **Divisional** level

3. **Functional** level

4. **Individual** level

These measures should be tied as closely as possible to the goals of developing distinctive competencies in efficiency, quality, innovation, and customer responsiveness. Care must be taken to ensure that the measures at different levels are not in conflict with each other.

Based on an organization's mission and goals, managers can develop a set of strategies to build the competitive advantage to achieve the goals.

The general rule is that individual measures should be in alignment with functional measures, functional measures to divisional/SBU measures, and divisional/SBU measures to corporate measures. The corporate measures, in turn, should resonate with the chosen strategy.

For example, a cost leadership strategy would focus on efficiency measures, particularly in operations and procurement. A differentiation strategy would focus on innovation and service measures. Since quality can lead to lower costs as well as differentiation, either strategy needs to include measures of quality.

Types of Strategic Control Systems

Based on an organization's mission and goals, managers can develop a set of strategies to build the competitive advantage to achieve the goals. Next, they need to establish an organizational structure which uses resources and capabilities to obtain a competitive advantage. Managers can evaluate how well their strategy and structure are working by developing key performance indicators for efficiency, quality, innovation, and customer responsiveness.

- **Efficiency** is synonymous with productivity (output/input, human productivity, material productivity, machine productivity, resource productivity).

- **Quality** denotes the number of defects in a given lot, product returns, reliability of product or service over time, service time, customer retention and defection rates.

- **Innovation** means the number of new products or services, patents obtained, revenues from new products as a percentage of total revenue, concept to market time, and innovation productivity (spending required to launch a successful product or service).

- **Customer Responsiveness** means the number and percentage of repeat customers, customer satisfaction levels which capture the totality of customer experience, response time, and service time.

As developers of the balanced scorecard, Kaplan and Norton have noted, managing an organization can be compared to flying an airplane. An aircraft needs to constantly monitor scores of parameters: fuel, airspeed, altitude, hydraulic systems, electrical and electronic systems, and safety. Similarly, organizations need to measure performance on multiple dimensions. Reliance on any one measure or indicator can be fatal. Thus, organizational performance has to be seen along:

- **Financial** lines (Return On Investment, Return on Assets, Return on Sales, Return on Capital Employed, Capital Turnover, Gross and Net Profit Margins);

- **Customer focus** lines (customer retention and defection, wait times, service times, customer experience, customer lifetime value, and elements of customer value);

- **Internal processes** (efficiency, resource productivity, and cycle time), and

- **Organizational capacity** (knowledge management, organizational learning, technology deployment, adaptation, and flexibility).

In addition to the financial, customer focus, internal process, and organizational capacity measures, organizations can use other types of control systems—personal control, output control, and behavior control.

Personal Control – aims to improve face-to-face interactions: between managers and their direct reports, between peer group members, between customer service personnel and customers, between directors and shareholders, between organizational buyers and suppliers, and other interactions. The goal of personal control is to ensure alignment between organizational, divisional, functional, team, and individual goals. Further, interactions are useful for providing appropriate feedback that can facilitate continuous improvement and organizational learning. Personal control provides opportunities to track and prevent free-riding or shirking.

Output Control – is a system for estimating or forecasting appropriate performance indicators for the organization, divisions, functions, teams, and individuals, and subsequently comparing actual performance about the estimates or forecasts. Reward systems are linked to outputs.

Thus, an output control system can be used for providing incentives such as compensation increases, benefits, profit sharing, and employee stock option plans. In establishing output controls at different levels, it is important to ensure that the measures do not conflict with each other at any time, and also to provide safeguards against manipulations that may give a distorted view of performance. Thus, the goal should be to achieve measurable outcomes at the organizational level. Measures at other levels should complement the achievement of organizational goals.

Behavior Control – is a system of establishing rules, procedures, and protocols that govern the actions of individuals, teams, functions, divisions, and the organization. The intent of behavior controls is not to specify the goals but to standardize the boundaries or the means of achieving the goals. Processes design ideally should make the outcomes predictable. If people at all levels follow the agreed-upon protocols, the expectation is that of system accuracy, repeatability, and predictability; features common to control systems.

The main elements of behavior control are budgets, standard operating procedures, rules, and regulations. Budgeting refers to the process of resource utilization design. While it is most common to have financial budgets, one can also look at other resources, including people and time. The goal of budgeting should be to use organizational resources efficiently. Standardization can be done at the level of inputs (for example, raw material standards), processes, or outputs. Over time, standardization can lead to predictable results. For example, fast food companies try to standardize all elements—from procurement to processing to delivery—with the overarching objective being the consistent fast food of a quality that customers expect and enjoy.

It is important to note that while rules and procedures are necessary to a point, their proliferation can lead to dissatisfaction, frustration, and increased bureaucratic costs. Too much reliance on standardization can stifle innovation and render the organization rigid. As organizations evolve and learn, they need to introduce flexibility in several areas to spawn creativity and innovation.

Strategic Reward Systems

Any strategic reward system needs to address four areas:

1. Compensation

2. Benefits

3. Recognition

4. Appreciation

The problem with most reward systems is two-fold: one or more elements are missing, and the included elements do not align with corporate strategies and goals.

A winning system should recognize and reward two types of employee activity—performance and behavior. Performance is easy to address because of the link between goals set and outcomes achieved.

Rewarding employees for behavior is more challenging than rewarding performance. Three questions are useful:

1. *What am I compensating employees for?*

2. *What are the behaviors that I want to reward?*

3. *How am I compensating employees?*

For example, are you compensating employees for coming in early and staying late, or for coming up with new ideas on how to complete their work efficiently and effectively? In other words, are you compensating people for innovation or creativity, or for sitting at a desk for a certain number of hours? There is obviously a big difference in the approaches.

The critical step is to identify behaviors that are important to your company. These could be enhancing the customer experience, fine-tuning critical processes, or expanding the range of one's knowledge and skills. While competitive compensation is a necessary condition, it is not sufficient by itself.

Benefits—be they health-related, leisure and vacations, retirement plans, or profit-sharing plans—must match those of competition. Otherwise, attrition will be high. Long-term rewards for key employees typically involve some form of equity ownership—open or restricted.

Recognition and appreciation do not receive the attention they deserve. Recognition is acknowledging someone before peers for specific accomplishments. Appreciation is expressing gratitude to someone for her or his actions. A strategic reward system that thoughtfully combines all the four components can lead to a high-performance organization. Failure to address one or more elements could be a recipe for failure.

Summing Up

Strategic control systems are tools to monitor and evaluate whether a chosen strategy and structure are working well. Control systems provide insights for improvement and change.

Strategic control systems are useful along all the four dimensions of creating and sustaining competitive advantage: Efficiency, Quality, Innovation, and Customer Responsiveness.

Control systems exist at all levels of the organization: Corporate level, Strategic Business Unit or Divisional level, Functional level, and Individual level.

The Balanced Score Card is an excellent tool for strategic control. Strategic reward systems complement strategic control systems.

Chapter 17

Strategic Planning Summary

Every organization has some strengths and some weaknesses. Strengths and weaknesses are internal to the organization. Every organization also has opportunities and threats. Opportunities and threats are external to the organization.

This section focused on planning highlights the following:

- The concept of planning
- The planning process
- Strategic planning—deliberate and emergent strategies
- Strategic decision making
- Strategic leadership
- Organizational structure
- Strategic control systems

As you read this section, hopefully, the following outcomes should be apparent:

1. **Understand** the concept of planning in general and strategic planning in particular.

2. **Appreciate** the notion of strategy as an emergent

process.

3. **Comprehend** strategic decision-making, challenges, and techniques for improvement.

4. **Recognize** the role of strategic leadership in achieving goals.

5. **Design** suitable organizational structures for achieving your stated goals.

6. **Understand** the role of strategic control systems in achieving your stated goals.

Reflection Questions

Reflection Question #1. Every organization has some strengths and some weaknesses. Strengths and weaknesses are internal to the organization. Every organization also has opportunities and threats. Opportunities and threats are external to the organization.

Think about your organization. What are its strengths? Weaknesses? Opportunities? Threats? Assume you are the CEO. Identify two or three steps that you would take to: leverage your strengths; address your weaknesses; exploit your opportunities, and mitigate your threats. Share your views with colleagues and get feedback.

Reflection Question #2. Nearly six decades after the term was introduced into management literature, strategy does not have a universally accepted definition. There are four different perspectives.

1. The first, called the *classical view*, looks at strategy

as a formal process and has its roots in economics and the armed forces. The objective is profit maximization. From this perspective, strategy is a zero-sum game. You can win only at the cost of others. The main proponents of this view include Alfred Chandler, Igor Ansoff, and Michael Porter.

2. The second, called the *processual view*, looks at strategy as a crafted process (that is, strategy can undergo changes) and has its roots in psychology. The objective is vague, and the approach relies on bargaining—trade-offs between competing alternatives and even between competing players. Proponents include Henry Mintzberg and Andrew Pettigrew.

3. The third, called the *evolutionary view*, looks at strategy as an efficient process (only the outcome matters) and has its roots in economics and biology. The objective is survival. The main proponent is Oliver Williamson.

4. The fourth, called the *systemic view*, looks at strategy as being embedded in every organizational process and has its roots in sociology. The goal is to create value for stakeholders and also care for the wellbeing of society. Mark Granovetter and Richard Whittington are the main proponents.

Identify at least one company that follows one of the four approaches to strategy. Which approach does your organization follow? If you were the CEO, would you continue with the present strategy or change it? Why or why not?

Case Study: When a Dream turns into a Nightmare

If you have traveled by air, one can say with near-certainty that you have traveled in a Boeing aircraft. Boeing designs, builds, and markets aircraft, helicopters, rockets, and satellites. The company employs over 150,000 people. Its 2016 revenues were $95 billion, and profits were $5 billion. Boeing's line of 737, 747, 757, 767, and 777 aircraft have an amazing record of safety and reliability.

In 2003, the company decided to launch the 787 and named the project "Dreamliner." Contrary to its strategy, Boeing outsourced the design and part of the manufacture of the 787. The project suffered from delays (5 years) and cost the company $5 billion. Over a ten-year period, the Dreamliner has cost the company over $20 billion. The aircraft has had quality and safety issues as well—with the huge engines, electronics, and lithium-ion batteries.

Why did such a great company make such an elementary mistake (outsourcing instead of designing and building in-house)? What lessons can be learned from the Dreamliner's perennial problems? Assume you are in charge of the next project—the Boeing 797. What would you do differently? Justify your answer.

Case Study: Staying In-Tune with Business at Elevations Credit Union

Pete Reicks, Senior Vice President for Enterprise Performance Excellence at Elevations Credit Union (ECU), described the credit union's historic strategic planning, review, and decision-making processes as "a lot of muscle power" that involved working longer, harder, and adding meetings to already-full days.[1] The challenge faced by ECU was that there were many good ideas on how to change and run the business but there was lack of alignment and consensus throughout the organization.

ECU's challenge is not unique. Strategic planning and implementation, essential to an organization's success, frequently end up in failed efforts and misdirected resources. Nearly 40 years have passed since the pioneering works of Michael Porter[2] and Henry Mintzberg[3] in business strategy began a rich tradition of thought and literature of what is good strategy. Yet the business world remains littered with examples of failed strategies.

Although there may be no cure-all method for developing and implementing strategy, ECU has developed and deployed a series of processes to ensure focused action on long- and short-term business needs while infusing agility. The addition of an *Operational Rhythm*, comprising three distinct meetings every month, helps achieve alignment of strategy and action. The approach integrates activities in the key strategic areas of ongoing business operations, ensuring product and service viability, and implementation of strategies.

Operational Rhythm Origins at ECU

ECU began its Baldrige journey in 2009 soon after Gerry Agnes took over as CEO. The Baldrige framework was seen as a roadmap to use for focus on continuous improvement

---

[1] Tyler Gaskill, "Elevating Excellence. Financial Institution Elevates Performance with Culture Change and Process Approach," *Quality Progress*, October 2015.

[2] Michael E. Porter, *Competitive Strategy: Techniques for Analyzing Industries and Competitors* (New York: Free Press, 1980).

[3] Henry Mintzberg, "Patterns in Strategy Formation," *Management Science* 24, no. 9 (1978).

and long-term sustainability. The credit union was fundamentally sound and moderately profitable at the beginning of the journey. At that time, however, the Great Recession was playing havoc and ECU, as a financial services organization, was facing strong headwinds.

As a part of the journey, ECU looked for ways to address two of the key criteria items in the Baldrige Excellence Framework. Elements of best-practice strategy are described in Category 2 of the Baldrige Framework.[4] The category calls out two key aspects of organizational strategy: how strategy is developed and how it is implemented.

The Framework provides guidance on several aspects of strategy. An overarching theme in all of the strategic elements and approaches to implementation is the use of systematic processes that are consistent over time yet allow for adaptation. Strategy is seen not as a fixed plan but a process of setting and adjusting direction.

As ECU developed greater understanding and use of business process management, an approach that evolved was a series of processes centered on developing and implementing strategy. The organization added a structured process of implementation meetings to a typical flow of strategic planning. The implementation approach created a segregation of activities around the separate meetings held on specific days of the month and focused on specific topic

---

[4] Baldrige Performance Excellence Program [BPEP], *Baldrige Excellence Framework. A Systems Approach to Improving Your Organization's Performance.* (Gaithersburg, MD: National Institute of Standards and Technology, 2017).

Meeting the Challenge of Aligning to Strategy

ECU's strategic planning process provides a structured planning process that is completed on an annual basis. The

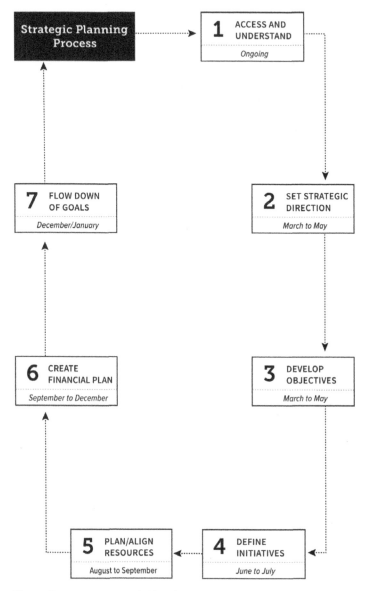

Figure 17.1. ECU's Strategic Planning Process.

steps and timing of each step are shown in Figure 17.1. The process follows a process of moving from direction to specific goals and a financial plan.

An innovation introduced by ECU was to create a specific focus on the elements of implementation. Some key challenges that organizations face in strategy implementation are the tyranny of the urgent—pressing operational items precluding action on strategic actions—and a narrow focus on limited (often financial) performance measures. The use of the *Operational Rhythm* with staggered meetings using set, but different, agendas was implemented by Elevations to meet these challenges.

The *Operational Rhythm* uses of three separate meetings as focal points: *Run the Business* (RTB), *Production*, and *Decide, Plan, Align* (DPA), each conducted on a consecutive Tuesday each month. RTB and Production meetings are considered as Analyze and Review forums to address management of ongoing operations. RTB links to ECU's business processes management by bringing in process owners' reports on process performance. Production meetings use the optic of looking at organizational performance from a more traditional and often financial perspective. Both RTB and Production meetings are used to identify improvement opportunities for business change.

DPA brings together proposals to allow senior leaders of ECU to act upon improvement recommendations and constitutes the main focal point for decisions for changing the business. Common areas of discussion in DPA include a review of change proposals and associated business cases.

Items discussed in DPA reflect both performance evaluations originating in RTD and Production and additional data suggesting the need for a change. The three meetings are depicted in Figure 17.2.

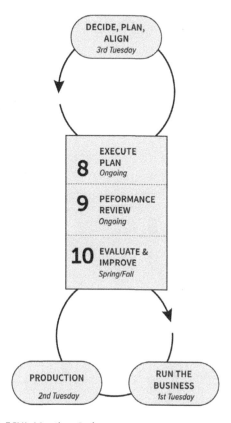

Figure 17.2: ECU's Meeting Cycle

Separation of the operational meetings into three separate days with differing agendas helps ECU to maintain focus on distinct aspects of performance management and strategy implementation. The separation is helpful to avoid the tyranny of the urgent and singular focus on financial results.

A unique aspect of the ECU system is the explicit integration of operational meetings into the strategic planning process. As shown in Figure 17.3, the operational meetings are clearly

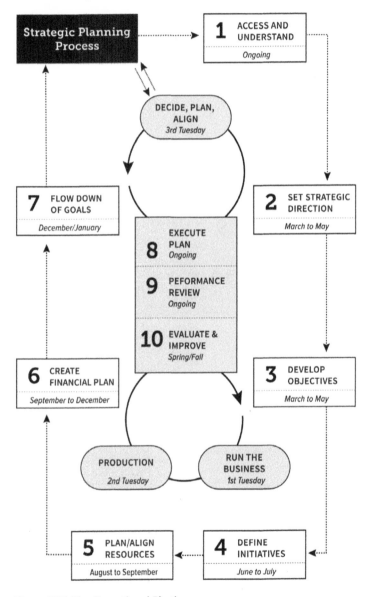

Figure 17.3. The Operational Rhythm.

linked to the annual strategic planning process. Plan execution and performance reviews are performed monthly. Formalized evaluation of improvements takes place in the spring and fall.

A Platform for Growth

As Elevations has grown its business geographically, with new services, and in overall size, the Operational Rhythm has provided a foundation to support the disciplined development of strategy followed by agile execution. The approach will be tested over time with more rapid rates of change and the need for more multifaceted decisions as business size and complexity grow.

Summing Up

Successful companies are in the habit of doing an analysis of its strengths, weaknesses, opportunities and threats via some form of a SWOT type of exercise. When companies keep abreast of what's happening within an industry—what changes have occurred or are incurring in the consumer, legal and governmental environments—and identify any emerging trends and products being introduced that could impact a product currently offered or in production, they can fine tune their own game plans, adding to success and avoiding costly mistakes.

References

Baldrige Performance Excellence Program [BPEP]. *Baldrige Excellence Framework. A Systems Approach to Improving Your Organization's Performance.* Gaithersburg, MD: National Institute of Standards and Technology, 2017.

Gaskill, Tyler. "Elevating Excellence. Financial Institution Elevates Performance with Culture Change and Process Approach." *Quality Progress*, October 2015, 32-41.

Mintzberg, Henry. "Patterns in Strategy Formation." *Management Science* 24, no. 9 (May 1978): 934-48.

Porter, Michael E. *Competitive Strategy: Techniques for Analyzing Industries and Competitors.* New York: Free Press, 1980.

Section 4
Focus on Your Customers

Some 80% of CEOs in a recent Gartner study said they provided exceptional customer service; however, only 8% of customers agreed. The huge difference between organizational perception and customer perception has a new name—the *experience gap*. Today, service is as important as the product. In many cases, service is more important than the product.

It is less expensive to retain existing customers than it is to create new ones. Despite all efforts, up to 20% of customers desert organizations every year.

The challenges for organizations are manifold:

1. How to optimize the customer acquisition process.

2. How to improve customer retention and loyalty.

3. How to reduce the costs of customer service.

4. How to increase customer share of wallet.

5. How to build brand awareness and equity.

This section aims to provide you with the tools and processes which address these questions. After reading and understanding this section, you will be able to:

1. Understand the drivers of superior customer service.

2. Deploy processes that lead to a great customer experience.

3. Measure key indicators of your efforts.

4. Develop a competitive advantage based on customer service.

Chapter 18

Defining
Your Customers

*The critical first step is to instill in every individual the
perpetual awareness, understanding, and appreciation
that customer service is everyone's business.*

Who are your customers? Where are they located? What do they want or expect?

These questions may appear simple. Most organizations have difficulty answering the questions. The retail giant Walmart receives 230 million customers in its stores every week. Should the company care equally about all 230 million? Or should Walmart categorize customers in some manner and serve the *best* customers in a *unique* way? This section provides you with the answers.

Defining your customers is the first step in running a successful business. Providing your customers with what they expect is the key to sustained success.

Defining Your Customers –
Internal and External Customers

Nearly 97% of executives surveyed by Gartner said that customers are external to the organization. While this is true from a revenue perspective, it fails to acknowledge—much less appreciate—the concept of the internal customer.

Internal customers are those within an organization that your work impacts. As an example, the customer service function is the internal customer of the sales function which, in turn, is the internal customer of the marketing function. Unless you satisfy your internal customers, it is unlikely that you will satisfy your external customers.

Satisfying internal customers demonstrates an organization's ability to facilitate teamwork across the organization. The critical first step in this is to instill in every individual the perpetual awareness, understanding, and appreciation that customer service is everyone's business.

The IT Company HCL Technologies took the concept of the internal customer to an unprecedented level. The company declared: "Employees first, Customers next." Anyone could log into an internal portal and log concerns or complaints about an individual, team, or department. Even the top executives and the CEO were part of the system. Within two years, the company forged ahead of the competition on customer service. The company also scored very low on employee attrition.

Promoting a sense of service within an organization is not an easy task. It requires developing a culture of trust, openness, empathy, and helpfulness—being ready to help and being ready to seek help.

While defining your external customers, three components are critical:

1. **Demographics** – what is your typical customer profile with regards to age, gender, ethnicity, geographic location, and economic status? Demographic factors are easy to define and relatively easy to collect. But they rarely convey buying behavior by themselves.

2. **Psychographics** – how do customers feel about products and services? Do they prefer quality without regard to price? Do they support products and services based on how the organization is committed to protecting and preserving the ecosystem? What drives customers?

3. **Behavioral** – past actions that may enable you to predict the future. Today, marketers typically track customers' social media activities with the intent to understand behavioral patterns.

A combination of the three components is necessary for a successful marketing strategy. B2B (business-to-business) organizations should also look at the following characteristics:

- The size of the buying organization.
- Revenue—to estimate the potential share of wallet.
- Geographies—to understand the impact of both geographic distance and cultural distance.
- Buying Center—to appreciate the role of the user, the influencer, the decision-maker, and the gatekeeper.

• Frequency (Capital Goods, Maintenance Goods, Consumables, Raw Materials, Spares)—to estimate average revenue per interaction and customer lifetime value.

It is useful to ask and answer the question: *Who is your ideal customer?*

Describe – based on demographics, psychographics, and behavior.

Locate – geographically and culturally—local, regional, national, or global.

Understand – the purchase process, the problem to be solved, the *job to be done* from the customer's perspective, quantity, frequency, value, and decision-making process (impulse, limited search, or extensive search; individual, family, team, or organization).

Connect – with current customers, gather insights, find out why they chose you, what do you have that others don't?

Create – customer profiles. The top 20% who typically account for 80% or more of revenues, the next 30% + 30%; the bottom 20%.

The *job to be done* construct is a powerful metaphor to understand customer expectations. When a fast food chain introduced a range of milkshakes, sales peaked early in the morning and quickly faded. Unable to understand the reason, the management team called in researchers to find the reason.

Companies need to understand everything
from the customers' perspective.

The researchers interviewed everyone who bought a milkshake over several weeks. To their surprise (and that of the company's management), they discovered that early morning commuters were the buyers. Typically, the group had a 25–30-minute commute and wanted something that they could consume easily but slowly over the entire commute. They had already tried everything from fruits to doughnuts to crackers with unsatisfactory results. The milkshake provided a *near perfect* solution to the *job to be done*. Since the milkshake was thick, it came up slowly through the straw. The ingredients were such that the user would have a *full* feeling for a couple of hours.

The same milkshake had no customers later in the day precisely because it took too long to consume. Parents picking up their children from school and stopping for a quick snack wanted a drink that the child could sip quickly. When the company changed the recipe and came up with a *thin* milkshake, children simply loved it, and sales soared.

The learning from this example is that the typical organization invariably comes up with a product or service, and then tries to find customers. If organizations only started with customers, the journey might be much easier and more satisfying to everyone.

Segmentation

Segmentation is the process of dividing a large heterogeneous market into relatively homogeneous parts or segments that you can reach efficiently and effectively with products and services matching their unique needs.

Geographic	Demographic	Psychographic	Behavioral
• Nations	• Age	• Social Class	• Benefits Sought
• Regions	• Gender	• Lifestyle	• User Status
• States	• Family Size	• Personality Traits	+ Ex-Users
• Counties	• Family Life Cycle		+ First Time
• Cities	• Income		+ Repeated
	• Net Worth		• Usage Rate
	• Occupation		+ Low
	• Education		+ Moderate
	• Ethnicity		+ High
	• Religion		• Loyalty Status
	• Generation		
	• Nationality		

Figure 18.1. Segmenting Consumer Markets.

Multiple Segmentation: PRIZM NE classifies American households into 66 unique segments and organized into 14 different social groups. These groups segment people and locations into marketable groups of like-minded consumers that exhibit unique characteristics and buying behavior based on a host of demographic factors.

Segmenting Business Markets: Besides the variables used in B2C marketing, business markets can be segmented by:

1. Customer Operating Characteristics (OEM, Raw Materials, Spare Parts, Consumables, Capital Goods)

2. Purchasing Approaches (New Task, Routine Re-buy, Modified Re-buy)

3. Situational Factors (Buying Center Characteristics, Decision-Making Approach)

4. Personal Characteristics (of organization and executives)

Requirements for Effective Segmentation: To be useful, a market segment should be: Measurable, Accessible, Substantial, Differentiable, and Actionable.

Measurable attributes include the size, purchasing power, and profiles of the segments.

Accessible refers to the fact that you can effectively reach and serve the chosen market.

Substantial refers to the fact that the markets are large and profitable enough to serve.

Differentiable refers to the fact that the markets are conceptually distinguishable and respond differently to marketing mix programs and elements.

Actionable refers to the fact that effective programs can be designed (product, price, promotion, and distribution) for attracting and serving the segments.

Identifying Your Target Market

Geographic segmentation—many multi-national corporations segment global markets according to geography. IBM, Accenture, Oracle, Cisco, and Adobe have North America, Europe, Middle East, South Asia, Asia Pacific, and Latin American segments.

Apparel manufacturers typically segment markets based on gender and age. It is also possible to segment based on income—Nordstrom, Saks, and Burberry aim to attract customers who don't mind high prices.

Insurance providers tailor their offerings based on family life cycles.

PC manufacturers segment markets based on use—students, executives, homemakers, gaming enthusiasts, and professionals (accountants, lawyers, and physicians).

Personal care products and fashion accessories lend themselves to psychographic segmentation. L'Oréal, P & G, Unilever, Estée Lauder, Neutrogena, Nivea, Lancôme, and Avon use psychographic segmentation.

Segmentation based on usage and loyalty is common in airlines, hotels, credit cards, and retailing.

Evaluating Market Segments - Segment Structural Attractiveness

The intensity of competition – the extent to which players are fragmented or consolidated. A fragmented industry typically means price rivalry and even price wars; a consolidated industry denotes relative stability but much higher entry costs. For example, the fast food industry is a fragmented industry with local, regional, national, and global players jostling for market share. The banking industry is a relatively consolidated industry with a few national and international players and some regional players.

Substitutes – the extent to which a firm's offering is perceived to be similar to competitors' offerings. The beverage industry has many close substitutes. When you are thirsty, you may settle for an available beverage if you cannot find your favorite beverage. Coffee and tea are close substitutes. So are the various brands of mineral water.

Buyer Power – is high when the industry has a few large buyers and a large number of suppliers, as in the case of automobile components. Buyer power is low when the industry has a few large suppliers and a large number of buyers, as in the case of convenience products and even some durables.

Supplier Power – is a mirror image of buyer power. Supplier power is high when the industry has a few large suppliers and a large number of buyers, as in the case of electric utilities. Supplier power is low when the industry has a large number of suppliers and a few large buyers as in the case of agricultural produce.

Entry and Exit Barriers – are a function of capital intensity, people employed, and whether the technology has alternative uses. For example, a player in the shipping industry is subject to high entry as well exit barriers. An industry with a strong union is subject to high exit barriers.

Evaluating Market Segments - Segment Size and Growth

Small versus Large segments – products and services tend to have segments that are inversely proportional to the value of the offering. Thus, convenience products such as bread and milk have mass markets.

In contrast, a product such as the VERTU mobile phone with embedded gemstones, a gold cover, and a price tag of $200,000 has a very small segment. The segment for technology products such as desktops and laptops grew rapidly in the 1990s and currently appears to have reached a plateau. The segment for large cars characterized as *gas guzzlers* dropped significantly due to a spike in oil prices. With increased awareness about health, beverage manufacturers have had to introduce new categories containing reduced sugar and salt content.

Growth potential – disruptive technologies and offerings tend to grow rapidly. Airbnb and Uber are examples of services that have grown exponentially. In contrast, mainframe computers have disappeared except for applications such as weather forecasting.

Ease of entry and exit – entry and exit are related to capital investment, the technology involved, brand equity, and loyalty. In a rapidly changing world, it is often much more difficult to exit a business than it is to enter a given sector.

Evaluating Market Segments - Company Objectives and Resources

Competitive advantage – one source of competitive advantage is the ability to compete in multiple markets and segments. McDonald's, Starbucks, and Walmart are examples of competing through sheer size and scale. Walmart's revenues are greater than that of its competitors put together.

Resource availability – growth requires resources—finance, technology, and people. The ability to generate cash and to use it to fuel growth differentiates great companies from the also-rans.

Consistency and alignment with mission and vision – organizations need to "stick to the knitting," to quote Peters and Waterman, or adhere to their "core competencies," in the words of Hamel and Prahalad.

For example, the mission of Walt Disney is to make people happy. Thus, Disney's suite of offerings such as theme parks, vacation spots, and movies aim to fulfill this mission. It is difficult to think of Disney getting into the computer business or the aircraft business.

Social responsibility and sustainability – Organizations that follow the Triple Bottom Line (TBL) of profits, people, and planet outperform competitors. Ikea pledges to plant and nurture ten saplings for every tree cut anywhere in the world for its products. Patagonia is committed to preserving the environment. Unilever aims to generate profits with a purpose.

Doing good to society is a proven method to enhance brand equity and customer loyalty. Caring for natural resources such as air and water show organizations in a positive light compared to organizations that either pay lip service to ecology or those that harm the environment.

Selecting Target Market Segments

Undifferentiated Strategy (mass marketing) – treats entire markets as one, and tries to address the market with one offering, one price, one type of promotion, and one type of distribution. Traditionally, commodities such as salt and sugar belong to this category.

Changing lifestyles and customer expectations mean even with commodities some differentiation is sought to be made. For example, low-sodium salt and packaged goods containing lower levels of salt, brown sugar, and sugar cubes are meant to create a kind of artificial differentiation.

Differentiated Strategy (multiple segments) – or multi-segment strategy is the most widely used segmentation approach. Most products and services today use multiple segments to cater to different classes of customers.

Laptops range from $100 to $5,000 based on function, speed, display, and other characteristics. Mobile phones range from a low of $50 to a high of $1,500 based on features. You can have food for $10 in a fast food outlet or spend $250 in a fancy restaurant. Airlines have configurations such as first class, business class, premium economy, and economy. Automobiles range from $12,000 to a few million dollars. Apparel range from a few dollars to a few thousand dollars. Sometimes the same product is packaged differently to cater to different segments.

Concentrated Strategy (focus on one segment) – the organization focuses on one segment of the market. Focus is a good entry strategy as it involves fewer resources—and therefore less risk—than trying to cater to multiple segments.

Focus is also useful at the highest end of the market such as in the case of designer jewelry, antiques, paintings, rare musical instruments, and *prestige* goods.

Micro-marketing Strategy (niche or part of one segment) –
looks at a part of a segment and is thus a refinement of the
concentrated strategy.

For example, Lefty's in San Francisco is a retail store that caters
to left-handed people only. Everything in the store caters to
left-handers. Lush is a cosmetics company (similar to The Body
Shop) that uses organic ingredients, does not do any animal
testing, and uses eco-friendly packaging. Square is a powerful
point-of-sale software that allows store owners to accept
credit card payments via phones or tablets.

Customization versus Standardization is a dilemma every
organization faces at some point. Standardization has the
benefit of exploiting scale economies and reducing costs.
Customization places the customer at the center and creates
a delightful experience. Customization comes at a price.

We can see a trend toward customization in a variety of
products and services. When you buy a computer, you can
choose the processor, the hard disk, display, screen size, and
application software based on your needs. Of course, you end
up paying a higher price than for a standard configuration. You
can configure web pages to your tastes and preferences—an
example of individual customization.

Positioning

Product position is the way customers perceive a product or
service on important attributes when comparing with other
products and services. Positioning is the combination of
emotional attributes that customers experience while looking
at a product or service.

*Of all the methods available for differentiation,
people represent the last frontier.*

For example, Mercedes-Benz conjures up the vision of a well-crafted engineering marvel with safety and precision as the defining attributes. Rolex and Omega bring to the mind notions of a legacy passed on from one generation to another. Walmart is synonymous with everyday low prices. Patagonia is known for its sustainability efforts. Singapore Airlines ranks consistently at the top for customer service. Google translates to a search engine. When you think of social media, names such as Facebook and Twitter instantly pop up.

Positioning Maps show consumer perceptions of brands versus competing products on important buying dimensions. Possible competitive advantages include:

- **Product differentiation** – a custom-built Ferrari costs a few million dollars whereas a car built on an assembly line costs a fraction of that.

- **Service differentiation** – a first-class or business-class ticket on any airline costs much more than an economy class ticket due to the additional features—reclining seats, choice of food and beverages, faster check-in, and more baggage allowance.

- **Channels** – at a time when the airline industry was full of intermediaries, Southwest pioneered the direct marketing concept in airlines. Today, all airlines offer direct booking even while allowing aggregators such as Expedia and Trip Advisor to sell tickets.

- **People** – of all the methods available for differentiation, people represent the last frontier. Highly motivated and engaged employees can create a lasting impression on customers. Employees who are not motivated or engaged can destroy an organization. Great Places to Work Institute publishes a list of companies where people matter the most – Google, The Boston Consulting Group, Baird, Edward Jones, Salesforce, and Quicken Loans were among the top ten in 2017.

- **Image** – corporate image, or what an organization stands for, can be a differentiator, too. The Body Shop pioneered the concept of responsible sourcing, organic materials, and no animal testing to create an image of a humane organization. Since the business model was quite visible, many others followed suit.

A difference (compared to the competition) is worth establishing to the extent that it satisfies the following criteria:

- **Important** – from the customer's perspective; for example, some hotels provide a 24-hour checkout instead of the standard noon checkout. For some customers, this may be an important attribute.

- **Distinctive** – firms often use colors to distinguish their offerings; Coca-Cola uses red while its main competitor Pepsi uses blue. The earthmoving equipment company Caterpillar has used yellow to make its machinery distinct and visible.

- **Superior** – Tesla became the most valuable automobile company in the U.S. in April 2017, surpassing GM and Ford. Tesla sold 76,000 cars in 2016 while GM sold ten million. The apparent anomaly makes sense through customers' and shareholders' perspective. Tesla is perceived to have superior technology in electric and autonomous cars.

- **Communicable** – any attribute becomes valuable only when a firm communicates the attribute effectively. The Walt Disney company has successfully communicated the image of happy families while promoting its resorts.

- **Preemptive** – Intel has consciously killed its products and replaced them with faster, more efficient processors. This strategy is seen right from the 8088 through the 286 and 386, Pentium, Celeron, and i-series of processors. The emphasis on innovation has had a preemptive effect on competition. The term *Intel Inside* is synonymous with personal computers.

- **Affordable** – refers to the *value for money* concept. Discount retailers offer the lowest possible price. A product or service is successful when customers believe they are getting good value for their money.

Value Proposition is the full mix of benefits upon which a firm positions its brands:

- **More for more** (unique features and attributes that command a premium price) – customers pay more for Apple's products in the belief they are getting a product with more features and greater reliability than competitors' products.

- **More for the same** (better than competition for the same price) – Toyota has positioned its Lexus and Prius as offering more features for the same price as that of competing cars.

- **Same for less** (attributes similar to competition but at a lower price) – Samsung and LG have followed this approach, using the Android operating system and claiming features similar to more expensive brands; in turn, Xiomi and Huawei have pushed the prices further down while claiming features similar to that of Samsung and LG.

- **Less for much less** (fewer attributes but at a much lower price) – deep discount auction sites such as eBay and Tophatter belong to this category. You may be getting a used product or a product whose value is difficult to determine at a very low price.

- **More for less** (superior attributes at a lower price—ultimate differentiator) – new products with fancy features may adopt this approach during the introduction stage. The firm is willing to undergo a short-term loss to gain market share. However, this value proposition model is difficult to sustain over the life-cycle of a product or service.

Recent Developments in Segmentation

During the first thirty years of the marketing era, segmentation relied on *a priori* approaches—that is, identifying customer groups by an accepted classification procedure related to variations in customer purchase or usage of the product category. Examples of *a priori* segments include such classification schemes as:

- **Standard Industrial Classification** (SIC) groups

- **Geographic** regions – Americas, Europe, Middle East, South Asia, Asia Pacific

- Basic **demographic** groups (rural, semi-urban, urban, household composition)

- **Values and Lifestyles** (VALS) classification – thinkers, achievers, experiencers, believers, strivers, makers, innovators, and survivors

- **PRIZM** or similar geodemographic classification systems

Post Hoc Segmentation Methods

Post hoc segmentation is empirically derived based on the results of a research study undertaken for the specific purpose of segmenting a market. The most critical question facing the researcher in conducting a post hoc segmentation is selecting the variables for the segmentation.

Examples include product attribute preferences, values, product purchase patterns, benefits sought, brand preferences, price sensitivity, socioeconomic status, lifestyles, self-image, attitudes, opinions related to the environment, and deal proneness. Four major classes of algorithms for *post hoc* segmentation studies are:

- Cluster analysis

- Correspondence analysis

- Search procedures, and

- Q-factor analysis

Details of these methods are available at the website of the American Marketing Association (http://www.ama.org).

Recent developments include:

- **Multi-dimensional segmentation** – uses many variables to segment—for example, stated needs, benefits, and purchasing capacity.

- **Artificial Neural Networks** – use a set of input variables and a set of known outcomes, an iterative process, and machine learning to find the best relationship between the inputs and the outcome.

- **Latent Class Models** – enable the user to simultaneously optimize a research function and find clusters within that framework. Proprietary software is available to run the algorithms.

- **Fuzzy and Overlapping Clustering** – allows researchers to look at the behavior of an individual in different situations. For example, the use of beverages in a social setting, at a bar, and with one's family may lead to the formation of multiple clusters within a demographic group.

Summing Up

This first section focuses on answering the following questions:

1. Who are your customers?

2. Where are they located?

3. What do they want or expect?

These questions may appear simple. Most organizations have difficulty answering the questions.

The retail giant Walmart receives 230 million customers in its stores every week. Should the company care equally about all the 230 million? Or should Walmart categorize customers in some manner and serve the *best* customers in a *unique* way?

Defining your customers is the first step in running a successful business. Providing your customers with what they expect is the key to sustained success.

Chapter 19

Customer Service and Loyalty

*A focus on service quality is the foundation
for meeting customer expectations.*

Great customer experience is at the heart of business success. Customer service is the lifeblood of the customer experience. Satisfied customers are likely to turn into loyal customers. Loyal customers become advocates and even evangelists.

Dissatisfied customers can cause havoc to any business.

Some studies show that it is much more expensive to create a new customer than it is to retain a customer. A focus on service quality is the foundation for meeting customer expectations.

This section explores the means to provide service that creates loyal customers.

Why is loyalty important?

Loyalty refers to customers' intention to continue doing business with a company, increase their spending, or say good things about the company (or refrain from saying bad things). The latest research shows that loyalty has a lot more to do with how well companies deliver on their basic, plain-vanilla promises than how dazzling the service experience might be. Most companies have failed to realize this and pay dearly in the form of wasted investments and lost customers. Key findings of research conducted globally and validated using isolating techniques, and conducting thousands of structured interviews:

- Delighting customers does not build loyalty; reducing their effort—the work they must do to get their problem solved—does.

- Acting deliberately on this insight can help improve customer service, reduce customer service costs, and decrease customer churn.

Conventional wisdom would suggest that customers are loyal to firms that go above and beyond the promise. Research shows that exceeding expectations during service interactions (offering a refund, a free product, or a free service such as next-day delivery) makes customers only marginally more loyal than simply meeting their needs. For leaders who swear by exceptional service, this is an alarming finding. The main reason for the exaggerated emphasis on exceeding expectations is that 80% of customer service organizations use customer satisfaction scores for determining the quality of the customer experience.

Managers assume that the more satisfied customers are, the more loyal they will be. Empirically, there is little evidence to suggest a relationship between satisfaction and loyalty.

- 20% of *satisfied* customers say they intend to leave the company.

- 28% of *dissatisfied* customers intend staying.

Thus, while customer service can do little to increase loyalty, it can (and does) do a great deal to undermine it. Customers are four times more likely to leave a service interaction disloyal than loyal.

Consider customer loyalty as two pies—one containing factors that drive loyalty and the other containing factors that drive disloyalty.

- The loyalty pie – product quality and brand; slice for service is small.

- The disloyalty pie – service accounts for most of this pie.

We buy from a company because it delivers quality products, great value, or a compelling brand. We desert a company, more often than not, because it fails to deliver on customer service.

Companies can reduce such interactions and measure the effects with a new metric, the Customer Effort Score (CES).

With this understanding, we can change the emphasis of customer service interactions. Framing the service challenge by making it easy for the customer can be highly illuminating, even liberating, particularly for companies that have been struggling to delight. Organizations can improve customer loyalty simply by reducing the time and effort that customers expend.

Instructing sales people to exceed customer expectations is likely to end up with confusion, wasted time and effort, and costly giveaways. Instructing them to *make it easy* gives a solid foundation for action. But, what exactly does *make it easy* mean?

REMOVE OBSTACLES. In particular, customers are frustrated by:

- Having to contact the company repeatedly.
- To be transferred to get an issue resolved.
- Having to repeat information.
- Having to switch from one service channel to another (for example, from a web-based service to a telephone call).

Most customers report having difficulties mentioned above. Companies can reduce such interactions and measure the effects with a new metric, the Customer Effort Score (CES), which assigns a value based on the effort required to solve a problem (for example, one can denote little or no effort while 4 or 5 can denote very high effort).

You can measure CES by asking a single question: *How much effort did you have to put forth to handle your request?* Use with other metrics such as repeat calls, transfers, and channel switching.

- Customers reporting low effort: 94% expressed intent to repurchase; 88% said they would increase spending.

- Customers reporting high effort: 81% expressed intent to spread negative word of mouth.

The superior predictive power of CES can be attributed to its transactional nature—as opposed to the holistic nature of NPS—and also its ability to capture negative as well as positive experiences.

A tool for Customer Effort Audit is available at: https://www.cebglobal.com/sales-service.html.

How to Ensure Minimal Customer Effort

Don't just resolve the current issue—head off the next one. Track repeat calls instead of using the first-contact-resolution (FCR) metric. Such tracking in due course will spot and eliminate sources of undue customer effort.

Bell Canada found that a high percentage of customers who ordered a particular feature called back for instructions on using it. The service reps now give a quick tutorial on the feature before hanging up. Result: Calls per event reduced by 16%; Customer churn reduced by 10%.

Fidelity offers *suggested next steps* on its website. Result: 25% generation of self-service transactions; 8% drop in calls per household.

Train your reps to address the emotional side of customer interactions. 25% of repeat calls stem from emotional disconnects between customers and sales reps. With some basic training, reps can eliminate many interpersonal issues and thereby reduce repeat calls.

A mortgage company teaches its reps to listen for clues to a customer's personality type. They assess whether they are talking to a *controller*, a *thinker*, a *feeler*, or an *entertainer*, and tailor their responses accordingly, offering a balance of detail and speed. Result: Reduction in repeat calls by 40%.

Osram Sylvania analyzes transcripts of calls to identify words that can trigger negative emotions and drive repeat calls—words such as *can't*, *won't*, and *don't*,—and coaches its reps on alternate phrasing. Result: Customer Effort Score lowered from 2.8 to 2.2—20% below the average for B2B companies.

LoyaltyOne, the operator of the Air Miles Reward program, teaches reps to offer alternatives instead of simply saying a particular flight is not available. Result: A 15% reduction in repeat contacts.

Minimize channel switching by increasing self-service channel *stickiness*. Nearly 60% of inbound calls come from customers who went to the website first. Companies pay little or no attention to simplifying their websites. In their anxiety to keep pace with competitors, companies routinely invest in technology without making a business case for it. With the profusion of self-service channels, customers are often confused. After spending considerable effort switching channels, they reach for the phone. Simplify the self-service experience.

Train your reps to address the
emotional side of customer interactions.

Cisco Consumer Products guides customers to the channel it determines will suit them best, by segment-specific hypotheses generated by the company's customer experience team. The language on the company's site nudges technology experts toward the online support community. Those with less technical expertise can access knowledge articles and simple step-by-step instructions. Further, they have eliminated the e-mail option. Result: Self-service handles 88% of customer contacts. The volume of calls has dropped accordingly.

Use feedback from dissatisfied customers to reduce customer effort. Companies frequently use post-call surveys to measure performance. Studies show that the data gathered neglects feedback from unhappy customers. The solution is to encourage salespeople to gather feedback from such customers and use the information to reduce the effort required in all future interactions.

National Australia Group encourages sales reps to call customers who have given it low marks. The reps solve the issue first and then collect information on improving the service. The process is used as part of organizational learning and is not used to penalize anyone. Result: Reduction in calls by 35%.

Empower the customer service employees to deliver a low-effort experience. The single biggest obstacle to reducing customer effort is an incentive system that values speed over quality. Customer service companies typically use metrics such as average handle time when assessing performance. They would be much better off removing the productivity governors that come in the way of making the customer experience easy.

A major telecom provider has eliminated all productivity metrics from its frontline reps' performance scorecards. The company evaluates its reps solely based on direct, short interviews with customers, essentially asking them if the service met their needs. Result: Although handle time has increased about 7%, repeat calls have fallen 63%.

South Africa's Nedbank has made low customer effort the cornerstone of its service value proposition and branding. The bank's *AskOnce* promise guarantees that the rep who picks up the phone will own the customer's issue from start to finish.

To sum up:

- Focus on mitigating disloyalty by reducing customer effort.

- Customer service preferences are changing—today's customers overwhelmingly are indifferent to the service channel.

- Self-service is the way forward for organizations to reduce customer effort.

Service Quality Principles

Definitions of quality have largely emanated from the goods sector. These range from the Japanese notion of *zero defects* to Six Sigma concepts (3.4 possible defects in a million opportunities) to *fitness for use* to *doing it right the first time* to *conformance to requirements.*

Knowledge about goods quality is not sufficient to understand service quality. The characteristics that render the measurement of service quality difficult are Intangibility, Heterogeneity, and Inseparability.

Because services are performances rather than objects, they cannot be counted, measured, inventoried, tested, and verified in advance of the sale to assure quality. The intangible nature of services also makes it difficult to understand how customers perceive services and evaluate service quality.

Services are heterogeneous in that their performance varies from provider to provider, from customer to customer, from day to day, and often from one part of the day to another. Consistency in delivery is hard to achieve, given that human behavior cannot be standardized.

Production and consumption of many services are inseparable. Quality occurs during service delivery, at the interaction between the customer and the contact person from the service firm.

- Service Quality is a comparison between Expectations and Performance.

- Quality Evaluations involve Outcomes and Processes
—service quality depends not only on the result (outcome) but also on the service delivery (process).

In their pioneering work, Professors Parasuraman, Zeithaml, and Berry (1985) introduced the Gap Model of Service Quality.

> "A set of key discrepancies, or gaps, exists regarding executive perceptions of service quality and the tasks associated with service delivery to customers. These gaps can be major hurdles in attempting to deliver a service which consumers would perceive as being of high quality."

GAP 1: Consumer Expectation – Management Perception Gap

While many of the executive perceptions about what customers expect in a quality service are aligned with customer expectations, discrepancies do exist between executive (management) perceptions and customer expectations.

Managers tend to think that a repair firm's size signals strength from a quality perspective. Customers, on the other hand, tend to associate small firms with high quality consistently.

Banking and brokerage service customers place privacy and confidentiality as vital quality attributes. Managers of such firms rarely treat these as essential requirements, focusing instead on revenues and profits.

Service firm executives do not always understand what features constitute high quality to customers in advance, or what features the service must have to meet customer needs.

GAP 2: Management Perception – Service Quality Specification Gap

Across service delivery firms, managers routinely express difficulty in matching customer expectations. Managers invariably cite constraints preventing them from delivering what the customer expects.

Repair firm managers are fully aware that peak demands for repairing air conditioners and lawn mowers occur during the summer months; precisely when many service personnel want to go on vacation. Thus, knowledge of customer expectations exists but the perceived means to deliver against expectations apparently do not.

> **Promising more than can be delivered will raise initial expectations but result in lower perceptions of quality when the firm fails to deliver on their promises.**

GAP 3: Service Quality Specifications – Service Delivery Gap

Even when guidelines exist for performing services well and treating customers correctly, high-quality service performance may not be a certainty. Executives bemoan the fact that *everything involves a person and it is hard to maintain standardized quality.* People are unique and have widely differing priorities. This translates to variable service quality.

A large majority of firms (77%) have guidelines for maintaining service quality in such ordinary aspects as answering phone calls (calls should be answered on the second ring, or within 7 seconds). But less than 12% can deliver on this because of variability in employee performance. Similarly, keeping error rates in documents and statements to less than 1% is a common goal. Most firms fail to achieve this.

GAP 4: Service Delivery – External Communications Gap

Media advertising and other communications by a firm can affect customer expectations. If expectations play a major role in customer perceptions of service quality (as the services literature contends), the firm must be certain not to promise more in communications than it can deliver in reality. Promising more than can be delivered will raise initial expectations but result in lower perceptions of quality when the firm fails to deliver on their promises.

A securities brokerage executive mentions an internal *48-hour rule* prohibiting employees from buying or selling securities for their accounts for the first 48 hours after the firm supplies the information. The firm does not communicate this information to its customers, perhaps contributing to the perception that *brokers make all the good deals.*

External communications can affect not only customer expectations about a service but also customer perceptions of the delivered service. The moral is simple: Deliver on your promise OR don't promise what you cannot deliver.

GAP 5: Expected Service – Perceived Service Gap

The cumulative effect of the gaps mentioned above is the inevitable difference between customer *expectations* of a service and customer *perceptions* of the delivered service.

Consider an employer issuing a payroll check payable the next day. The employee wants the cash immediately. The bank declines to honor the check. When a friend points out the legal constraints preventing the bank from cashing her check, the customer responds: "Well, nobody in the bank explained that to me." Because they did not receive an explanation in the bank, the customer perceived the bank to be unwilling rather than unable to cash the check. The bank's inability to honor a post-dated check results in a perception of poor service quality.

Service Quality Components

Regardless of the type of service, customers use similar criteria while evaluating service quality. These criteria appear to fall into ten key categories that may be called service quality components or service quality determinants. Please note that the components may well have overlapping characteristics.

- **RELIABILITY:** Reliability means consistency of performance and dependability. Also, it means that the firm honors its promises. Accurate, correct, timely.

- **RESPONSIVENESS:** Willingness or readiness of employees to provide service. Prompt, timely.

- **COMPETENCE:** Knowledge and skill of contact personnel. Knowledge and skill of support personnel. Capabilities of firm.

- **ACCESS:** Ease of contact and approachability. Convenient hours. Convenient location.

- **COURTESY:** Politeness, respect, consideration, friendliness of contact personnel. Contact personnel appear clean and neat.

- **COMMUNICATION:** Keeping customers informed in a language they can understand; listening; explaining the service, the cost, and trade-off between service and cost. Assuring customers that problem(s) will be solved.

- **CREDIBILITY:** Trustworthiness, honesty; always having the customer's interest at heart; the reputation of the firm. Characteristics of contact personnel. The degree of hard sell involved in interactions with the customer.

- **SECURITY:** Freedom from danger, risk, or doubt. Physical safety, financial security, and confidentiality.

- **UNDERSTANDING THE CUSTOMER:** Learn the customer's specific requirements. Provide individualized attention. Recognize the regular customer.

- **TANGIBLES:** Physical evidence of service facility. The appearance of personnel. Tools or equipment used to provide service. Physical presentations of the service (example: a credit card).

The properties for evaluating quality include:

- **Search Properties** – attributes which a consumer can determine before purchasing a product; include attributes such as color, style, price, fit, feel, hardness, softness, and smell.

- **Experience Properties** – attributes which can only be discerned after purchase or during consumption; taste, performance, and dependability.

- **Credence Properties** – attributes which the consumer may find impossible to evaluate even after purchase and consumption. For example, consider the brake linings of an automobile. When replaced, the customer is unable to determine whether the replacement was indeed necessary and whether the new linings fit properly.

The quality determinants discussed earlier can be arrayed along a continuum ranging from *easy to evaluate* to *difficult to evaluate*. In general, offerings high in search properties are easiest to evaluate, those high in experience properties are more difficult to evaluate, and those high in credence properties are the hardest to evaluate. Most services contain few search properties and are high in experience and credence properties, making their quality more difficult to evaluate.

Only two of the ten determinants of quality—tangibles and credibility—can be known in advance of the purchase, thereby making the number of search properties few. Most of the determinants of service quality are experience properties: access, courtesy, reliability, responsiveness, understanding/ knowing the customer, and communication. Each of these can only be known as the customer is purchasing or consuming the service.

Because of the heterogeneous nature of services, customers may choose to reevaluate these determinants every time they make a purchase. Two of the determinants probably fall into the category of credence properties: competence and security. Consumers are probably never certain of these attributes, even after consumption of the service.

Because few search properties exist with services, and because credence properties are extremely difficult—if not altogether impossible—to evaluate, we can say that consumers typically rely on experience properties when evaluating service quality.

Based on the GAP Model of service quality, and insights gathered from research, perceived service quality can be suggested to exist along a continuum ranging from ideal quality to totally unacceptable quality, with some point along the continuum representing satisfactory or acceptable quality. The position of a customer's perception of service quality on the continuum depends on the nature of the discrepancy (gap) between the expected service and perceived service.

Summing Up

Great customer experience is at the heart of business success. Customer service is the lifeblood of the customer experience. Satisfied customers are likely to turn into loyal customers. Loyal customers become advocates and even evangelists.

Dissatisfied customers can cause havoc to any business.

Some studies show that it is much more expensive to create a new customer than it is to retain a customer. A focus on service quality is the foundation for meeting customer expectations.

This section provided guidelines for creating loyal customers by providing quality service that meets customer expectations.

Chapter **20**

The Elements of Value

*Products and services must attain
a certain minimum level, and no other elements
can make up for a significant shortfall
on perceived quality.*

The value in marketing is also called customer-perceived value. Customer-perceived value is the difference between a customer's evaluation of the benefits and costs of a product or service in comparison with others.

Traditionally, the concept of value relates to the Unique Value Proposition (UVP) or Unique Selling Proposition (USP). A compelling UVP or USP is the building block of differentiating your offering in relation to others.

Some notable examples of USP:

- AVIS – We are number two. We try harder. The USP helped Avis increase market share from 11% to 35% in four years when the company was struggling for survival.

- FedEx – synonymous with *overnight delivery*.

- DeBeers – A diamond is forever.

- Domino's – Your pizza delivered to your door in 30 minutes or less, or it is free.

Recent research suggests that there is more to value than a catchy slogan. This chapter explores a new concept called the *elements of value.*

Understanding the Elements of Value

This segment draws inspiration from the work of Eric Almquist, John Senior, and Nicolas Bloch of Bain and Company.

Customers evaluate products and services by comparing perceived value against price. Firms routinely focus on price because it is the most flexible of the marketing mix elements. Increasing prices can increase revenues, assuming that volume does not change. Decreasing prices can increase volumes but may not increase revenues. Price analytics have sufficiently evolved to provide managers with a range of options.

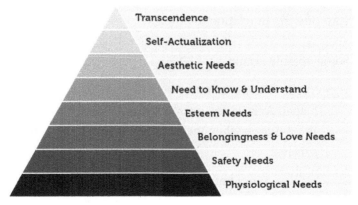

Figure 20.1. Maslow's Hierarchy of Needs.

How does one measure value? Value, being at least in part a psychological construct, is difficult to define and measure. A useful baseline to use is the Maslowian Needs Hierarchy. Maslow proposed different levels of needs that people tend to go through as they progress in life.

Drawing on this model, and looking at it from a marketer's perspective, you can design products and services to deliver value along the following dimensions:

1. **Functional Elements** – saving time, reduce effort, sensory appeal.

2. **Emotional Elements** – reduces anxiety, nostalgia, attractiveness.

3. **Life-Changing Elements** – provides hope, heirloom, affiliation & belonging.

4. **Social Impact Elements** – transcendence, value to society, global impact.

Bain and Company's research identifies 30 fundamental attributes. The elements of value approach extend Maslow's insights by focusing on people as consumers—describing their behavior as it relates to products and services.

It is important to remember that the hierarchical representation of needs is the work of later scholars. Maslow himself took a more nuanced view that numerous patterns of fulfillment can exist and there is certainly an overlap between successive levels.

For example, rock climbers achieve self-actualization in unroped ascents of thousands of feet, ignoring basic safety considerations. The Indian leader Mahatma Gandhi often went on a fast, thus voluntarily depriving himself of a basic need such as food, in the quest for social impact—the fight for independence. Thus, he can be construed to have reached transcendent goals even while neglecting physiological needs.

The research found the following to be the most important elements in different types of businesses:

- Apparel Retail – Quality, Variety, Aesthetics, Saves Time, Avoids Hassles.

- Grocery – Quality, Variety, Sensory Appeal, Reduces Cost, Rewards Me.

- Smartphones – Quality, Reduces Effort, Variety, Organizes, Connects.

- Consumer Banking – Quality, Access, Reduces Effort, Avoids Hassles, Heirloom.

It is interesting to note that across all industries studied; perceived quality seemed to affect consumer advocacy more than any other element. Products and services must attain a certain minimum level, and no other elements can make up for a significant shortfall on perceived quality.

After quality, the critical elements differ with industry type. In food and beverages, sensory appeal runs a close second. In banking, access and heirloom (something that appreciates in value from one generation to the next) vie for the second spot. In financial services as an industry, heirloom appears crucial because of the connection between money and inheritance. Well-designed online businesses make many consumer interactions easier and more convenient. Mainly digital companies thus excel on *saves time* and *avoids hassles*. Omnichannel retailers win on some emotional and life-changing elements. They are twice as likely as online-only retailers on *badge value, attractiveness*, and *belonging*.

Companies have begun to use this method in several practical ways, instilling a *hunt for value* mentality in their employees. Many successful entrepreneurs instinctively find ways to deliver value. As companies grow, this process becomes harder. The leaders of most organizations spend less time with customers, and innovation inevitably slows. The elements can help them identify new value once again.

The broadest commercial potential of the elements of value model lies in developing new types of value to provide. Additions make the most sense when the organization can deliver them while using its current capabilities and making a reasonable investment, and when the elements align with the company brand.

Some guidelines may be helpful:

- **Structured Listening** – meet with customers individually and in groups to understand their priorities for a product or service. List the elements and find out the top attributes that customers look for in the product or service.

- **Ideation Sessions** – explore where improvements in value may resonate with customers. Use all customer-touching functions and domains to determine the elements with the greatest potential.

- **Customer-centric Design of Prototypes:** Use design thinking to build prototypes that are likely to meet customer expectations of the elements of value. Each concept that a project team comes up with is likely to yield a different mix of attributes, price, and level of customer service. Remember that perceived quality should always be at the top. No other element can make up for a significant shortfall on quality.

- **Rigorous Choice Modelling** – After designing prototypes, test them on as many customers as possible using discrete choice analysis. This analysis requires people to make a sequence of explicit choices when presented with a series of product or service options. The objective must be to arrive at a winning combination of attributes.

The elements of value have been found to be particularly useful in:

- New Product Development and additions to existing products.

- Pricing – any discussion about pricing must include a discussion about the elements of value.

- Customer Segmentation – whenever a firm adds new elements of value, it may be very useful to look at their impact on customer segments.

The elements of value have an organizational dimension too. Someone in the company needs explicitly to think, manage, and monitor value.

The concept of value remains rooted in psychology. The elements of value can make it much less amorphous and mysterious. The elements can help managers creatively add value to their brands, products, and services and thereby gain an edge with customers—the true arbiters of value.

Examples:

- The life-changing element of *motivation* is at the core of Fitbit's exercise-tracking products.

- The functional element *organizes* is central to Intuit's TurboTax because it helps customers deal with complexities.

- The social-impact element of *transcendence* is the key to Tom's—the company donates a pair of shoes to a child for every pair of shoes purchased by a customer.

- The life-changing element of *self-actualization* is at the heart of a $10,000 Leica—the pride of owning a camera that famous photographers have used for a century.

- Zappos scores twice as high as traditional apparel competitors on the elements of *saves time* and *avoids hassles*.

- Apple excels on 11 elements in the pyramid, several of them high up, which allows the company to charge premium prices.

- The emotional element of fun and entertainment is at the heart of Walt Disney's success.

- The functional elements of simplifies and connects explain the phenomenal success of Facebook, Twitter, Instagram, and WhatsApp.

- Rolex and Omega address the life-changing element of heirloom while promoting their watches.

- Loyalty programs of airlines, credit cards, and hotels cater to the emotional element of *reward me.*

- UNICEF and the Red Cross are examples of the life-changing element of providing hope.

Summing Up

Going beyond the traditional notions of customer-perceived value and unique value or sale proposition, the elements of value model develops a framework against the backdrop of Maslow's hierarchy of needs.

Customer-perceived value has four levels or dimensions:

1. Functional level.

2. Emotional level.

3. Life-changing level.

4. Social impact level.

At each level we can divide customer expectations into elements:

1. The functional level includes such attributes as saves time, reduces effort, simplifies, reduces cost, organizes, integrates, and informs.

2. The emotional level includes attributes such as wellness, therapy, entertainment, design and aesthetics, nostalgia, and attractiveness.

3. The life-changing level includes attributes such as motivation, affiliation, belonging, hope, and self-actualization.

4. The social impact level deals with transcendence—actions taken for the greater good of society, actions taken without any selfish motive, and actions that might transform the quality of life for large sections of people.

The more elements of value a product or service can capture, the higher the probability of success. Similarly, the higher the level of perceived value, the greater the opportunity to charge premium prices.

Chapter 21

The Service Profit Chain

Organizational culture, policies, and support structures determine employee satisfaction, motivation, loyalty, and productivity.

Michael Porter popularized the value chain concept—the notion that an organization creates value through an orchestrated integration of primary and support activities. The concept is useful in understanding value creation in manufactured goods. When we study services, the concept falls short in explaining value creation in services.

James Heskett and Earl Sasser propose the service profit chain to explain the value creation process in services. The model is a series of propositions, each cascading into the next.

- Customer loyalty drives growth and profitability.
- Customer satisfaction drives customer loyalty.
- Value drives customer satisfaction.
- Employee productivity drives value.
- Employee loyalty drives productivity.
- Employee satisfaction drives loyalty.

- Internal quality drives employee satisfaction.
- Leadership is at the heart of the chain's success.

This section explains the service profit chain.

Defining the Service Profit Chain

The lifetime value of loyal customers can be very high when one considers the impact of repeat purchases, purchases of related products and services, and the value of referrals.

For example, the lifetime revenue stream from a loyal pizza-eater can be $8,000, a car owner over $300,000 and a corporate buyer of passenger or cargo aircraft billions of dollars.

James Heskett, Earl Sasser, and colleagues at Harvard Business School proposed the Service Profit Chain as a means to capture service value explicitly. The Service Profit Chain proposes the following:

- Growth and profits are primarily a function of customer loyalty.
- Loyalty derives from customer satisfaction.
- The value of services provided influences customer satisfaction.
- Satisfied, motivated, loyal, and productive employees are at the heart of value creation.

Organizational culture, policies, and support structures determine employee satisfaction, motivation, loyalty, and productivity.

PROPOSITION 1:

Customer loyalty drives growth and profitability.

Frederick Reichheld and Earl Sasser have shown that a 5% increase in customer loyalty can produce profit increases from 25% to 85%. Loyal customers turn into advocates and evangelists or apostles.

PROPOSITION 2:

Customer satisfaction drives customer loyalty.

Organizations typically measure customer satisfaction on a scale from extremely dissatisfied to extremely satisfied. Such qualitative measures may be missing the point.

Consider a Likert scale of 1–5 or 1–10. Scott Cook has shown that customers who rate a service at 5 or 10 (highest levels on scales) are six times more likely to repurchase than customers who rate a service at 4 or 8.

Just as important is the effect dissatisfied customers have on the product or service. A dissatisfied customer is likely to reach out to at least six acquaintances and prevent them from buying the product or service. In this age of social media, a particularly dissatisfied customer can potentially reach out to hundreds of acquaintances.

PROPOSITION 3:

Value drives customer satisfaction.

Customers are value-oriented. What is the value? Value is the result that customers receive in relation to the cost they incur in acquiring the service. Cost includes both explicit and implicit costs (time, effort, and convenience). The result is the experience that customers have while making use of the service.

For example, when you travel from one place to another, on-time departure and arrival, comfort, courtesy of staff, cleanliness, and fellow passengers combine to make you feel satisfied or otherwise with the experience. You compare the experience with the costs incurred and decide whether you want to fly the same airline again or not.

PROPOSITION 4:

Employee productivity drives value.

Of all the determinants of organizational performance, human productivity is easily the most critical.

Consider Southwest Airlines. Turnaround times for a significant majority of flights is 15 minutes or less. As a result, Southwest has 40% more pilot and aircraft utilization than its competitors. Consciously having just one type of aircraft (the fuel-efficient Boeing 737) reduces maintenance, spares, and enhances productivity. There are no seat assignments, and the airline does not offer meals on its flights. Southwest did away with intermediaries long before the industry adopted the initiative as a means to save costs.

Customer perceptions of value are very high because of frequent departures, on-time service, friendly employees and low fares. The Federal Aviation Administration's tracking shows that Southwest achieves the highest level of on-time arrivals, the lowest number of complaints, and the fewest lost-luggage complaints per 1,000 passengers. The high employee productivity drives value as perceived by customers.

PROPOSITION 5:

Employee loyalty drives productivity.

Most organizations measure the loss incurred by employee turnover by estimating the cost of recruiting, hiring, and training replacements. However, the real cost in service jobs is the loss of productivity and decreased customer satisfaction. A study of the automobile industry suggests that the average monthly cost of replacing a sales representative who had five to eight years' experience with an employee with less than a year's experience can be as much as $40,000 in sales.

In the financial services industry, the consequences can be still more dire. Studies have estimated that it takes nearly five years for a broker to rebuild relationships with customers that can return $1 million in commissions to the brokerage house —a cumulative loss of at least $2.5 million in commissions.

It is vital for organizations to foster loyal employees.

PROPOSITION 6:

Employee satisfaction drives loyalty.

While some attrition is inevitable, organizations would do well to minimize turnover. For all industries and sectors in the U.S., the attrition rate is 10% every year. When you look at dissatisfied employees, that figure jumps to 30%.

One of the common features that companies tracked by the Great Places to Work Institute have is a low turnover. Alphabet, Edward Jones, Pal's Sudden Service, and Ritz Carlton have turnover rates significantly lower than their industry average —as low as 3–4% a year.

Deliver on your promise OR
don't promise what you cannot deliver.

What drives employee satisfaction? Is it salary, perks, plush workplaces, or great colleagues?

PROPOSITION 7:

Internal quality drives employee satisfaction.

Internal quality is the emotion that we have toward our jobs, colleagues, and the organization. In the services sector, the ability and authority to achieve results for customers are the most important attribute of internal quality.

Job-related training and development are equally important —Google typically devotes up to 350 hours a year per employee on training and professional development. Internal quality is also characterized by the attitude people have toward one another and the way people serve each other inside the organization.

For example, ServiceMaster, a provider of a range of cleaning and maintenance services, aims to maximize the dignity of the individual service worker. The *importance of the mundane* is repeatedly emphasized throughout the organization. No job is considered to be superior or inferior to any other job.

PROPOSITION 8:

Leadership is at the heart of the chain's success.

Leaders who understand and appreciate the significance of the service profit chain develop and maintain a corporate culture that emphasizes service to customers and fellow employees.

Such leaders show a willingness and ability to listen. Successful CEOs like Herb Kelleher of Southwest, Ken Iverson of Nucor, John Martin of Taco Bell, and Bill Pollard of ServiceMaster spent considerable time with customers and employees.

Taco Bell:

- Taco Bell's management tracks profits daily by unit, market, manager, zone, and country.

- Taco Bell integrates the daily information with the results of exit interviews that the company conducts with a million customers each year.

- Result: Stores in the top quadrant of customer satisfaction ratings outperform the others by all measures.

- Taco Bell links 20% of all operations managers' compensation in company-owned stores to customer satisfaction ratings, realizing a subsequent increase in both customer satisfaction ratings and profits.

- Taco Bell examines employee turnover records for individual stores. Taco Bell has discovered that the 20% of stores with the lowest turnover rates enjoy double the sales and 55% higher profits than the 20% of stores with the highest employee turnover rates.

As a result of this self-examination, Taco Bell has instituted financial and other incentives to reverse the cycle of failure associated with poor employee selection, subpar training, low pay, and high turnover.

Also, Taco Bell monitors internal quality through a network of 800 numbers created to answer employees' questions, field their complaints, remedy situations, and alert top-level management to potential trouble spots. The company conducts periodic employee roundtable meetings, interviews, and a comprehensive company-wide survey every other year to measure satisfaction.

As a result, Taco Bell's employee satisfaction program features a new selection process, improved skills training, increased latitude for decision-making, and automation of unpleasant *back office* labor.

Relating all the links in the service-profit chain is a tall order. However, profitability depends not only on placing hard values on soft measures but also on linking the individual measures together into a comprehensive service picture.

Service organizations need to quantify their investments in people—both customers and employees. The service-profit chain provides the framework for this critical task.

Source: Heskett, James L. et al. Putting the Service Profit Chain to Work. *Harvard Business Review*. Reprint 94204.

Summing Up

Michael Porter popularized the value chain concept—the notion that an organization creates value through an orchestrated integration of primary and support activities. The concept is useful in understanding value creation in manufactured goods. When we study services, the concept falls short in explaining value creation in services.

James Heskett and Earl Sasser propose the service profit chain to explain the value creation process in services. The model is a series of propositions, each cascading into the next.

- Customer loyalty drives growth and profitability.
- Customer satisfaction drives customer loyalty.
- Value drives customer satisfaction.
- Employee productivity drives value.
- Employee loyalty drives productivity.
- Employee satisfaction drives loyalty.
- Internal quality drives employee satisfaction.
- Leadership is at the heart of the chain's success.

Service organizations need to quantify their investments in people—both customers and employees. The service-profit chain provides the framework for this critical task.

Chapter 22

Focus on Your Customers Summary

Customer service is critical to business success.

Customer service is critical to business success. This section examines concepts related to customer service and provides guidelines to meet customer expectations and create loyal customers. In particular, the section focuses on:

- Defining your customers

- Segmenting and targeting your customers

- Creating compelling value propositions

- The relationship that exists between customer service, quality, and loyalty

- A new model of value creation based on the Maslowian hierarchy

- The service profit chain denoting linkages between different components of service value creation

Reflective Questions

Reflection Question #1. Ritz Carlton is an example of outstanding customer service. A customer leaves his laptop charger in his room. He learns about it only when he is in the air. He decides to call back from his office the next day. When he arrives in his office the next day, he has a surprise waiting for him. An overnight package from the Ritz Carlton contains his charger. An accompanying note says that the charger is important to the customer and hence is being sent by the fastest means possible. That is not the end of the story. The package contains an extra charger—just in case! Every employee at the Ritz Carlton, irrespective of the level in the organization, is independently authorized to spend up to $2,000 per day to enhance the guest experience.

What lessons can you learn from this example? What does the example tell you about empowerment and engagement? How would you apply the lessons in your organization?

Reflection Question #2. Warby Parker has disrupted the vision glasses industry in ways that are hard to imagine. You can browse their collection of frames in the comfort of your home. You can try them on through a Virtual Reality (VR) app. You can order five frames. The frames are delivered to you free of charge—no obligation whatsoever. You can decide to retain one or two or three and return the rest—again at no cost to you. You pay only for those you decide to keep. Of course, you can have the frames fitted with prescription glasses, sunglasses, or many other varieties. A customer recounts forgetting his reading glasses on a train. He orders a new, identical pair. He receives not one, but two pairs of reading glasses by overnight mail. The accompanying note says that since the glasses had a few scratches, they have been replaced with new ones.

This situation is one of those rare coincidences. The person sitting across him in the train happened to be the General

Counsel of Warby Parker. Besides the glasses, the General Counsel thoughtfully includes a relevant and eminently readable book. Getting a book gifted isn't in the customer service manual—it's one of those happy surprises that companies do in a variety of ways to enhance experiences for those who buy products from them. The end result is that the customer says he is loyal to the company for life and has encouraged many of his colleagues and friends to switch as well.

How can you apply some or all of the principles in your organization? Outline three steps you would take to improve customer loyalty.

Case Study:

Tata Group

The Tata Group is one of the largest conglomerates in India, with over 100 businesses spread across the world. One of the businesses is automobiles. Tata Motors is one of the flagship companies in the group, making automobiles in India and also owning Jaguar Land Rover in the UK. Ratan Tata, the chairman of the holding company, would see people riding two-wheeled vehicles (motorcycles and scooters) often with three (two adults and a child) and sometimes four (two adults and two children). Ratan Tata wanted to provide a solution.

In 2008, Nano was born, a small car propelled by a two-cylinder engine and designed to seat two adults in the front and two children in the rear; the car was hailed as the ultimate in *reverse innovation*. At a pre-launch price of $2,500, the Nano was easily the most affordable car in the world. The initial enthusiasm was unprecedented. Waiting time stretched into months. The Nano could easily be classified as a disruptive innovation.

In theory, the Nano should have been a success beyond imagination. The company has tried everything possible—compressed air engine (with a capacity of 120 miles on one charge), electric vehicle, and a bi-fuel variant. Unfortunately, the expected success has never materialized. The plant has never been used to full capacity. Meanwhile, due to a raw materials price increase, the price of the car also has steadily increased and currently stands at just over $4,000. For comparison, a Volkswagen Beetle made in Mexico in 1990 would be about $10,000 in today's pricing. The Ford Model T had an initial price of $850, equivalent to $22,500 today. The Nano was launched as an alternative to motorcycles and scooters.

In a developing country, with over 350 million *middle-class* citizens, you would think that the Nano would be a huge success, particularly because of the strength of the Tata Brand—a brand synonymous with the Triple Bottom Line, a brand that had always espoused pro-social goals long before corporate social responsibility became fashionable. The Tata Brand is also well-known for its exemplary HR practices, ethical leadership, and great customer service.

How do you explain the lukewarm response to a great idea and a well-engineered product? If you were Ratan Tata, what would you do differently? Why?

Case Study:

Dream Jobs—Aiming for the Stars at Stellar Solutions

Introduction

In 1995 Celeste Ford had a vision to create a company that tackles only high impact projects—critical customer needs—with an exceptionally engaged workforce. The idea from its start was to align the dream jobs of employees with customers' critical needs. This philosophy has been key to Stellar's success allowing the company to grow from a boutique consulting operation at founding to a major player in delivering high-impact professional systems engineering and technical management services in the aerospace industry. The trajectory of pursuing a strategy combining intense customer focus and high employee engagement has landed Stellar on Fortune Magazine's "Great Place to Work" list for three years running. In 2017 Stellar was a recipient of the Malcolm Baldrige National Quality Award, the U.S. presidential quality award.

Stellar Solutions is a provider of high-impact engineering expertise to customers across a range of professional and technical disciplines to help deliver successful capabilities and achieve mission success. The company has several service lines across the five points of the star:

- Intelligence
- Defense
- Civil space
- Commercial space
- International space

The company is based in Palo Alto, California, with corporate locations in Colorado, Virginia, the UK, and France. The company has a distributed workforce with most employees working on client sites, often in top-secret and secure locations. Stellar has over 200 employees who are typically deployed to larger teams within other organizations. The working environment of the employee is often determined by the hosting client organization.

The Dream Job Worksheet—Simple yet integral

The dream job worksheet is, at its core, a very simple instrument. The key elements of the worksheet fit onto one page and ask two essential questions as a part of employee goal setting. The first question asks the employee to identify their dream job. In answering this question employees are guided by supervisors to develop a robust statement of their dream jobs. A key to this discussion is identifying the passion of the employee.

The second question that an employee is asked involves next steps. If the employee is in their dream job, the discussions with supervisors might involve identification of next steps in a career path. If the employee is not in their dream job, the discussion can involve how to transition to such a job. Employees not in dream jobs may choose a path forward that includes a different type of assignment, serving different clients, or even leaving the company.

Most of Stellar's workforce are highly experienced professionals who have worked in other companies in similar customer sectors or who have completed a career in the U.S. military. This mature nature of the workforce means that employees have an understanding of the industry and the types of jobs available. Often employees are hired to work on projects or in teams of major contractors where they have previously worked.

Stellar views the concept of the dream job and the use of the worksheet as central to its competitiveness. As a company whose main product is services delivered by a skilled workforce, the company leverages workforce engagement in two of its three core competencies (CCs), shown below.

CC1. Maintaining intimate relationships with our customers to keep a pulse on their most critical needs and identify the areas where we can have the highest impact.

CC2. Hiring and retaining "Stellar" employees by maintaining a high level of employee engagement, which results in a workforce that is motivated to deliver high impact services to the customer.

CC3. Aligning the dream jobs of our employees with customer critical needs so that our employees are positioned to help our customers achieve success for their mission.

The dream job worksheet is fundamental to strategy, planning, and operations at Stellar. The concept of the worksheet is that matching employee passion for work with critical customer needs holds the potential to produce outstanding customer results. The worksheet is integrated into Stellar's strategic planning processes and is an integral part of the operations of the business. The Dream Job Worksheet is one of the critical inputs to the strategic planning process of the company as shown in Figure 22.1.

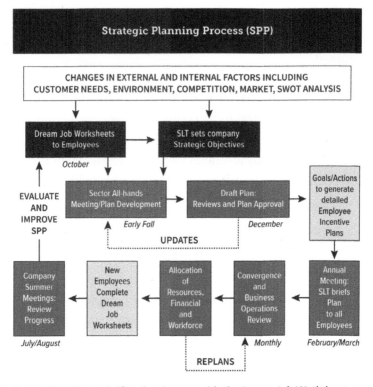

Figure 22.1. Strategic Planning Process with the Dream Job Worksheet.

A unique feature of Stellar's model is the use of employee input through the dream job worksheets to define annual strategic objectives. Rather than taking a human resources approach to workforce under which personnel services are acquired to meet needs in projects sold to customers, Stellar's approach integrates the desires of employees with the understood needs in its markets.

Matching Critical Customer Needs to Dream Jobs

The concept of critical customer needs is foundational to Stellar and dates to the company's formation in 1995. The concept is one that allows the company to provide client services to clients in areas of perceived high value and importance. Pinning down a critical need is a complex task that involves many inputs.

A key element in the critical needs identification is hiring and keeping supervisors who are experienced and knowledgeable in the areas served. Rather than using a process of selecting supervisory personnel solely based on performing the functions of jobs well, Stellar has supervisory employees who have both a deep knowledge of the client areas served and the ability to manage professionals. This balanced experience allows for those in leadership positions to learn of and interpret key changes in the client areas. Emerging critical areas of need also are surfaced through dialogue with customers and key thought leaders in Stellar's semi-annual all-company retreats.

Dream Jobs in a Distributed and Remote Workforce

Most of Stellar's client-facing employees work in client sites and not at a Stellar facility. This distributed and remote nature of the workforce creates challenges in managing workforce engagement and performance. To meet these challenges Stellar uses a workforce management process involving frequent check-ins by supervisors with employees.

Each employee and customer site is visited by a senior leader at least once each month. This touch base activity involves ensuring a match of the employee's performance and satisfaction to critical customer needs. Supervisors are expected to conduct these visits on site and document results.

Increasingly the results of these discussions are captured both in notes for the employee as well as client notes. The latter are now input into a customer relationship management system, Salesforce.com, and can allow for better analysis of trends in customer interactions.

Conclusions

Stellar's process of explicitly asking employees about dream jobs and then acting on that input represents an approach to supporting high performance and employee engagement. As the company grows in size and complexity, one may ask whether the system is scalable and sustainable. Another area of concern is how dream jobs can be identified in areas that the company does not yet serve.

Reflection and Discussion Questions

Consider the following when discussing this case.

1. Is the dream job worksheet an effective tool to assess workforce capability and capacity?

2. Does the dream job worksheet approach truly support the learning and development needed to support future needs of the company? Why or why not?

3. Is the dream job worksheet an effective element of a workforce first strategy? Why or why not?

4. Is the concept of a dream job worksheet transferrable to companies providing products other than professional services?

5. Are there elements of Stellar's use of the dream job worksheet that are transferable to your organization?

6. Can the dream job worksheet substitute for many of the organizational assessments used in companies?

7. What supervisory skills might be required to use a dream job worksheet effectively?

8. What facets of Jim Collins' *Good to Great* organizations might the dream job worksheet support?

Section 5
The Workforce

Get ready to build an irresistible organization.

Business leaders rate employee retention and engagement as the No. 2 issue for business success, second only to global leadership. Gallup's research shows that only 13 percent of all employees are highly engaged, and 26 percent are actively disengaged.

Glassdoor, a company that allows employees to rate their employers, reports that just 50% of employees recommend their company as a place to work. In the technology sector, two-thirds of all employees believe they could find a better job in less than 60 days if they only took the time to look. Some 80% of organizations believe their employees are overwhelmed with information and activity at work, yet fewer than 8% have programs to deal with the issue.

According to Deloitte, more than 70% of millennials expect their employers to focus on pro-social goals; 70% want to be creative at work, and more than two-thirds believe it is management's job to provide them with accelerated development opportunities to retain talented employees.

The employee work contract has changed. People are operating more like free agents than in the past. The balance of power has shifted from employer to employee, forcing business leaders to learn to build an organization that engages employees as sensitive, passionate, and creative contributors. Deloitte calls this shift from improving employee engagement to a focus on building, an irresistible organization.

This section on the workforce explores how to build an irresistible organization. After reading and understanding this section, you should be able to:

1. **Understand** the importance of workforce engagement in an organization.

2. **Appreciate** the principles of effective workforce engagement.

3. **Apply** the principles to build an *irresistible organization*.

Chapter **23**

Workforce Engagement

*The work environment is highly complex—
where we once worked with a team in an office,
we now work 24/7 with email, instant messages,
conference calls, and mobile devices that have
eliminated any barriers between our work
and personal lives.*

The concept of employee engagement has been with us for many years. More than 30 years ago, Gallup and other organizations pioneered the concept of the *engagement survey*. Today there are hundreds of survey providers, and most offer validated surveys and benchmarking tools to help organizations assess employees' level of engagement.

While this may be a good starting point, it is certainly not enough. A typical employee engagement survey does not measure all the variables, it is not in real time, and it does not consider all the issues which drive employee engagement. Most importantly, engagement surveys rarely provide actionable solutions. How can we address the problem of employee disengagement?

The Changing Nature of Employee Engagement

Every year, employee engagement surveys are a one-billion-dollar business. Gallup, the pioneer of such surveys, uses 12 factors that statistically predict retention. Other survey providers try to measure leadership, management, career opportunities, and other work environment elements.

The models are not wrong, but they do not provide actionable results. The deficiency has much to do with the changing work environment itself. Employees today operate in a transparent job market where in-demand staff find new positions in their inboxes.

Organizational structures have become relatively flat, giving people less time with their managers. Younger employees have increased the demand for rapid job rotation, accelerated leadership, and continuous feedback.

The work environment is highly complex—where we once worked with a team in an office, we now work 24/7 with email, instant messages, conference calls, and mobile devices that have eliminated any barriers between our work and personal lives. These changes have radically altered the engagement equation.

A large pharmaceutical company found that executive turnover in its China operations was unusually high. The annual engagement survey gave no clues to help diagnose the problem.

By running a statistical analysis on all variables affecting executive turnover, the company found out that in China, unlike in some other parts of the world, high rates of increase in compensation was the expectation and the norm. The job market was very competitive, and competitors routinely poached talented executives with significant increases in compensation.

Today more and more companies are deploying analytics solutions to predict retention, correlating factors such as compensation, travel, demographics, and location to understand why certain people are less engaged than others.

High technology companies throw benefits at employees to see which ones have the largest impact—vacations, free food, fitness centers, stock options, flexible timings, and fun offices. Do any or all of these result in high engagement?

Most companies do not have an answer. The challenge is well-defined, but difficult to address in organizations.

How can we create an organization in today's changing, complex, and ambiguous environment that is attractive, creates a high level of passion and performance, and has a built-in real-time monitoring mechanism to fix problems?

You need to be clear about four issues:

1. What does *employee engagement* mean today?

2. How can you develop tools and protocols that measure feedback and employee sentiment in real-time?

3. How can you customize the practices to suit local cultures and aspirations?

4. How can you transform employee engagement to a routine HR function to a core business strategy?

The Irresistible Organization: Deloitte's irresistible organization model has five key elements and twenty underlying strategies. Organizational culture binds the elements and the strategies.

Most studies show that compensation is an important factor in employee satisfaction. Aon Hewitt's research shows that compensation ranks among the top five drivers (but is not number one). We do not discuss compensation because research shows that pay is a *hygiene factor*, not an *engagement factor*. In most cases, if compensation is not high enough, people will leave—but increasing compensation does not directly increase employee engagement (with a few exceptions).

Among the highest-potential employees in large organizations, there is a direct correlation between pay increases and retention. Among the remaining 90% of the workforce, compensation simply needs to be competitive and fair within job categories. Once compensation is competitive and fair, the issues we discuss have a much greater effect on employee engagement.

Element #1:

MAKE WORK MEANINGFUL

The most important part of employee engagement is job/person fit. We need to make sure that jobs are meaningful, people have the tools and autonomy to succeed, and that we select the right people for the right job. Selecting the right people for the right job is not a simple undertaking.

Technology has changed and transformed nearly every job. Today's driving force for success is to do more with less. Organizations constantly look for technology solutions, outsourcing, and a general propensity to produce more output with less expensive human input.

Improving productivity is important. However, research suggests that when we enrich jobs, give people more autonomy, decision-making power, and support, the organization makes more money.

Psychologist Daniel Pink writes that autonomy, mastery, and purpose drive people. MIT Professor Zeynep Ton shows that retailers like Whole Foods and Costco deliver higher profitability per employee by giving their employees above-average wages and greater control over their jobs. The idea of *lowering the cost of labor* to save money is self-defeating because people become less productive as their workload goes up.

At Costco, cross-trained people handle many positions. Employees manage cash registers, stock shelves, rearrange the store, develop promotions, and manage others. The result is both a set of highly empowered teams that have the training and freedom to be autonomous and productive as well as above-average retention and engagement rates.

As we design jobs to be meaningful, we must also carefully select the right person for each job. Fewer than 40% of all hiring teams use any form of formal pre-hire assessment. Most managers look for education, GPA, and experience. When organizations study the characteristics of high performers, they find that other *fit factors* drive success and happiness on the job.

> **Giving people time away from the workplace lets them relax, engage, and perform better.**

Creativity expert Sir Ken Robinson calls the critical success factor *The Element*. The Element combines aptitude and attitude with passion.

For example, theater employees who drive the highest levels of customer satisfaction are not those with good grades or strong experience. Rather, they are people who *like to have fun* and *love to serve others*.

An insurance company found that the best salespeople were not from top schools but rather those who had experience in the automobile industry and zero mistakes on their resumes. When we hire people who fit, they perform well, and they love their work.

Organizational culture has become an important part of job fit. Zappos, a company that prides itself on culture as strategy, uses its ten core values to assess people for cultural fit in the early stages of the application process.

By getting to know candidates well (through online and phone meetings) before people even apply for jobs, Zappos can assess fit and help people decide if they should even apply for a job. This type of assessment has helped Zappos maintain a high level of engagement, low turnover, and its place among one of the best customer-service providers in online retail.

Research also shows that meaningful work takes place in small teams. Jeff Bezos, the CEO of Amazon, observes that "if there are more than two pizzas in the room for lunch, then the team is too big." Small teams feel empowered, make decisions faster, and people get to know each other and can lend a hand when one of the teammates needs help.

Engaged people need time to think, create, and rest.

At Google, the policy is called *20 percent time*, a time set aside to work on something new or outside your normal job function. A well-known retailer sends employees home when the store is relatively empty of customers. The employees are free to run errands, have lunch with their families, or just relax. When things get busy, they return to the store. This company is one of the most profitable in its industry, in part, because slack time gives its workforce the freedom to take care of their home lives and put more effort into their work.

It may seem counterproductive to let people take time off during the week, but in fact, the opposite is true. Over-worked people tend to burn out, produce lower-quality output, provide lower levels of customer service, become depressed, and sometimes just flail around in their exhaustion.

Giving people time away from the workplace lets them relax, engage, and perform better.

Element #2:

FOSTER GREAT MANAGEMENT

The second element of an irresistible organization is management. We use the word *management* here, not leadership, to refer to the daily, weekly, and monthly activity managers use to guide, support, and align their people.

Management is the most important capability we have.

CEOs can create strategies, investors can optimize capital, and marketers can create demand, but when it comes to building products and offerings, serving clients, and developing internal processes, middle managers make things happen. We each strive on our ability to contribute to a greater good, and management's job is to set goals, support people, coach for high performance, and provide feedback for continuous improvement. Investment in fundamental management practices has a tremendous impact on engagement, performance, and retention.

In reviewing engagement issues, the first area we find is the importance of simple, clear goals. When people have defined goals, and the goals are shared freely, everyone feels comfortable, and more work gets done. Goals create alignment, clarity, and job satisfaction—and they must be reviewed and discussed regularly.

Goal setting is a challenge. Only 51 percent of companies even attempt to develop aligned goals, and, among these, only 6 percent regularly revisit the goals. Too many companies write down annual goals and look at them at the end of the year. Companies that revisit goals quarterly have a threefold greater improvement in performance and retention than those that revisit goals yearly.

Nothing makes a person feel better about work than being able to be highly successful.

Google uses an agile goal-setting process called OKR (objectives and key results). Intel originally developed the concept and Google has adopted the concept. The process is simple and effective. Each individual (from the CEO down) sets ambitious and measurable objectives (like launch Gmail Version X by year end) and defines *key results* that monitor progress. Everyone's OKRs are public, so it is easy to see what the CEO or your peer is holding herself or himself accountable for in the organization. At Google, this creates alignment because employees can see who is dependent on their work. People feel comfortable that they know what to do, they see what others are working on, and the measurement of their performance is clear.

Coaching is the second management practice that drives engagement. A coaching culture is a practice that has the highest correlation with business performance, employee engagement, and overall retention. When people get into supervisory positions, they often think their job is to direct and evaluate other people. While the direction is important, it is the coaching and development role of management that is the most valuable.

What makes a great coach? Marcus Buckingham describes that great coaches understand people's strengths, move them into positions and rearrange work to leverage their strengths, and coach them to build on their strengths. Nothing makes a person feel better about work than being able to be highly successful.

The third aspect of great management is leadership development. Organizations with high levels of employee engagement focus on developing great leaders. They invest heavily in management development and ensure that new leaders get ample support.

High-impact organizations invest 1.5–3.0 times more on management development than their peers. The continuous focus on building leaders, connecting leaders to each other and giving leaders the coaching they need is critical to building a highly engaged workforce.

The fourth issue of great management is the need to simplify and re-engineer the performance measurement process. Seventy-five percent of companies have institutionalized the process. Performance measurement is among the most damaging and disheartening process employees face each year. Only 8 percent of employees think the process is worth the time they put into it, and the focus on rating and ranking takes the focus away from the coaching and development that people often desperately need.

In many companies, the process does not involve enough continuous feedback, places too much weight on the rating, and often does not encourage exceptional performers to perform at an even higher level.

The concept of *forced ranking*, popularized in the 1960s, is now falling away because it takes away the autonomy and judgment of leaders, discourages very high performers, and rewards those in the middle.

Management's job is not to manage work but rather to develop, coach, and help people. Rewarding managers only for making their numbers incentivizes *talent hoarding*; i.e., attracting good people and holding onto them for years.

Forward-thinking companies reward managers for *talent production*, developing people who leave their teams. High-engagement companies use the culture of continuous development in management.

Element #3:
ESTABLISH A FLEXIBLE, HUMANE, INCLUSIVE WORKFORCE

The third element of an irresistible organization is the need to build a flexible, humane, and inclusive workforce. Most employees today have complicated lives. Some 68% of women would rather have more free time than make more money.

While 40% of professional men work more than 50 hours per week, 80% would like to work fewer hours. Given the nature of work today, if leaders want people to engage with their organizations, they have to give them a flexible and supportive work environment.

SAS, the No. 2 place to work for the last 15 years, has an in-house daycare center, fitness center, and pool, and the company's turnover rate is below 2 percent (against the industry standard of 20% or more).

Google has multiple food centers, a bowling alley, a fitness center, and yoga rooms.

Free food, yoga and meditation classes, happy hours, commute buses with internet access, and free laundry service are now commonplace in high-pressure companies across a wide range of industries. These are no longer *perks*, they are essential elements of making work fit into our lives.

In addition to such benefits and employee wellness programs, research shows that open, flexible workplaces have a major impact on engagement. Open workplaces enable people to meet easily—the new spaceship-shaped Apple campus is designed to encourage groups to meet others. Open workplaces also give people highly flexible places to work, depending on the way employees feel on a given day.

Zappos lets people work from local restaurants, and the company pays for Wi-Fi. Introverts still want a quiet office. Considering that one in three people is an introvert, workplaces can be designed to provide privacy when required and an open environment for interaction.

Another key engagement driver is the need for continuous and ongoing recognition. Just saying *thank you* is an extraordinary tool for building an engaged team. High recognition com-panies have 31 percent lower voluntary turnover than companies with poor recognition cultures. High-engagement companies foster a culture of recognition through social reward systems (tools that give people points or kudos to reward to others), weekly or monthly thank-you activities, and a general culture of appreciating everyone from bottom to top. The key to success is to create a social environment where recognition can flow from peer to peer, freeing managers from being the judge and jury of employee recognition. Organizations that build a culture of recognition see the tremendous impact.

When JetBlue implemented a peer-to-peer recognition system focused on company values, employee satisfaction surged 88 percent. There are physiological effects as well. When you thank someone, it releases oxytocin, a hormone that makes people more relaxed, happy, and collaborative.

Highly engaged workplaces are also inclusive and diverse. People feel comfortable being themselves. While 71% of organizations state that they foster diversity and inclusion, only 11% have such an environment today. Worse, only 23% of organizations hold their CEOs accountable for building a diverse and inclusive environment. Instead, leadership often delegates this work to a director within HR. The lack of diversity plagues some of the fastest-growing companies in the world.

Diversity and inclusion is not an HR strategy; it is a business strategy. Not only do diverse workplaces attract people from a wider sample, but research also shows that teams that operate in an inclusive culture outperform their peers by a staggering 80%.

How do organizations become more inclusive? Inclusion usually comes from the top. Inclusion, unlike diversity, is a cultural issue—one that requires support from top-level leaders as well as all levels of management.

*Building opportunities for growth
is a complex and systemic challenge.*

Leaders must overcome their unconscious biases and make every effort to listen, create open forums for discussion, and promote people with varied backgrounds (gender, nationality, race, age) who embrace listening and inclusive values.

Element #4:

CREATE AMPLE GROWTH OPPORTUNITIES

When top performers leave a company, the most frequent comment they make is, "I just didn't see the right opportunities here." We often go to work with selfish interests. If we don't feel we are going to progress in our chosen role or career, we are likely to look elsewhere.

Engagement research shows that learning opportunities, professional development, and career progression are among the top drivers of employee satisfaction. Employees under the age of 25 rate professional development as their number one driver of engagement. Professional development is the number two priority for employees up to age 35. As employees get older, their focus on development shifts away from mobility and upward progression in favor of aligning a job with long-term career goals.

Building opportunities for growth is a complex and systemic challenge. First, there must be developmental opportunities, both formal and informal, that let people learn on the job, take developmental assignments, and find support when they need help. This means designing onboarding and transition management programs, developing a culture of support and learning, and giving people time to learn.

Second, a company must support and honor facilitated talent mobility. Most people will not be promoted every year or two (although high-potential millenials often expect it), but they want to feel that they are growing and can take on new assignments in their chosen area. Managers, and the company as a whole, need to support and facilitate internal mobility, giving people the freedom to try something new and move from a role where they are highly productive to one where they may become a trainee again.

Third, organizations must look at their management and leadership behaviors to make sure that learning, development, and mobility receive due recognition. Organizations mostly reward leaders for *making their numbers*. While goals are important, it is equally important to reward leaders for developing people, moving people into the best role, and keeping retention high.

Organizations with a strong learning culture are 92% more likely to develop novel products and processes, 52% more productive, 56% more likely to be the first to market with their products and services, and 17% more profitable than their peers. Their engagement and retention rates are also 30-50% higher than peers.

Element #5:

ESTABLISH VISION, PURPOSE, AND TRANSPARENCY IN LEADERSHIP

The final and perhaps the most important element in the irresistible organization is leadership. Research suggests that four leadership practices most directly impact employee engagement.

The first is to develop and communicate a strong sense of purpose. When organizations define their success through the eyes of their customers, stakeholders, or society, people come alive. Mission-driven companies have 30% higher levels of innovation and 40% higher levels of retention, and they tend to be first or second in their market segment.

How do you create purpose, mission, and soul? Define your company regarding all of its stakeholders—employees, customers, investors, and partners. When all stakeholders benefit, the business performs well. When you offer people a mission and purpose greater than financial return, you attract passionate individuals who want to contribute. And that brings a level of commitment and engagement no compensation package can create.

NASA is a mission-driven organization. During the heat of the space race, a group of reporters visited NASA. As they headed to the meeting room, they saw a janitor working with a broom in hand. The reporters took out their cameras and asked the janitor, "So what is your job at NASA?" The janitor immediately looked into the camera and said, "It's my job to help put a man on the moon." How many of your employees can answer a question like this?

The second important element in leadership is transparency. Due to social networks, the internet, and mobile technology, the news spreads faster than thought. Therefore, whether it is bad news (a rough quarter, an unintentional mistake, an accident, a legal battle, or a compliance violation) or good news (a good quarter, someone achieving something significant, or a great customer experience) be sure to share promptly and truthfully.

Whole Foods goes so far as to release every employee's total salary and bonuses from the previous year in its annual wage disclosure report. If employees are concerned about their compensation, they are encouraged to meet with HR executives to discuss their issues.

Transparency is particularly difficult for traditional leaders. Traditional leaders often believe they can *manage the truth* through PR, communications specialists, or timed release of information. Today, this approach typically fails, and people immediately see the deception. Among millenials, transparency from leadership rates is among the most important drivers of company loyalty.

Third, leaders must continuously invest in people. High-engagement companies have executives who invest in learning, meet with teams and provide feedback, and genuinely care about each other. Research spanning over a decade shows that companies that *overinvest* in Learning and Development (investment per employee) rate the highest in employee retention, innovation, and customer service and outperform their peers three-fold in long-term profitability. Investment in people matters a lot during both good times and bad.

Fourth, senior leaders must continuously focus on inspiration. Through their words, communications, and actions, it is the top executives who ultimately engage everyone in the organization. By talking about the future, sharing the vision, and translating the business strategy into meaningful, personal concepts, leadership can be one of the most important drivers of engagement.

A Focus On Simplicity

As we illustrate at the bottom of the model, highly engaged companies work very hard to make work simple. They remove administrative overhead (compliance processes, formal check-off processes, and multi-step processes) in favor of trust, autonomy, and a focus on cooperation.

Simplicity—or the removal of formal bureaucratic overhead —can have a dramatic impact on work satisfaction. A series of worker-productivity studies by the University of Rotterdam shows that workers who operate in highly complex environments have increased levels of cardiovascular and other illnesses unless they have extraordinary autonomy and local support. Without increased amounts of empowerment and local control, complexity can lead to high levels of error and stress.

Southwest Airlines, one of the top 20 rated employers in the U.S., has honed simplicity and empowerment in its business model. Southwest uses a single airplane model (Boeing 737), thus driving down maintenance and inventory costs. Southwest empowers the local team (the airplane crew) to make all decisions they need to run safely, on time, and on budget. Online reservations and common boarding for every flight simplify operations. It is not surprising that the company has reported profits for 43 consecutive years and continued to score among the highest in customer satisfaction year after year.

Capturing Real-Time Feedback

How do organizations implement workforce engagement practices in an integrated and holistic way? First, leadership and HR must develop a complete understanding and mindset of these factors and how they relate to one another. Almost every management practice has an impact on employee engagement. While we focus on performance, growth, and innovation, we must simultaneously focus on the impact of each strategy on individuals.

Second, it is important to obtain regular, unbiased, and anonymous feedback. People always want to talk about what is working and what is not working in their company. An annual employee survey is too slow and limiting. Today pulse survey tools, sentiment monitoring tools, and employee sensing tools give employees a variety of ways to express their feelings and provide direct feedback to managers and peers. Consider using one or more anonymous *heartbeat monitors* of your business.

Placing Employee Engagement at the

Center of Everything We Do

If we don't have teams committed to our mission, passionate about their work, and willing and ready to work together, we cannot possibly succeed over time. Nearly 90% of executives understand the importance of employee engagement; fewer than 50% understand how to address the issue.

Today's technology-driven world of work is complex, demanding, and integrated into our lives. Even though 79% of companies today find it daunting and difficult, they can plot their path to the future and design organizations that will thrive with passion, performance, and engagement by focusing on the five elements of irresistible organizations.

Summing Up

The concept of employee engagement has been with us for many years. More than 30 years ago, Gallup and other organizations pioneered the concept of the *engagement survey*.

Today there are hundreds of survey providers. Most offer validated surveys and benchmarking tools to help organizations assess employees' level of engagement. While this may be a good starting point, it is certainly not enough. A typical employee engagement survey does not measure all the variables, it is not in real time, and it does not consider all the issues which drive employee engagement. Most importantly, engagement surveys rarely provide actionable solutions. How can we address the problem of employee disengagement?

Chapter **24**

Strategies to Improve Employee Engagement

Satisfied, loyal, and productive employees create value. Businesses must, therefore, create the environment in which employees are satisfied and engaged.

Contrary to popular belief, employee engagement is not the same thing as job satisfaction, nor does it mean job happiness. All engaged employees are, to varying degrees, content, but the reverse is not true. Employees may be content and not be engaged.

> *Employee engagement is the extent to which people are personally involved in the success of the business.*
>
> —Emma Bridger, Award-winning author
> and employee engagement expert

Engaged employees will go the extra mile because they feel a strong emotional connection to the organization. Engaged employees want the business to succeed because they identify with their company's mission, purpose, and values at a personal level. This section explores strategies to improve employee engagement in an organization.

Improving Employee Engagement

Engagement affects every person in your organization. Every person in your organization affects your bottom line. Your employees are your first and most important customers.

Professor James Heskett and others popularized this concept through their service-profit chain. The researchers established links between profitability, customer loyalty, and employee engagement.

High
Quality
Leadership

- Leadership
- Internal Service Quality
- Employee Satisfaction

Enhanced
People
Outcomes

- Employee Satisfaction
- Discretionary Effort
- Intent to Stay
- Productivity
- External Values

Enhanced
Business
Impact

- Customer Satisfaction
- Customer Loyalty
- Revenue Growth
- Profitability

Figure 24.1. Improving Employee Engagement, adapted from Heskett, Jones, Loveman, Sasser & Schlesinger (2008).

Satisfied, loyal, and productive employees create value. Businesses must, therefore, create the environment in which employees are satisfied and engaged. In turn, engaged employees create valuable, loyalty-inspiring experiences for customers. Loyal customers drive business profits.

While employee engagement creates value, employee disengagement destroys it. Disengaged employees are not only unhappy and unproductive, but their negativity also rubs off on the people around them, turning potentially engaged employees into non-engaged employees. The Gallup Organization estimates that disengaged employees cost U.S. companies $550 billion each year.

Strategy #1: Values and Purpose

Why does your company exist? Most companies find this terrain hard to navigate, and hard to articulate. Human beings still carry certain tribal tendencies. We have an innate desire to be a part of something bigger than ourselves.

A sense of purpose is one way of doing that because it connects us to a common, higher mission and inspires us to place the needs of others before our own. Arming your employees with a sense of purpose is critical to creating the emotional bond between your employees and their work, thus enhancing their engagement. A company's core values are an extension of *why the business exists*.

The core values of Google are:

- Focus on the user and all else will follow.

- It's best to do one thing really well.

- You don't need to be at your desk to find an answer.

- You can make money without being or doing evil.

- The need for information crosses all borders.

- Great is just not good enough.

Why values matter—the Inside-Out Effect of Culture

Your organization's culture is the sum of the beliefs and behaviors that guide interactions between employees and other key stakeholders. Culture manifests in observable things like hours, dress code, benefits, workspace, turnover, hiring, and customer care and satisfaction.

Culture is also something less tangible—it is a feeling, the mood, and energy people bring in each day, the language they use, the mindset they adopt, and the methods they use to solve problems. An inconsistent culture can create a disconnect within your organization, which can have negative consequences for current and potential customers, and cost your business significantly in the long run.

Assessing an internal culture is a difficult task. The following questions might help: Do you and your employees socialize outside of work? Do most of your employees have a best friend at the office? Are your employees likely to accept responsibility for their mistakes or pass the blame to others? Are your employees likely to recommend a friend to work at your company? Do you observe certain undesirable behaviors, like employees frequently coming in late or leaving early?

There is no concept of work-life balance here. It is all just life.

—Erica Javellana, Zappos

For retail innovator Zappos, the why of their brand has just one word—happiness. The concept of delivering happiness is the foundation of the company's culture and values, and informs everything they do, from the way they hire to their famously responsive customer service and free shipping.

All new employees (irrespective of level) go through a four-week training process. Two weeks are devoted to fielding customer service calls—the touchpoint of the business. At the end of the four weeks, the new employee can quit with pay and a $2,000 bonus. The cash incentive to leave helps weed out any potential mistakes in the hiring process.

Note: Zappos is now a wholly owned subsidiary of Amazon.

Action Steps:

1. Why does your organization exist? Can you write this down in one sentence or a phrase?

2. Create a mission statement and values that align with the reason for your existence.

3. Use the values and mission statement to form the basis of your organization's culture.

4. Create activities and recognition programs that capture your values.

5. Be consistent and make sure you are authentic. Reflect your culture in all your activities—internal and external.

Strategy #2: Communication

Good communication establishes trust and legitimacy between leaders and employees, and between managers and their direct reports. Effective communication should be:

1. Frequent and consistent

2. A two-way street

3. Consistent with the brand and culture

4. Multi-channel

5. Fully inclusive

Communication channels: For small offices, the morning meeting/team huddles can be a relaxed, efficient means to be on the same page every day. The *all-hands meeting* is effective in organizations with over a hundred employees. A town-hall style platform is recommended, with senior executives outlining key aspects of strategy and purpose, and everyone having an opportunity to raise questions.

Many CEOs are taking a leaf out of the academic setting, and make themselves available during specific hours on specific days. Senior managers can replicate the process for their teams.

Enterprise social networks that provide everyone a snapshot of current activities and projects is a great tool for collaboration and staying on top of everything. The suggestion box, often considered outdated, can be valuable in eliciting anonymous feedback, concerns, and questions.

Action Steps:

1. Start by listening—gauge the organization's communication needs.

2. Audit communication channels—what channels make sense?

3. Select and deploy the right mix of communication channels.

4. Organize a morning or weekly meeting (ideally not more than 10 minutes daily or 30 minutes weekly).

5. If your organization employs over a hundred people, hold town-hall style meetings (once a quarter) and listen to what people have to say.

6. Collect and use feedback, and engage in dialogue (a *dialogue* facilitates understanding each other's viewpoint, even when these are different; a *conversation* is a zero-sum game—after a while, the executive higher in the organization usually *wins*).

7. Strive for authenticity and transparency at all times.

The Four Seasons group of hotels has a reputation for exemplary service and high levels of engagement. Any employee at any level can bring up an important issue for consideration, and a dialogue follows almost immediately. Each employee has a discretionary budget for enhancing the customer experience. The organization learns continuously through open forums where people relate both positive and negative experiences and outcomes.

Strategy #3: Health and Wellness

Employee health and well-being is a significant factor in productivity and employee engagement. Nearly 62% of engaged employees feel their work positively affects their physical health. The number drops to 39% among non-engaged employees and to 22% among employees who are actively disengaged. Likewise, 54% of self-assessed disengaged employees say their work has a negative effect on their health, while 51% see a negative effect on their well-being.

Caring about employee health is not just a perk or nice gesture; there is also a strong business case for employee health and wellness initiatives. Organizations who invest in health and wellness save money in the long run by curtailing healthcare costs and reducing productivity-loss due to illness-related absenteeism.

A Harvard Business School study estimates that on average, employers who invest in comprehensive health and wellness initiatives derive a nearly 3-to-1 return on money saved. Health and wellness campaigns also play a role in creating that important emotional connection between employers and employees.

Group fitness challenges also promote teamwork, camaraderie, and bonding, and gives individuals in your organization the sense that you are all in it together. The key is not to focus on one-off perks, but rather to create a lasting, long-term health and wellness strategy that aligns with the company's fabric and culture.

How does an effective wellness strategy look? Your health and wellness strategy should be voluntary, long-term, physical, fun, and competitive. It should also include access to good nutrition and mental health support.

The logistics company Hassett Express has two mission statements—one geared toward customers, and the other committing to employee well-being. The company launched a group fitness challenge—the goal was to collectively walk the distance equal to the distance between the company's headquarters and their farthest satellite office, about 2,000 miles away. The company handed out pedometers and created a custom web portal where employees could log steps, distance, and time. The company provided information on safe walking routes and the distance between major landmarks. The objective was to complete the 2,000-mile walk collectively within six weeks. The team rose to the challenge and completed the distance in five weeks. The benefits of the program included a fitter, healthier team, and a strong sense of camaraderie.

The company which has completed greater challenges and well-being is as much a part of the mission as providing great service to customers.

Action Steps:

1. Bring in personal trainers or yoga instructors to conduct onsite fitness classes.

2. Incentivize health-conscious choices, like biking or walking to work, or getting a flu shot.

3. Organize company-wide fitness challenges to inspire physical activity while promoting teamwork and bonding.

4. Get employees off their seats; reduce the sedentari-ness of office life by providing *active desk* options.

5. Provide easy access to nutritious meals, snacks, and beverages.

6. Make sure that wellness activities are voluntary, never mandatory. Employees need to feel that they are free to choose their level of participation.

7. Harness the power of technology by providing your employees with digital fitness trackers.

8. Open a dialogue about mental health and make confidential services available.

Strategy #4: **Workspace and Environment.**

The best office workspaces authentically reflect their company's brand and cultural values and are conducive to the type of behavior and activities supporting the business. Phenomenal spaces are both functional and inspirational, create a sense of pride, and are places where employees want to spend their time.

For example, if you value a flat organization where ideas can come from anywhere, from the mailroom assistant to the CEO, try taking down the walls. An open plan, in which there are no cubicles or offices, will help create an environment that is non-hierarchical, where open communication and radical ideation are the norms.

The software company New Relic values creativity and col-laboration so much that the company has a music rehearsal and recording studio at their headquarters. Employees can relax, create, and bond through the music they love.

A big part of having the right space for your team
is showing them you care about them
and want to make a place that they will enjoy
and can promote their growth.

Google's Tel Aviv office features floor to ceiling slides, an indoor orange grove, and a heritage floor with curated pieces from the city's markets and bazaars. Since innovation and collaboration are highly valued, fifty percent of the interior consists of communal space, like cafes and lounges.

Planning your spaces to include open layouts, spaces for collaboration, as well as places for focus and solitude is important. Additionally, affordable niceties like ping-pong tables, iced coffee machines, and thoughtfully placed puzzles (where each employee can collaborate on ideas that will add to their workplace) can do wonders for morale and engagement. Some companies (like Enplug) allow employees to build their furniture—DIY is way cheaper than buying ready-to-use furniture.

The trend today is to make your space as residential and *homey* as possible, which reinforces the idea that the work-life distinction is less meaningful than it used to be.

Enplug buys used, worn-in couches on Craiglist rather than expensive new ones. They are much more affordable and give your office a comfortable, livable quality.

Overall, the goal should be to create an authentic space within your means that reflects your unique culture and values, is conducive to the types of behaviors your company needs to be successful, and where employees want to spend time. If you can do that, you will be well on your way to creating an engaged workforce.

Action Steps:

1. Clarify your company's mission and codify it in core values. Make these values visible and apparent in your office.

2. Create a space that reflects the culture your business needs and is authentically you, whatever that means.

3. Create spaces for serendipitous interaction, like game rooms, lounges, cafes, and reading rooms.

4. Turn your lunch/break room into a hub for collaboration, connectivity, and community.

5. Create a mix of spaces that reflect the entire spectrum of values and behaviors your business needs, including open spaces, collaborations, and spaces for solitude and focus.

6. Make it fun! Simple perks can go a long way to upping the fun factor, giving your office the balanced atmosphere it needs to create engaged employees.

7. A big part of having the right space for your team is showing them you care about them and want to make a place that they will enjoy and can promote their growth.

Strategy #5: Create Well-Defined Roles.

You cannot have an engaged workforce without clarity at the organizational level. Your company needs a mission statement, core values that support the mission, and a culture that embodies your values and enables your mission.

Many companies fall into a trap when they neglect to connect the big picture with the individual and their specific role within the company. A prerequisite for employee engagement is that employees need to know that their work matters, and that it is both valued and valuable. Employees need well-defined roles.

Defining job roles is about connecting the organizational mission with each employee's day-to-day activities. Ultimately, the role should be a clear framework for how the employee's efforts contribute to the company's overall mission. Without the framework, employers risk confusion, disengagement, and burnout.

At Toyota Motor, the roles are visible through posters at the employee's workstation. Thus, each employee knows what to do every day, and how that action relates to the organization's mission of "Leading the way to the future of mobility, enriching lives around the world with the safest and most responsible ways of moving people; through our commitment to quality, constant innovation, and respect for the planet, we aim to exceed expectations and be rewarded with a smile; we will meet our challenging goals by engaging the talent and passion of people, who believe there is always a better way."

Action Steps:

1. Clarify organizational objectives and drill down from there. Every employee should know how her/his role fits into the company's overall mission.

2. Write an accurate job description, and update as needed when an employee assumes additional responsibilities.

3. Use assessment testing to find the right fit for the right role.

4. Set goals, and check in frequently. Roles and objectives change over time, so reassess as often as necessary.

Strategy #6: Relationships with Colleagues.

Fostering a sense of community, loyalty, and friendships in the workplace can and should be a strategic component of your company culture that gives your business a competitive advantage.

Gallup reports that close work relationships boost employee satisfaction by 50%, while people with a self-described best friend at work are seven times more likely to be fully engaged at work. Employees experience higher levels of happiness and satisfaction in their work when they have friends in the workplace.

The culture of work has evolved in the last few decades from a top-down, paternal model to more of a partnership model. Executives are more relaxed and more willing to let their personalities and personal interests shine through at work. The executives' action has a trickle-down effect on the rest of the organization. The shift from work-life balance to work-life integration also means that employees are more comfortable exhibiting their *true selves* in the workplace. Personal relationships help build emotional bonds that inspire positive feelings toward the company and mission.

Many companies choose to build company game rooms in their offices. Online gaming giant Zynga has a world-class arcade-style game room which is a favorite congregation spot for employees. Research shows that gaming for as little as 20 minutes per day with coworkers elevates the mood, strengthens social bonds, and builds trust.

Company retreats off-site are another fantastic way to nurture personal connections between individuals and teams.

Remember, not everyone will be friends at work, and not everyone has to be friends. Don't force it!

Action Steps:

1. Create an environment where friendships will form naturally by injecting a sense of fun into your company culture and values.

2. Incorporate *personality fit* into the hiring process.

3. Make meetings personal—take a few minutes at the start of meetings to encourage personal sharing.

4. Reward company performance with company retreats, offsite activities, or bonding activities.

5. Don't force it. Your goal is to create the right environment so you can reap the rewards of higher engagement, not to mandate friendships.

Strategy #7: Employee Recognition and Incentives.

Princeton economist Angus Deaton and psychologist Daniel Kahneman demonstrate that money is a threshold rather than a scorecard. Beyond a threshold, money does not contribute to overall happiness.

> **Work toward a culture of recognition,**
> **not just a recognition program.**

The finding has serious implications for employee engagement. This information helps reinforce the notion that it is the less quantifiable personal and emotional factors—not the financial ones—that matter the most. That's where recognition programs come into play. Create avenues for team-wide or company-wide recognition, such as monthly or quarterly awards for team members who demonstrate outstanding work ethic or display exemplary leadership.

SnackNation creates company points or dollars that peers can award at any time. Employees can redeem the points or dollars for exclusive company merchandise. The approach allows employees to give and receive recognition throughout the day and fosters a spirit of appreciation.

Action Steps:

1. Integrate weekly individual recognition activities into your overall engagement strategy.

2. Create monthly or quarterly awards that embody your core values.

3. Consider profit sharing, bonus structures, or equity. Remember that it is more about enabling employees to identify with the big-picture company goals and creating a sense of vested interests than remuneration.

4. Work toward a culture of recognition, not just a recognition program. Ingrain appreciation in your daily interactions.

Strategy #8: Creating an Organization of Amazing Managers.

Senior leadership is important in engagement strategy. CEOs and senior leaders set the vision and strategy for any organization.

In most organizations, middle managers have an even bigger influence on engagement than senior leadership. Managers are the direct link between the C-suite and the rest of the organization. Managers make daily contact with employees and execute strategy. They are a critical factor in the effectiveness of your engagement strategy.

Gallup reports that managers account for at least 70% of the variance in employee engagement scores across business units. A Dale Carnegie study suggests that the immediate supervisor is the chief emotional driver in the workplace; reactions to her or him explain 84% of how employees feel about their organization.

Good managers need vision, decisiveness, team-building skills, accountability, self-awareness, empathy and emotional intelligence, and their direct reports' best interest at heart.

Action steps include:

1. Select managers with the right mix of skills for leadership. Work with them to develop any fundamental skills they lack.

2. Do not simply promote star performers—remember the Peter principle: *In a hierarchy, every employee tends to rise to her/his level of incompetence.*

3. Educate your managers on both the company vision and on the importance of engagement.

4. Hold your managers accountable—developing their direct reports should be a Key Performance Indicator (KPI) for managers.

5. Appoint a dedicated engagement manager to guide and execute your engagement strategy. Without someone leading execution, your strategy is at great risk of remaining a paper tiger.

Strategy #9: Cultivating Personal Growth and Development.

Talented people are your most precious resource. The growth and development of your employees is a foundational concept in employee engagement. Employees need to feel that they are continuously growing and developing, both personally and professionally. If your workforce feels it is stagnating or treading water in a dead-end job, they will disengage and look for outside opportunities.

An atmosphere of continual growth is no longer just a desire; it is a necessity for companies that don't want to experience high turnover. Organizations today are moving away from a human resources model to a human capital model.

The human resources model treats talent as a finite, exhaustible asset. The role of the HR professional is to enhance the asset through strategic hiring and allocate the resource like any other resource.

Human capital implies that talent is something that we can nurture and grow; therefore, HR professionals invest in and develop talent, not just acquire it. Nurturing and growing human capital includes subsidizing education, time for passion projects (employees can pursue any project they like, and the company gets the first shot at any business potential), and vacations and sabbaticals.

Examples:

- Google employees can devote 20% of their time (effectively one day every week) pursuing a pet project. On the face of it, 20% may appear to be a huge chunk of time away from business-related work, but the policy has paid off. Many of Google's best-known products such as Gmail, Google maps, and Adsense are a direct result of *passion time projects.*

- Media Temple is a tech company providing cloud hosting solutions. Each employee gets a paid, one-month sabbatical every three years, during which time they can travel anywhere, engage in service projects or learn a new skill. The benefits far out-weigh the costs.

Action Steps:

1. Educate leaders on the difference between human capital and human resources, and how it relates to engagement.

2. Subsidize education—with MOOC (massive open online courses), you no longer have to spend huge amounts to learn. As long as the focus is on learning and not necessarily on getting a degree, the costs are within reach of most organizations.

3. Encourage passion projects—allocate a percentage of work time for this. Alternatively, allow employees to compete in a *hackathon*—a time-bound activity within which each team must come up with a business idea and justify it.

4. Allow employees to take *sabbaticals* during which they can travel, experience new cultures, or participate in a service project that reshapes their perspective.

5. Leverage the expertise of your company by holding seminars, workshops, and intense discussion sessions.

Strategy #10: **Completing the Puzzle.**

Consider an 8-week plan for enhancing employee engagement:

- Week 1: Articulate your organization's sense of purpose and ensure that everyone understands the purpose. Address some *low-hanging fruit* issues to enable everyone to see immediate results. Activities can include an audit of communication channels, and providing access to healthy snacking options.

- Week 2: Dedicate Week 2 to listening—get employees' feedback on engagement, find out their interests, generate ideas on reorganizing workspaces, and clarify individual roles.

- Week 3: Use the data to develop your values, finalize your strategy, and make sure your communication channels work well.

- Week 4: Hold a company all-hands meeting. Answer questions and start basic projects immediately (reorganizing workspaces, changing some of the furniture, providing space for solitude, and dedicating areas for discussion).

- Week 5: Launch your wellness campaigns. Bring in trainers to impart training, and harness the power of interdepartmental competition with wellness challenges. Prominently display your values and mission. Make sure employees have access to healthy snacks and beverages.

- Week 6: Take stock—start business meetings with 3-minute personal anecdotes. Assess employee roles and change where necessary. Set business and personal goals. Begin weekly company-wide communications on issues that matter.

- Week 7: Open your fun and game room. Make socializing a part of the work by reserving the last hour on Fridays for an informal get-together, either at the office or a nearby restaurant. Hold your first education session—leverage the expertise that already exists in your organization before bringing in external experts.

- Week 8: Devote the week to recognition, rewards, and loyalty programs. Recognize wellness achievers. Start planning a future offsite activity or retreat. Measure the effectiveness of your strategy and adjust as necessary.

May your employee engagement journey blossom and flourish!

Summing Up

Contrary to popular belief, employee engagement is not the same thing as job satisfaction, nor does it mean job happiness. All engaged employees are, to varying degrees, content, but the reverse is not true. Employees may be content and not be engaged. Engaged employees will go the extra mile because they feel a strong emotional connection to the organization. Engaged employees want the business to succeed because they identify with their company's mission, purpose, and values at a personal level.

This section has explored strategies to improve employee engagement in an organization.

Chapter **25**

The Workforce Summary

The balance of power has shifted from employer to employee, forcing business leaders to learn to build an organization that engages employees as sensitive, passionate, and creative contributors.

Business leaders rate *retention and engagement* as the No. 2 issue for business success, second only to global leadership. Gallup's research shows that only 13% of all employees are *highly engaged*, and 26 percent are *actively disengaged*.

Glassdoor, a company that allows employees to rate their employers, reports that just 50% of employees recommend their company as a place to work. In the technology sector, two-thirds of all employees believe they could find a better job in less than 60 days if they only took the time to look. Some 80% of organizations believe their employees are overwhelmed with information and activity at work, yet fewer than 8% have programs to deal with the issue.

Research by Deloitte indicates that more than 70% of millennials expect their employers to focus on pro-social goals; 70% want to be creative at work, and more than two-thirds believe it is management's job to provide them with accelerated development opportunities to retain talented employees.

The employee work contract has changed. People are operating more like free agents than in the past. The balance of power has shifted from employer to employee, forcing business leaders to learn to build an organization that engages employees as sensitive, passionate, and creative contributors. Deloitte calls this shift from improving employee engagement to a focus on building, an irresistible organization.

Reflective Questions

Reflection Question #1:

How far are your employees engaged? Would you consider administering an anonymous survey to determine the engagement level of your organization? Assume that the survey shows a low (less than 40%) level of employee engagement. How would you address the issue in the short-term and the long-term? If your survey shows employee engagement to be higher than 75%, what would you do to maintain and, if possible, to improve that level?

Justify your answer based on the following:

1. Resources that you are willing to invest in the process.

2. Results that you expect from implementing changes.

3. A business case for your proposal and its implications.

Reflection Question #2:

Develop a wellness program for your organization. Address issues related to fitness, emotional well-being, nutrition, and psychological safety separately. Outline the steps to achieve tangible goals on each dimension. Specify a time-frame within which you will achieve the desired results. Justify your answer.

Short Case Study: **IDEO's Employee Engagement Formula by Duane Bray (Partner, IDEO).**

David Kelley founded IDEO with a simple goal—to create a workplace made up of his best friends. Some 30 years later, IDEO is a global design company with 650 people.

Four elements of IDEO's culture stand out:

1. Permission to play: We encourage experimentation. We have brainstorm kits, Post-It notes, crayons, drawing paper, scissors, clips, and tape in every meeting room. We encourage people to express themselves in a variety of ways. Employees create their work environments—including furniture, layout, workstation, and anything they need. We constantly try to find ways to turn the mundane into the engaging. We insert animated GIFs into office-wide e-mails so that they have a narrative, build community, and encourage dialogue.

2. A common purpose: IDEO's purpose statement— "Positive and disproportionate impact in the world through design"—is ambitious and intentionally broad. We connect the dots for our associates worldwide by providing them the autonomy to tailor the purpose statement to suit their environment. In large offices, each part of the business may create its purpose statement. For example, the Food and Beverage Studio's purpose is "Bridging the worlds

of culinary and science to solve the world's food problems." The flexibility allows creativity and alignment.

3. A social contract: Seven common values bind us together: *be optimistic, collaborate, learn from failure, embrace ambiguity, talk less and do more, take ownership,* and *make others successful.* These values are the behaviors that drive our social contract. They allow teams to govern themselves without needing oversight and management, and they help people understand what success looks like. We have found that they are also a great aid in development. The employees we hire rarely struggle with the skills of their jobs, but sometimes they do need support in adhering to the values.

4. Bottom-up innovation: We have learned that the most promising new ideas and capabilities are best incubated from the bottom-up through someone's energy and commitment. When someone generates an idea and is passionate about it, we always try to understand the needs, alignment with our purpose, and a clear sense of the desired outcome. The best strategies are ones that people can make their own.

In a world where great talent is hard to find and harder to retain, companies succeed by keeping their employees engaged, happy, and fulfilled. There is no silver bullet. But the four principles listed above have helped IDEO go a long way in achieving that goal.

Questions:

1. Write a commentary on IDEO's employee engagement model.

2. Would you use the model in your organization, without or with changes? What are the changes you feel to be necessary to your organization? Why?

3. If you believe you cannot apply this model, please explain the reasons.

Section 6
Performance Management

A Gartner study shows that 70% of managers of 500 large corporations equate performance management with measuring individual performance.

Performance management does not have a universally accepted definition. A Gartner study shows that 70% of managers of 500 large corporations equate performance management with measuring individual performance.

Unfortunately, this view misses the point.

The competitive environment of the 21st century has three key components—complexity, ambiguity, and rapid change. Product life cycles have shrunk dramatically. Organizational mortality is at an all-time high, with life-spans in many industries being less than five years.

While human capital is critical to business success, we need to measure much more than individual performance. We need holistic measures which look at organizations for what they are—dynamic systems capable of anticipating and embracing change instead of merely *reacting* to change.

This section on performance management introduces you to such holistic measures. After reading this section, you should be able to:

1. **Understand** the concepts of enterprise performance management.

2. **Appreciate** the different approaches to performance management, such as the Balanced Scorecard, strategy maps, activity-based costing, and customer lifetime value.

3. **Apply** appropriate methods to your situation or organization.

4. **Measure** results.

5. **Learn** from your results and start the journey of continuous improvement.

Chapter **26**

Understanding Performance Management

Performance management is all about improvement.

An organization must grapple with three major choices constantly:

1. Market and customer choices – which segments and types of customers to serve and not to serve.

2. Product or service choices – what/what not to offer.

3. Sustainability choices – how to keep winning, how to keep learning, and how to meet stakeholders' expectations.

While performance management can provide insights into all three, its usefulness is the most in achieving the third dimension—continuous adaptation, agility, and successful execution of strategies. Performance management is particularly useful in managing uncertainty and complexity. This section explores the contours of performance management.

What Is Performance Management?

If we remove all the technicalities, performance management is all about improvement.

1. How do we create value for our customers?

2. How do we create an eco-system with employees, suppliers, distribution channels, regulators, and society; where each stakeholder group perceives its expectations as having been met?

3. How do we anticipate and embrace change?

Digital Equipment Corporation (DEC): At its zenith, DEC was a powerhouse that could do no wrong. Founded by Ken Olsen, and managed with an obsession for engineering precision, the company grew to $14 billion in sales and employed 130,000 people worldwide in the 1970s. When the personal computer arrived on the scene, DEC was unable to adapt and failed spectacularly. In 1998, Compaq bought DEC. Of course, HP acquired Compaq later.

The rise and fall of DEC have three important lessons for leaders and managers.

First, be constantly watchful of disruptive innovations. DEC's failure was one of the starting points for innovation expert Professor Clayton Christensen to develop his theory of disruptive innovation. Here's how Professor Christensen put it:

> "Every disruption has three components: a technology enabler, a business model innovation, and a new commercial ecosystem. In computing, the technology enabler of disruption was the microprocessor. It so simplified the design of a computer that Steve Jobs and Steve Wozniak could put one together in a garage. It transformed the fundamental technological problem of computing

from a problem that took hundreds of people
several years to solve into one that could be
solved by a few people in weeks, or even days."

Next, the simplified technology had to be tied to a business
model which would place a cost-effective and convenient
computer on the market. DEC had produced a microprocessor, but its warring business divisions could not agree on a
computer for less than $50,000. The technology trapped in a
high-cost business model was irrelevant, and the market killed
DEC. Companies (like IBM) which could adapt to the new
commercial ecosystem (democratization of computing)
placed the personal computer at $2,000 and still managed
to generate a 20% margin.

Even a *culture of innovation* can become dysfunctional as
markets change. Edgar Schein, an emeritus professor at the
MIT Sloan School of Management and an expert on organizational culture analyzed DEC's rise and fall through the
lens of corporate culture in his book *DEC is Dead, Long Live
DEC: The Lasting Legacy of Digital Equipment Corporation*.
He said:

> "Olsen created a 'culture of innovation' that
> empowered employees and was characterized by
> expressly stated values such as *Do the right thing*,
> an oft-cited maxim. But, as DEC grew bigger, the
> values and culture that helped it thrive as a younger,
> smaller organization led to an environment
> that felt more and more chaotic and out of control
> when compared to its glorious days. A corporation's
> founding values, if they lead to success, tend to
> ossify as a set of tacit assumptions about successful

strategy. When the business environment shifts, the organization may not be able to adapt, rejecting plans or ideas that don't fit its preconceived notions. The illusion that organizations can control their fate stems from the failure to understand how technology and culture limit what is possible."

In a recent interview, Schein argued that DEC would probably have survived and even flourished if it had been split into three separate units: one for the search engine Alta Vista, the second for computers, and the third for microprocessors. Olsen's error might have been his inability to see the writing on the wall and clinging on to notions that were no longer valid.

The competitive environment is complex, uncertain, and volatile.

Paul Kampas, the coauthor of the book on DEC, has argued that technology-driven companies need to shift from a *product*-innovation culture to a *process*-innovation culture as their markets mature.

Intel has nearly perfected process innovation. By relentlessly focusing on Moore's Law and processes to pack more and more circuits on a wafer of silicon, the company has stayed ahead of the curve. Intel represents a classic case of technology driving markets instead of markets driving technology.

In an age when company mortality is at an all-time high, perhaps an executive's lasting legacy may be how she/he treats people. As one former DEC executive observed on Olsen's passing away in 2011, "I feel indebted because it was the golden era of corporate culture done right, and this was all Ken Olsen's values."

And Curt Nickisch noted: "Ken Olsen was certainly one of the titans of the computer industry. But he was also a personal titan to most of the employees in the organization that he co-founded, DEC. They knew him for his humility and the culture of fun and excitement he created."

Why is responding to changes so critical? The competitive environment is complex, uncertain, and volatile. The sheer speed of change renders calendar-based planning and long-term planning unsuitable. Strategies cannot be static. They need to be dynamic. Managers need to adapt and refine in real-time.

Suppose managers and indeed, employees at all levels, could answer the following questions every day:

- What if my plan or decision is wrong?

- What are the consequences if I am wrong?

- If I am wrong, how can I correct it?

Performance management helps answer these questions. Performance management enables organizations to anticipate, adapt, and respond rapidly.

Consider two scenarios—one in which managers and employees are provided with relatively precise information about the short-term (one to three months) and relatively less precise information about the future (six months to a year and more). The second scenario provides the opposite characteristics—which one should they prefer? Since short-term information is likely to be more precise, managers cling on to this and focus on short-term goals. Long-term information is likely to be ambiguous and hence managers find it difficult to create long-term value.

It is useful to think of performance management as an umbrella concept that encompasses and integrates the following:

- Operational information
- Financial information
- Strategy mapping
- Balanced Score Card (BSC)
- Activity-Based Costing (ABC)
- Budgeting including Financial Modeling
- Forecasting
- Capacity Requirements Planning (includes Materials Requirement Planning, Enterprise Resources Planning)
- Supply Chain Management (SCM)
- Customer Relations Management (CRM)
- Risk Management and Risk Mitigation
- Human Capital Management
- Lean Management

- Organizational Design, and

- Six Sigma, Zero Defects, and Related methodologies

- Descriptive and Predictive Analytics

Practical Models for Performance Management

Performance Management provides the technological and social integration of different elements that make up an organization.

Performance Management makes strategy execution everyone's business. Deployed holistically, it makes employees at all levels feel and act like owners and creates a synergistic effect that is crucial to sustained business success.

The first step is to develop a clear mission and strategic direction.

Google's mission is to organize the world's information and make it universally accessible and useful. Why is this mission compelling and powerful? Google's mission addresses extraordinary problems in a way that may not require any change in the next hundred years.

First, by including the term *universal*, Google implies that everyone on the planet is a potential customer. Second, Google organizes information—in myriad ways. Third, Google provides access to anyone—there is no fee for accessing information. Fourth, Google constantly refines information to make it useful. The genius of the mission is that it does not require a separate vision.

Objective	Activity	Process	Output	STRATEGIC SUCCESS
TO ESTABLISH CLEAR STRATEGIC DIRECTION	Strategic Review Exercise	• Information Dissection Framework • Internal/External Analysis • Customer Analysis • Environmental Analysis	• Revised 5 Year Vision • Finalized Organization Mission • Identified Financial Results • Established Key Strategies	
TO DEVELOP OBJECTIVE LINKAGES REVISED	Strategy Map Development Exercise	• Customer Value Proposition • Objective-to-Objective • Result and Driver Analysis • Environmental Analysis	• Linked Objective from One Perspective to Another • Established Strategic Themes • Corporate Strategy Map	
TO DEVELOP CORPORATE PERFORMANCE METRICS REVISED	Corporate Balanced Scorecard Development Exercise	• Objective to Measure Analysis • Initiatives Analysis	• 1st Draft Corporate BSC • Identified Unit Type of Target to Each Measure • Identified Tracking Instrument • Finalized Initiatives	
TO TRANSLATE STRATEGIC GOALS INTO OPERATIONAL OUTPUTS	Cascading & Alignment Exercise	• Unit Operation Performance Analysis • Measure-to-Measure Mapping	• Operating Unit Measures Are Strategic Linked to Corporate Measures • Finalized Corporate BSC • Operating Unit Action Plan	
TO RELATE INDIVIDUAL PERFORMANCE MEASURES TO CORPORATE PERFORMANCE	KPI Development Exercise	• Job Type Analysis • KRA/KPI Analysis	• Identified Company-Wide KPIs • Established Individual KPIs and Linked to Unit BSC	

PERFORMANCE RESULT LINKAGE

Figure 26.1. Organizational Culture Transformation Initiative, adapted from Detert, Schroeder, & Mauriel (2000).

Information and knowledge are infinite. There will always be room for improvement. Hence, Google's mission is a perpetual *work in progress*. Of course, Google is a business. The company earns its revenue through advertisements across the millions of websites that it serves.

In a simple sentence, Google articulates why it exists, what it does, and how it creates value. Once the mission (and vision) is clear, we need to translate it into meaningful objectives.

Objectives can be strategic (growth, market share, time horizon) and financial (return on investment, return on assets, return on equity, earnings per share, and compounded annual growth rate). In a single business, there may be just one set of objectives.

In businesses with multiple products or services, we need to translate corporate objectives into business-level objectives. Business-level objectives lead to functional objectives— what to achieve and how to achieve the desired goals in marketing, operations, accounting and finance, human capital, technology, quality, logistics, innovation, service, supply chain, and customer relations.

Functional objectives lead to team-based objectives and finally to individual performance. Thus, individual performance is the final piece of the jigsaw which is the totality of organizational objectives.

An alternative method of deploying enterprise performance management is shown in Figure 26.2.

Figure 26.2. Key Elements of Enterprise Performance Management.

The key elements are purpose, processes, and people. The underlying elements are models, measurement, and information.

From this perspective, a performance management system is a subset of a knowledge management (KM) system—a virtuous cycle of transforming data into information, information into knowledge, and knowledge into wisdom.

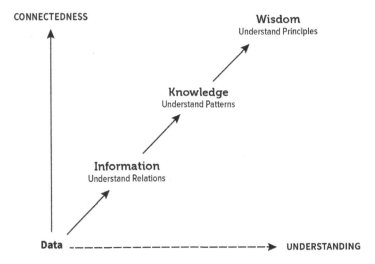

Figure 26.3. A Knowledge Management System.

Knowledge has two dimensions—how much do we understand and what are the relationships between the various aspects of knowledge? In its fundamental form, we start with data. Data by itself has little value.

For example, if we say we have a million customers, it does not convey much. To make this information meaningful and relevant, we need to slice and dice a million customers into active and dormant, loyal and occasional, high-potential and low-potential, geographies, demographics, and psychographics.

Information becomes knowledge when we understand patterns—trends, cycles, expectations, and changing environments. Knowledge becomes wisdom when our experiences and learning lead to an understanding of principles: stage in an industry life cycle, competencies, macroeconomic forces, social forces, competitive forces, regulatory forces, and how we can leverage our strengths/mitigate threats while adhering to core values and ethical foundations.

A well-designed and deployed performance management system has the potential to drive the organization toward the ultimate differentiating principle of more for less. It can create value for all stakeholders that cannot be achieved by any stand-alone methodology.

Most organizations define performance measures quite well. They fail to provide the necessary culture; in particular, they fail to provide psychological safety. Psychological safety is an environment that encourages divergent views to be expressed without the fear of ridicule or retribution.

As Professor Amy Edmondson of Harvard Business School has shown empirically, a performance-oriented system embedded in an organizational culture of high psychological safety leads to organizational, team, and individual learning and enrichment.

A low-performance orientation with low psychological safety leads to apathy; maintaining the status quo becomes the dominant goal.

A high-performance orientation with low psychological safety leads to anxiety and stress; both are detrimental to the organization.

A low-performance orientation with high psychological safety leads to complacency; people perform at the minimum level.

Only when a high-performance orientation is combined with high psychological safety do we achieve learning at all levels. The organization becomes vibrant and dynamic, with every activity being seen as an opportunity to excel and to improve.

There is a shift in the source from which organizations realize their financial ROIs—from tangible assets to intangible assets of employee knowledge and information. That is, the shift is from spending on equipment, computer hardware, and the like to knowledge workers applying information for decision-making.

In the initial stages of an organization's evolution, the emphasis is on transactional data and information. For example, accounting is focused on historical information. There is no attempt to study the present, much less to look into the future and make corrections and adaptations.

In retrospect, a significant approach to the Y2K problem can be termed reactive. The transition, from traditional systems to much-touted techniques such as MRP and ERP, provided snapshots of the past and no foresight into the future. It should not come as a surprise that hundreds of millions of dollars invested in such software failed to yield the expected results.

Any attempt to adapt systems quickly has to be grounded in the present and the future. The goal of Business Intelligence (BI), Performance Management (PM), and Analytics is to develop descriptive models.

For example, Activity-Based Costing (ABC) is a modeling technique that categorizes expenses into costs of processes, work activities, and the types of outputs, products, service-lines, channels, and customers that consume an organization's capacity. A strategy map and its associated performance indicators is a model of how an organization defines its linked strategic objectives and plans to achieve them.

In either case, data is transformed into information. At this stage, people can know not only what happened but also why it happened. In the next stage, organizations make the transition to what-if scenarios and rolling financial forecasts, to which organizations are proactive. Organizations shift their management style from after-the-fact post-mortem and control-based on an examination of the variance from plans, budgets, and expectations to an anticipatory management style where they can adjust spending and capacity, as well as projects and initiatives before changes in work demands arise.

Information is used to create knowledge. People can know not only what happened and why it happened but also what can happen next. In the final stage that can be called the optimizing stage or the continuous-learning stage, tacit knowledge is the basis of decision-making.

Summing Up

This section has examined the contours of performance management.

An organization has to grapple with three major choices constantly:

1. Market and customer choices – which segments and types of customers to serve and not to serve.

2. Product or service choices – what/what not to offer.

3. Sustainability choices – how to keep winning, how to keep learning, and how to meet the expectations of various stakeholders.

While performance management can provide insights into all three, its usefulness is the most in achieving the third dimension—continuous adaptation, agility, and successful execution of strategies. Performance management is particularly useful in managing uncertainty and complexity.

Chapter 27

Performance Management Tools

An integrated advantage can lead
to sustained superior performance.

Several tools are available to facilitate a value-creating performance management system. This section introduces a few tools:

1. Balanced Scorecard and Strategy Map

2. Activity-Based Costing

3. Supply Chain Management

This chapter also introduces a Systems framework for Performance Management.

Identifying the Performance Management Tools

Balanced Scorecard and Strategy Map: Robert Kaplan and David Norton pioneered the Balanced Score Card and Strategy Map concepts. The Balanced Score Card looks at organizational performance through four prisms:

1. Financial – Irrespective of industry or sector or country, organizations need to create value. Value is a multi-dimensional construct. Part of it can be measured. Part of it is intangible and hence difficult to measure.

A common denominator for measurement is finance. Peter Drucker famously said that Return on Investment is the best indicator of firm performance. Other common measures include Return on Assets, Return on Capital Employed, Return on Sales, and Return on Net Assets.

Shareholders are interested in the stock price. Acquirers and institutional investors may be interested in market capitalization. In the final analysis, organizations need mechanisms to increase revenues and decrease costs. Michael Porter has argued that Cost Leadership and Differentiation are the two generic strategies which can lead to superior performance.

A cost leader tries to reduce costs to a level lower than that of comparable competition. Southwest Airlines, Nucor Steel, and discount retailers (such as Walmart) are examples of cost leaders. A differentiator tries to build and include unique characteristics or features into the offering and thereby charge a premium price. Apple, BMW, and Rolex are examples of differentiators.

Many scholars have argued that cost leadership and differentiation are not mutually exclusive. Although difficult, firms can aim for an integrated strategy that includes cost leadership and differentiation. If and when achieved, an integrated advantage can lead to sustained superior performance. Toyota in the automobile industry is an example of successful integration of cost leadership and differentiation.

Customers are willing to pay a high price
for the true to life sound quality.

Michael Treacy and Fred Wiersema have proposed an alternative model for framing value propositions: Operational Excellence (sometimes referred to as the best total cost), Product Leadership, and Customer Intimacy (sometimes referred to as customer solutions).

2. Operational Excellence aims at providing offerings at low prices; the low prices are an outcome of having the lowest total cost; the offerings do not provide any unique features or characteristics; the customer experience focuses on the low price and does not expect personalized or superior service. The *same for less* and *less for much less* value propositions can be mapped into this strategy.

3. Product Leadership focuses on unique features and the notion of *best in category* offerings; the price is set high; customer experience meets expectations; the value proposition tends to be *more for more*.

4. Customer Intimacy also aims to charge premium prices with offerings meeting expectations of quality but with an enhanced or memorable customer experience. *Much more for more* is the value proposition.

Ikea in furniture, Bose Corporation in acoustics, and Four Seasons among hotels represent the three value propositions.

Ikea's mission and vision: "At IKEA our vision is to create a better everyday life for the many people. Our business idea supports this vision by offering a wide range of well-designed, functional home furnishing products at prices so low that as many people as possible will be able to afford them." Ikea's 2017 figures of 36.1 billion euros in revenues and 2.5 billion euros in net profits demonstrate the success of the strategy.

Bose acoustic systems have been known for their exceptional quality for over 50 years. Customers are willing to pay a high price for the *true to life* sound quality.

Four Seasons has been ranked consistently among the best hotels in the world and one of the best companies for employees.

Operational excellence requires organizations to lead the industry in price and convenience. *Product leadership* requires constant innovation (can be within or procured) and agility in speed to market. A product leader must be willing to disrupt itself. *Customer intimacy* requires the willingness to do almost anything to satisfy customers. The firm is interested in customer lifetime value, not the value of each transaction.

Strategy Mapping is a six-step process that addresses the following:

1. An **overarching objective** to be achieved:

    • Return on capital employed

    • Profit margin

    • Shareholder value (dividends and stock price)

- Growth

- Market share

2. Determining the **value proposition** (generic models of cost leadership/differentiation OR operational excellence/product leadership/ customer intimacy).

3. Choice of **financial strategies**:

   - Capital budgeting

   - Investment

   - Dividend

   - Revenues

   - Productivity (technological, asset, and human)— cost controls, cost allocation, and cost reduction

   - Utilization (plant, equipment, time, people, inventory)

4. Choice of **customer-centered strategies**:

   - Customer experience (capture, measure, and enhance)

   - Internet of Things (IoT) and design thinking

   - Customer retention

   - Customer growth

   - Increase revenue per customer

   - Reduce cost per customer

   - Customer lifetime value

5. Implementing **internal perspective strategies:**

- Focus on cost or differentiation
- Focus on operational excellence, product

6. Implementing **learning and growth strategies:**

- **Organizational capital** – goal alignment, organizational structure (flattening, empowerment, wholeness, teamwork, and collaboration, culture, shared vision, leadership, trust, psychological safety, and accountability)

- **Information capital** – data, analytics, networks, security, and infrastructure, information systems, decision support systems, and expert systems

- **Human capital** – creation, acquisition, sharing, and dissemination of knowledge, engagement, service quality, creativity, goal alignment, camaraderie, and productivity

The primary goal of any organization is to create value for stakeholders—shareholders, customers, employees, suppliers, regulators, government, community, society, and the planet.

Strategy maps help articulate the value creation process. By focusing on critical areas—cost, features, operational excellence, innovation, and customer experience—strategy maps facilitate clear communication with stakeholders. Strategy maps force organizations to formulate strategies before implementing them. In the process, they make it possible for organizations to jettison redundant measures of performance. Strategy maps allow the seamless integration of the four components of the balanced scorecard framework—customer, financial, internal, and learning and growth—and thus provide a complete framework for measuring organizational performance.

Strategy maps need to cascade to different levels if they are to guide improvement and learning at every stage. The real value of strategy maps is in aligning corporate, strategic business unit or divisional, functional, team, and individual goals.

When deployed with authenticity and commitment, they can help the creation of organizational synergy. Strategy maps can be used equally effectively by for-profits, not-for-profits, and public service entities.

To be instruments for purposeful change, strategy maps should:

1. Be a part of the strategy formulation process.

2. Include all key stakeholder groups.

3. Cascade down from mission and vision to value propositions and objectives along financial, customer, internal, learning and growth dimensions.

4. Articulate corporate, divisional, functional, team, and individual key performance indicators.

5. Link objectives to action plans—for example, how to reach zero defects, or how to measure and enhance the customer experience, or how to speed up the concept-to-market cycle.

6. Facilitate timely decision-making in critical areas—financial, marketing, operational, technological, and human.

7. Provide a roadmap for organizational learning and growth.

8. Lead to constant reflection, renewal, and optimism.

9. Adapt rapidly to changing environments in industry, competition, economy, and global trends.

Activity-Based Costing (ABC)

Activity-Based Costing may be considered as a refinement of absorption costing. ABC traces resource consumption to the source and allocates costs to final outputs. Resources are assigned to activities and activities to cost objects. Cost objects use cost drivers to allocate activity costs to outputs. Absorption costing focuses on volume-related drivers (for example, machine hours or labor hours) whereas ABC focuses on transaction-based drivers (such as orders received, processes required). Thus, long-term variable overheads that are considered to be fixed costs can be traced back to individual offerings, forming the basis for value-based decisions.

The main advantage of ABC is that it provides a more meaningful picture of product or service costs, and thereby can lead to better pricing decisions. By focusing on cost drivers, ABC isolates activities that do not create value and paves the way for managers to either eliminate them or at least to reduce such costs.

ABC can also be used for profitability analysis for offerings and customers. Thus, it can be a valuable complement to the Balanced Score Card, Continuous Improvement, and related Performance Management techniques.

Supply Chain Management

Supply Chain Management (SCM) is the oversight of materials, information, and finances as they move in a process from supplier to manufacturer to wholesaler to retailer to consumer. Supply chain management involves coordinating these flows both within and among organizations.

The objective of an effective SCM system is to minimize inventories at every stage. In other words, the concepts of Just in Time (JIT) and supply chains go together.

SCM flows are comprised of:

- Product or Service flow
- Data and Information flow
- Finance flow

Vertically-integrated partnerships or value-adding partnerships are a set of independent organizations working closely together to manage the flow of goods and services along the entire value chain. In the most successful models, value-adding partnerships are comprised of small companies, each of which performs one part of the value-added chain and coordinates its activities with the rest of the chain.

An excellent example of value-adding partnership is that of McKesson Corporation, the American company distributing pharmaceuticals at a retail sale level and providing health information technology, medical supplies, and care management tools. The company had revenues of $179 billion in 2015. Over the last thirty years, the company has built enduring relationships across the value chain. The McKesson partnership is so powerful that competitors have been forced either to emulate the business model or withdraw from the business altogether. The key to McKesson's success is the understanding that each player in the value-added chain has a stake in the others' success.

Today, McKesson offers a proprietary system for supply chain management and analytics as reported on its website. The module provides actionable insight into a hospital's supply chain with business analysis and performance models, plus valuable data tools to organize and interpret the data. Among the benefits of the module are:

- Actionable insights into supply chain with business analysis and performance models.

- Organization and interpretation of data via valuable data tools.

- Evaluation of current and potential contracts with extensive contract analysis.

- Trending information associated with key business drivers to directors, managers, and human resource and finance executives.

- Focus managers' attention on important business goals with relevant, actionable workforce measures.

- Improved salary management process with real-time earnings information.

- Detailed turnover analysis to promote employee retention.

Other examples of successful implementation of value-adding partnerships can be found in the textile industry (Italy, India), the construction industry, the automobile industry (Toyota), and the movie industry.

In a value-adding partnership, each small operating company focuses on doing just one step of the value-added chain. Each unit can design all aspects of the organization to the single task. People, plant and equipment, compensation, career progression, accounting and finance, and management ethos—all vary according to the work to be done. Focus results in low overheads, lean staff, and few middle-level managers. Response time is short because of limited or no hierarchy and rapid decision-making. Creativity blossoms and more employees are directly in touch with the customers.

Key success factors are those activities, attributes, competencies, and capabilities seen as critical prerequisites.

Since each entity can be different from the others, the system has built-in diversity that can be a powerful seeding ground for innovation. Marketing orientation flows naturally and not as an edict. Despite some pitfalls arising from mutual dependencies, the economic value of value-adding partnerships is compelling. They can result in the simultaneous pursuit of cost leadership and differentiation for the value system as a whole.

System Framework for Performance Management

A system framework for performance management includes the following 12 considerations:

1. What is the **vision** and **mission** of the organization and how is this brought to the attention of managers and employees? What mechanisms, processes, and networks are used to convey the organization's overarching purposes and objectives to its members?

2. What are the **key factors** believed to be central to the organization's overall future success and how are they brought to the attention of managers and employees?

3. What is the **organization structure** and what impact does it have on the design and use of performance management systems (PMS)? How does it influence and how is it influenced by the strategic management process?

4. What **strategies and plans** have the organization adopted and what are the processes and activities that will be required to ensure its success? How are the strategies and plans adapted, generated, and communicated to managers and employees?

5. What are the organization's **key performance measures** deriving from its objectives, key success factors, and strategies and plans? How are these specified and communicated and what role do they play in performance evaluation? Are there significant omissions?

6. What level of performance does the organization need to achieve for each of its key performance measures (identified in the previous question), how does it go about setting appropriate performance targets for them, and how challenging are those performance targets?

7. What processes, if any, does the organization follow for evaluating individual, group, and organizational performance? Are performance evaluations primarily objective, subjective, or mixed; and how important are formal and informal information and control in these processes?

8. What rewards—financial and non-financial—will managers and other employees gain by achieving performance targets or other assessed aspects of performance? Conversely, what penalties will they suffer by failing to achieve them?

9. What specific information flows—feedback and feedforward systems—and networks does the organization have in place to support its PMS operation?

10. What type of use is made of information and the various control mechanisms in place? Can these uses be characterized in terms of various typologies in the literature? How do controls and their uses differ at various hierarchical levels?

11. How has the PMS altered in the light of the change dynamics of the organization and its environment? Have the changes in PMS design or use been made in a proactive or reactive manner?

12. How strong and coherent are the links between the components of the PMS and how they are used (as denoted by the above 11 questions)?

The Performance Measurement System Framework aligns mission, vision, strategy, objectives, key indicators, metrics, and actions.

Key capabilities of the Framework are:

- **Leverage** an agile, self-service performance solution for business users.

- **Build** strong alignment between strategies and operations, creating a seamless path to performance execution.

- **Gain** deep insight into performance, and the factors that impact performance.

- **Enhance** communication and collaboration by making it easy to share details about strategies, goals and objectives, initiatives, and metrics.

- **Balance** performance, risk, governance, and compliance.

- **Empower** business users at all levels to engage in performance management.

- **Strengthen** relationships with stakeholders—customers, suppliers, and business partners.

Mission outlines the *overriding purpose of the organization in line with the values or expectations of stakeholders.*

Vision sets out the *desired future state; the aspiration of the organization.*

Vision and Mission are part of belief systems, and they embody core values and purposes. However, vision and mission have importance only so far as they are communicated and acted upon. While communicating vision and mission, it is important to outline the behavior that is expected of organizational participants. Top management also needs to be clear as to how the behavior of organizational participants would be observed and acted upon.

Key success factors are those activities, attributes, competencies, and capabilities seen as critical prerequisites for the success of an organization at a certain point in time. Their identification and monitoring are essential for the fulfillment of strategic goals. Key success factors (KSF) are those perceived to be important by the managers concerned, rather than representing any objective or external point of view. Key success factors are a codification of the vision and mission in more concrete terms and in a more compressed time frame. For example, managers may regard growth of revenue in a foreign market as a KSF for a vision of becoming a global market leader. Similarly, outsourcing of certain activities or processes to countries with lower operating costs could be the KSF for a vision of becoming a cost leader.

Organizations are formed to carry out activities which could be carried out by markets to increase efficiency through the reduction of transaction costs. Organization structures are then formed as a means of formally establishing the specification of individual roles and tasks to be carried out. Organization structures involve choices regarding decentralization/centralization of authority, differentiation/standardization, and the level of formalization of rules and procedures, as well as configuration (structures, processes, and relationships).

Structures include the simple, functional, divisional, holding company, transnational, geographic, matrix, team-based, project-based, and web. Processes include planning, supervision, and market processes. Relationships refer to internal relationships and external relationships—strategic alliances, supplier relations, channel relations, networks, and virtual organizations. Structure and strategy are closely linked. On one hand, strategy drives structure. On the other hand, the structure can determine strategy.

The relationship is complex, with the balance of power leaning toward corporate and business strategy in affecting organization structure, but toward organization structure in affecting operating strategy. It is also likely to be associated with whether the organization is experiencing an evolutionary or revolutionary stage of development. Strategy is likely to follow the structure in an evolutionary stage, and structure is likely to follow the strategy in a revolutionary stage. Strategy and structure are mutually interdependent in that they support and constrain each other.

Strategy is the direction that the organization chooses to pursue over the long term as a means of achieving organizational objectives. The strategy literature argues that the organization needs to develop the strengths that match its KSFs to achieve the desired outcomes that it sets for itself. A key element of this involves translating strategic goals into operating goals to attain alignment. Research also suggests that a match between the environment, strategy, and internal structures is associated with superior performance. Various strategy typologies have been proposed:

- Defender, prospector, and reactor strategies

- Cost leadership and differentiation strategies

- Conservative and entrepreneurial strategies

- Build, hold, and harvest strategies

- Operational excellence, product leadership, and customer intimacy strategies

All these typologies represent a useful way of looking at an organization's strategy and a way to reflect on how they are translated into the Performance Management System. The emphasis of the question on strategies and plans is on the actions that are thought likely to achieve outcomes—that is, the relationship between means and ends.

It is possible that an organization has clear goals and objectives, identified KSFs, but has not thought through what actions will be necessary to achieve such goals (a strategic planning failure). Or an organization may decide not to go through a detailed planning process and instead adopt a flexible, adaptive approach to respond to environmental uncertainties.

In other words, forecasting is believed to be so unreliable, that it is thought better not to plan, but to have the capacity to respond quickly to events as they unfold (such as in agile manufacturing and software development). Beyond strategies, the important issue in this question is about communicating to all levels. Failure to communicate strategies and plans to organizational members may result in a lack of understanding of how individual actions contribute to the overall strategy.

Key performance measures are the financial or non-financial measures or metrics used at different levels in organizations to evaluate success in achieving their objectives, KSFs, strategies, plans, and satisfying the expectations of different stakeholders. They are specifically included in the performance management system framework to reflect both the importance that is attached to performance measures in today's organizations as well as the influence such measures have on individual behavior.

The question is explicit about whether performance measures are derived from objectives, KSFs, strategies, and plans to the extent that identification of suitable performance measures is part of the strategic management process. The number of such key measures is also important, because managers' limited attention spans mean that the use of many performance measures reduces their impact. Kaplan and Norton (Balanced Score Card) recommend a maximum of 25 performance measures in total. The explicit development of causal relationships between measures in some form of the causal model (such as strategy maps) also provides evidence of how an organization views its performance measures.

The process of target setting (participation, consultation, imposition) may be as important as the outcome (perceived target difficulty). Research has found target levels have effects on performance, with moderately difficult or stretch goals enhancing team performance. The embedding of continuous improvement into targets appears inescapable, as organizations face competitive and global markets. The use of benchmarking, particularly the use of best practices benchmarking, appears to provide greater legitimacy for targets and has been strongly advocated by the beyond budgeting movement.

Performance evaluation represents a critical nexus in control activities. Both formal evaluation practices and informal indications of what is considered to be important are covered in this question. It is particularly important to distinguish between performance evaluation routines (often orchestrated by the human resources function) and those operated by senior managers. This is an area where subordinates' perception of what they believe to be the situation is more important than the formal situation.

This question includes individual performance as well as the performance of teams, departments, and divisions, and the organization as a whole. Performance evaluations of business units using balanced scorecards place greater emphasis on common measures than on unique measures. Research shows that managers evaluated by organizational profits achieve higher joint outcomes when following a team orientation than an individualistic orientation. Cooperation and integrative problem solving among executives occur more frequently when performance evaluations focus on corporate profits rather than on divisional profits. Performance evaluations may be objective, subjective, or fall in between these two extremes. The cautionary notes provided earlier deserve consideration.

Rewards are typically the outcome of performance evaluations. As such, reward systems are the next logical aspect to be considered in the analysis of performance management systems. Rewards may range from expressions of approval and recognition to financial rewards such as bonuses, salary increases, and stock options, long-term progression, and promotion.

The question also opens up the issue of the distinction between positive (rewards) and negative (punishment or penalty) control activities. Issues of equity, fairness, and inclusiveness between different managers also loom large in many organizations. The issues covered by this question relate strongly to the processes and structures of accountability and corporate governance.

Group reward practices have attracted increased attention in recent years. The use of group rewards faces some challenges, including the potential for free-riders and the tendency of the mediocre becoming the norm. Group rewards may indeed be the answer in organizations that view themselves as a complex network of interdependent relationships.

Information flows, systems and networks are essential enabling systems of any performance management system—they are the binding agents keeping the whole system together. The question notes the difference between feedback information—that is, information used to enable the undertaking of corrective and/or adaptive courses of action—and feed-forward information—that is, information that is used to enable the organization to learn from its experience, to generate new ideas, and to recreate strategies and plans.

In other words, it distinguishes between information flows aimed at the correction of past shortcomings, from those which attempt to anticipate future events and respond in advance of their occurrence. Feedback and feed-forward information flows are directly related to the notions of single-loop and double-loop learning.

Single-loop learning entails a response to a signal of deviance from a pre-defined course of action that does not question the initial objectives or strategies; it sees the deviance as the product of a deficient operationalization. Hence, its association with ubiquitous feedback information flows.

In contrast, double-loop learning involves questioning the role of the framing and learning systems which underlie actual goals and strategies. Hence, their association with feed-forward information flows.

The use made of information and controls is a cornerstone of performance management systems. Feedback information flows are fundamental to diagnostic use as they enable single-loop learning, while feed-forward information, with its double-loop function, can provide a check for strategic validity. The alignment between strategic intent and strategic action is unlikely to persist in dynamic environments, and strategic dissonance will then result.

Dissonance becomes strategic at key moments typified by *the giving way of one type of industry dynamics to another; the change of one winning strategy to another; the replacement of an existing technological regime by a new one.* The role of strategic validity controls is to signal the need to review strategies. Such revisions can be facilitated by frank, open discussions between managers and employees. It is the use of strategic validity controls that primarily serves the important role of identifying the failure of intended strategies and the rise of emergent strategies.

Change and its dynamics are an important part of the framework. Environments change, organizations change, and performance management systems also need to change to sustain their relevance and usefulness. The idea of change in performance management systems applies to both the design infrastructure and the way performance management information is used.

The question draws the attention to the antecedents (causes) and consequences (outcomes) of change in the performance management system, leaving issues of process aside. This is an area of major importance as the rate of change increases. The incorporation of change dynamics into the analysis of performance management system design adds to our understanding of how different components of the system interrelate. In particular, it draws attention to the issue of lags in performance management systems, which can result in an extant system appearing incoherent. It is also important to consider the scope of strategic change in the increasingly competitive environment faced by contemporary organizations. Strategies are a core component of a performance management system, and a strategic change can be expected to send ripples across the entire system.

Like any other system, a performance management system is greater than the sum of its parts. There is a need for alignment and coordination between the different components for the whole to deliver efficient and effective outcomes. Although the individual components may be apparently well-designed, evidence suggests that when they do not fit well together (either in design or use), control failures can occur.

The 12 preceding questions of the PMS framework make clear the key links between the components and thus provide a good starting point for questioning, critical analysis, and assessment of the balance, harmony, consistency, and coherence of the links in the whole system.

Judgments should be made about the extent to which the control system: considers multiple stakeholders; measures efficiency, effectiveness, and equity; captures financial and non-financial outcomes; provides vertical links between strategy and operations, and horizontal links across the value chain; provides information on how the organization relates to its external environment; and has an ability to adapt.

The Performance Management System Framework, as depicted in the form of 12 questions (ten *what* and two *how* questions), is a very useful tool for examining the structure, operation, and use of performance management systems in a holistic manner. It can be employed to describe the structure and use of the package of controls deployed by management to ensure that an organization's strategies and plans are effectively implemented.

Summing Up

Several tools are available to facilitate a value-creating performance management system. This section has introduced a few tools:

1. Balanced Scorecard and Strategy Map

2. Activity-Based Costing

3. Supply Chain Management

The section has also has introduced a Systems framework for Performance Management.

Chapter 28

Performance Management Challenges

*Retaining and enhancing the capabilities of people
is a better strategy than allowing churn and constantly
being on the lookout for candidates.*

We have seen a holistic view of performance management.

Organizations continue to view performance management primarily at the individual and occasionally at the team level. Few organizations view performance management from a systems framework. The transition from traditional frameworks to radically different approaches is a painful process. Some of the leading corporations have given up the individual measurement.

This chapter looks at the current practices and challenges.

Evolution of Performance Management

Professor Peter Cappelli of the Wharton School has argued that historical and economic contexts have played a critical role in the evolution of performance management. When the human capital was plenty, the emphasis was on whom to let go, whom to keep, and whom to reward.

Under those circumstances, appraisal, with its focus on individual accountability, was a useful tool. But when people with the required skill set are in short supply, as they are now, developing people is a more important goal than assessing people and letting them go. Hiring new people is expensive, and there is no guarantee that recruits can do a better job than the people they replace. Retaining and enhancing the capabilities of people is a better strategy than allowing churn and constantly being on the lookout for candidates.

The principle is similar to marketing—satisfying and retaining customers is a much better option than allowing customer defection and chasing new customers.

Appraisals can be traced back to the U.S. military's *merit rating* system, created during World War I to identify poor performers for discharge. During and after World War II, the U.S. Army devised *forced ranking* to identify enlisted soldiers with the potential to become officers. By the early 1950s, about 60% of U.S. companies were using appraisals to document workers' performance and allocate rewards. By the 1960s, the figure had risen to 90%. Improving performance appeared to be an afterthought.

The social psychologist Douglas McGregor argued for engaging employees in goal setting and assessments. His *Theory Y* approach assumed that employees wanted to perform well and would do so if supported adequately. This was in sharp contrast to the then-prevailing *Theory X* which postulated that people were primarily motivated by rewards and punishments.

Companies, led by General Electric, began splitting appraisals into separate discussions about accountability and growth, to give development its due. In the 1970s, inflation rates shot up, and merit-based pay took center stage in the appraisal process. Annual wage increases mattered. Getting no increase represented a substantial reduction in wages/salaries.

There was immense pressure on organizations to award pay objectively. Thus, accountability became a higher priority than development for many organizations.

Three changes reinforced the shift:

- Jack Welch became the CEO of General Electric and championed the forced ranking system—a military creation. Whereas the Army's goal was to quickly identify a large number of officer candidates, Welch used the process primarily to shed people at the bottom. Other companies followed suit.

- The 1933 legislation on compensation capped salaries but exempted performance-based pay. This led to an increase in outcome-based bonuses for corporate leaders. A trickle-down effect enabled the process to permeate to other levels including frontline supervisors and even hourly employees. Appraisal became the main tool to assess merit.

- A flawed McKinsey research project, *War for Talent*, suggested that some employees were inherently more talented than others. However, nothing in the study showed that fixed personality traits made certain people perform better.

Thus, by the turn of the century, organizations were using performance appraisals mainly to hold employees accountable and to allocate rewards. One-third of U.S. companies and 60% of the Fortune 500 reportedly used forced ranking. Other factors feeding into this retrograde step were the flattening of organizations and the resultant increase in the span of control—the number of subordinates that supervisors had to manage increased from six in 1960 to twenty in 2000. This also heralded a greater move toward lateral hiring to fill managerial positions; two-thirds of corporate jobs were filled from outside in contrast to just 10% a generation earlier, reducing the need for internal development.

In 2002, Colorcon, the private pharma company that supplies advanced coating systems, modified release technologies and functional excipients to leading pharmaceutical companies, announced that it was not bothering with annual reviews anymore. The company's head of global human resources explained in his presentation at the Wharton School that Colorcon had found a more effective way of reinforcing desired behaviors and managing performance. Supervisors were giving people instant feedback, tying it to individuals' own goals, and handing out small weekly bonuses to employees they saw doing good things. Many companies have since adopted what has become known as Feedback Fridays every week.

In 2005, a few years after Jack Welch left GE, the company backed away from forced ranking because the process fostered internal competition and undermined collaboration. More and more companies began questioning how useful it was to compare people with one another or even to rate them on a scale. The move toward team-based work often conflicted with individual appraisals and rewards. Low inflation and small budgets for wage increases made appraisal-driven merit pay seem futile.

The appraisal process has been at the receiving end of criticism from employees at all levels. Research shows that people detest numerical scores; they would rather be told they are *average* than to be rated three on a five-point scale.

58% of the executives polled said that their current performance management approach drove neither employee engagement nor high performance.

People hate forced ranking in particular. Iwan Barankay has demonstrated that performance declines when people are rated relative to others. Also, research has shown that appraisal scores have as much to do with the rater as they do with performance. A study by Willis Towers Watson has shown that 45% of managers intensely dislike doing reviews and do not see any value in appraisal systems. Deloitte reports that 58% of HR executives consider reviews an ineffective use of supervisors' time. The advisory firm CEB found that the average manager reported spending 210 hours—close to five weeks—doing appraisals each year.

Simultaneously with the growing dissatisfaction with traditional processes, technology firms in general and software development firms, in particular, started using new methods to ensure projects were completed on time, within budget, and delivered high quality. The Agile Manifesto for software developers favored responding to change as being more important than adhering to a plan. The manifesto emphasized principles such as collaboration, self-organization, self-direction, and regular reflection on how to be more effective, with the aim of prototyping more quickly and responding in real time to customer feedback and changes in requirements.

Adobe was one of the first companies to drop annual appraisals altogether. The company was already using agile concepts to develop software. The process involved breaking down projects into *sprints*, modules that could be developed quickly, and immediately followed by debriefing sessions to capture mistakes made and lessons learned. Adobe explicitly brought the agile method to the performance management process; constant assessment and feedback replacing annual appraisals. Microsoft, Dell, and Juniper Systems followed suit.

Deloitte reported in 2015 a large majority of U.S. companies were in the process of changing their performance measurement systems. PWC reports that two-thirds of large companies in the U.K. are in the process of changing their systems.

In the Deloitte survey, 58% of the executives polled said that their current performance management approach drove neither employee engagement nor high performance. There appears to be a dire need to design something nimbler, real-time, and individualized; something squarely focused on fueling performance in the future rather than assessing it in the past.

A Business Case for Dropping Appraisals

Why is there a shift away from traditional appraisal systems? Three reasons are apparent.

First, today's competitive landscape demands treating human resources as the primary source of distinctive competencies and competitive advantage. The real cost of capital is close to zero and capital is in abundance. Resources and even capabilities can/will be replicated, and the traditional bases for differentiation are no longer valid.

Upgrading talent management efforts is the most critical need. This is particularly true of knowledge-based industries—high technology, consulting, and professional services. Organizations need people who are deeply motivated by the potential for learning and advancement. People should ideally be in charge of their growth. Such an approach demands rich and immediate feedback from supervisors as opposed to post-fact, semi-annual, or annual ritualistic reviews. Retaining good people is critical to business success.

One of the key requirements is to eliminate *dissatisfiers*—practices that employees abhor and that is the prime reason for attrition. Annual reviews, forced rankings, and numerical ratings are on top of the list. Managers need to provide constant feedback, coaching, and assessment to ensure their direct reports are on a learning curve.

Among the professional service firms, Kelly Services was the first to drop appraisals in 2011. After beginning with a pilot group in 2013, PWC quickly discontinued annual reviews for all 200,000-plus employees. Deloitte followed in 2015, and Accenture and KPMG made similar announcements after that. Besides the hundreds of thousands employed by these firms, one should remember that the firms provide management advice to thousands of organizations. Thus, their actions have a cascading effect on the largest corporations in the world.

Second, today's organizations need the ability to adapt and change rapidly. They need the courage to disrupt themselves and create new business models if they have to survive. Across industries, the business mortality rate has dramatically increased, and many organizations struggle to survive five years. Given these dynamics, planning for only a year is often self-defeating.

When organizations don't want their people doing the same things, it doesn't make any sense to hang onto systems built mainly to assess and hold people accountable for past or current practices. As the head of human resources at GE points out, projects tend to be both short-term and to change along the way. Therefore, employees' goals and tasks can't be plotted out a year in advance with much accuracy.

GE has eliminated individual ratings and annual reviews. Its new approach to performance management is aligned with its FastWorks platform that borrows heavily from agile techniques. The goal now is to have frequent conversations (called *touchpoints*) and keep asking two basic questions: *What am I doing that I should keep doing? What am I doing that I should change?* Annual goals have been replaced with short-term *priorities*.

Third, teamwork is a key factor in organizations. It is as true in knowledge-based organizations as it is true within service organizations or project-based organizations. Retailers like Gap who were among the earliest adopters of appraisal systems realize that customer service requires exceptional collaboration between front-line and back office employees. Traditional systems do not enhance team performance, nor do they help track collaboration. Gap supervisors discuss performance with their direct reports through the year. Goals now are typically short-term (every quarter). Two years into the system, Gap reports far more satisfaction with its performance process and the best-ever completion of store level goals. The company nevertheless feels that further improvements are needed in setting stretch goals and focusing on team performance.

Challenges That Persist

The journey from a formal, mechanistic, annual review to an informal system of continuous feedback requires a cultural shift. This system of feedback is difficult to sustain if it does not happen organically. The greatest resistance to abandoning appraisals comes from HR itself. Processes that revolve around performance ratings—standardization, objective criteria, metrics and measurement, and documentation—have evolved over decades. Taking away appraisals flies in the face of conventional wisdom and does not necessarily solve every problem.

Some of the challenges that organizations still grapple with while making the transition from traditional performance management to new approaches are:

- **Aligning** individual and organizational goals: Traditional models have a top-down approach: organizational mission and goals; divisional goals; functional goals, and individual goals. Each goal is aligned with the one above. What happens when business goals for a year cannot be articulated and short-term, project goals take their place? How does one cope with changes in intra-project and inter-project goals? These are challenges that have to be addressed. Data currently available isn't adequate to draw conclusions.

Organizational learning holds the key.

- **Rewarding** performance: Appraisals provide a clear way for managers to reward individual contributions. Organizations switching to continuous feedback and coaching have to figure out how to link rewards to performance. Managers now use qualitative judgments in the place of numerical scores. Where the organization has reached Level 4 or Level 5 on the Learning Organization continuum, the change may not pose serious difficulties. When such maturity is lacking, qualitative judgments may do more harm than good.

- **Identifying** poor performers: Traditional performance management systems are supposed to identify poor performers, but they often fail. The problem is the reluctance of managers to flag failing employees, particularly where these same managers have been involved in the hiring process. And the problem does not go away merely by changing the frequency of feedback. Many issues causing poor performance can't be solved through management interventions. Unless managers are willing to be objective, problems will persist. Teams may have some poor performers, and top management may be blissfully ignorant of what is going on. Organizational learning holds the key. But organizational learning is not easy, and it cannot be taken for granted.

- **Avoiding** legal hassles: HR managers often worry discrimination charges may increase if pay increases are based on continuous feedback and evaluation instead of numerical ratings once a year. It is worth noting that appraisals haven't prevented discriminatory practices. Cognitive biases such as fundamental attribution error, the halo effect, and stereotyping can all lead to discrimination whether the appraisal is done continuously or once a year. Gap has reported that getting rid of performance scores has improved fairness in pay and other decisions. However, the data is insufficient to conclude.

- **Managing** the feedback spiral: Traditional systems require managers to provide feedback and consequences once a year. Refined systems may provide feedback twice a year. Large organizations use online tools to collect feedback—particularly from customers and peer groups. The IT firm HCL Technologies pioneered a unique feedback system—anyone in the organization could provide feedback on anyone else based on specific interactions and experiences. Even the CEO was included in this process. At the time of writing, the system had over 6,000 responses that were posted in one week. HCL also came out with a new tag line: "Employees First, Customers Next."

For all the upside, the glaring downside is obvious—operating in a hypercompetitive industry with low entry barriers while being dependent on large corporations for orders, it's difficult for the organization to reward its employees in line with the competition. This comes out clearly in the frustration expressed by employees. In other words, in the absence of a business model based on achieving superior performance, grand initiatives at transparency and democratization will be seen merely as platitudes lacking meaningful substance. Other organizations have tried technology with varying degrees of success:

- GE has an app called PD@GE (PD stands for Performance Development) that allows managers to call up notes and details from earlier conversations and summarize the information. Employees can use the app to seek direction when they need it.

- IBM has a similar app that also enables employees to provide feedback to peers and choose whether the recipient's supervisor gets a copy.

- Amazon's Anytime Feedback tool does much the same thing. While these tools help managers gauge performance in real-time, they can also lead to distortions. For example, Amazon's cutthroat culture encourages employees to be critical of one another's performance, and forced ranking creates incentives to push others to the bottom of the heap. The more emphasis placed on peer feedback, the more likely the problem.

- **Leadership** matters: Like in any new initiative, success in an enlightened approach to performance management is a function of leadership. No initiative —whether performance management, innovation, quality, continuous improvement—can succeed without a firm and sustained commitment of the leadership team.

  - At Intel, a two-year pilot was conducted in which employees received continuous feedback but no formal appraisal. Supervisors had no problems differentiating performance or distributing performance-based pay without the ratings. The company reverted to formal appraisals because the leadership believed appraisals created healthy competition and clear outcomes.

  - At Sun Communities, a manufactured-home company, senior leaders oppose eliminating appraisals because they believe formal feedback is essential to accountability.

  - At Medtronic, which gave up ratings several years ago, the appraisal system is back after the acquisition of another company which uses a more traditional view of performance management.

  - Deloitte has taken a step backward from having no ratings at all to having employees assigned to one of four categories every quarter.

- PWC's move backward is comprised of substituting a single rating every year with scores on five competencies. This practice adds to the confusion. The pushback emanated from senior leadership —the partner track—who wanted to know how they were doing.

- At New York Life, after the elimination of formal ratings, the company started sharing merit-pay increases internally and interpreted them as performance scores. These became known as *shadow scores* and the ensuing frustration brought about a return to formal appraisals.

Summing Up

In this section, we have seen a holistic view of performance management.

Organizations continue to view performance management primarily at the individual and occasionally at the team level. Few organizations view performance management from a systems framework. The transition from traditional frameworks to radically different approaches is a painful process. Some of the leading corporations have given up the individual measurement. We have looked at the current practices and challenges.

Chapter **29**

Risk-Based
Performance Management

*Risk management is closely associated
with enterprise performance management.*

L ooking to the future is essential to the success of an organization. Enterprise Performance Management is a part of a wider concept of Enterprise Risk Management (ERM). There is growing evidence of a convergence of three related concepts—Governance, Risk, and Compliance.

Governance is about responsible and responsive stewardship. Formulating an appropriate strategy, executing the strategy ethically, providing a safe work environment, and creating engaged human capital is at the heart of governance.

Compliance means operating according to the law of the land; multinational enterprises need to be sensitive to the laws of every country in which they operate. Governance and compliance are part regulatory and part ethical concepts. Risk management is closely associated with enterprise performance management. This section provides an introduction to risk management.

Enterprise Risk Management

Risk management and performance management are grounded in two principles:

1. The less uncertainty there is about the future, the better.

2. If you cannot measure it, you cannot manage it.

The popular notion of risk is that it is a threat. Agile leaders and managers view risk as an opportunity. The objective of risk management is less volatility, greater predictability, fewer surprises, and the ability to bounce back rapidly after a risk event occurs.

It is important to remember that more things *might* happen than *will* happen. Both risk and opportunity have a common feature—both are about the future. Organizations have difficulty in quantifying risk because they don't have a common basis for evaluating risk appetite relative to their risk exposure.

Risk appetite is the level of risk an organization is willing to accept and absorb to generate the returns it expects to gain. The goal is not to eliminate all possible risk, but to match risk exposure to risk appetite.

Risk management has three steps:

1. What is the probability of an event occurring?

2. What is the severity of the impact of the event?

3. What is our capability to respond to the event?

Based on the three factors for various risks, risk management evaluates alternative actions and associated costs to potentially mitigate or take advantage of each identified risk.

Precise execution is essential for success.

We can categorize risk in several ways: strategic, tactical, and operational; external and internal; controllable and uncontrollable.

It is useful to categorize risk along six dimensions:

1. *Price risk* – the risk of an increase in supply or aggressive price reduction by competitors leading to lower prices and therefore lower profits.

2. *Market risk* – the risk of sudden changes in customer preferences and expectations.

3. *Credit risk* – the risk of not meeting obligations, inability to collect receivables, or entities failing to settle a legal obligation.

4. *Operational risk* – the risk arising from failed processes, inadequate people performance, or technological failure/redundancy.

5. *Strategic risk* – the risk resulting from poor strategy selection or execution.

6. *Legal risk* – the risk of liquidity failure, insufficient net positive cash flow, and regulatory penalties.

Of the six types of risk, strategic risk and operational risk are the most critical.

Strategic risk can occur at the strategy formulation stage or the implementation stage. The strategy must be clearly defined to be followed: cost leadership, differentiation, broad market or focus, product leadership, customer intimacy, segments, target markets, and positioning. Precise execution is essential for success.

Operational risk can occur out of potential benefits from risks taken and the missed opportunities of risks not taken. Operational risk includes quality, hiring, training, development, retention, succession planning, supply chain, logistics, disaster management, innovation risk, and competitor actions.

A risk-based performance management involves four steps:

1. Risk management: What is our strategy? How can it go wrong? What are the corresponding probabilities? What are the key risk indicators? How can we quantify the outcome of each possible major event—competitor moves, changes in the environment, or changes in the market? How can we develop a system to constantly monitor the gaps between expected and actual performance?

2. Strategy and value management: Which markets should we address? Which markets should we avoid? Which offerings should we make to customers?

Which offerings should we avoid? How do we create value for different stakeholders? What measures can we use to track performance? Drawing a strategy map and following the steps is useful during this stage.

3. Investment evaluation: This step is about strategy execution. We should treat all resources as being scarce. The challenge is to improve value creation in every process. Customer expectations and shareholder expectations are at odds with each other. How do we balance the opposing forces? Similarly, employee expectations and shareholder expectations can be at odds with each other. Divergence in expectations is inevitable. Managing differing expectations is one of management's biggest challenges.

4. Performance management: This step is about monitoring and control. We can deploy all the tools discussed—balanced scorecard, activity-based costing, supply chain management, customer retention, and continuous improvement initiatives. How are we doing along critical dimensions? What can we do better? The virtuous cycle of measurement, corrective and preventive action, improvement, realignment, and renewed monitoring is a continuous loop. The goal is to monitor risk and to realign strategy whenever required.

Summing Up

Enterprise Performance Management is a part of a wider concept of Enterprise Risk Management (ERM). There is growing evidence of a convergence of three related concepts: Governance, Risk, and Compliance.

Governance is about responsible and responsive stewardship. Formulating an appropriate strategy, executing the strategy ethically, providing a safe work environment, and creating an engaged human capital is at the heart of governance.

Compliance is operating according to the law of the land —multinational enterprises need to be sensitive to the laws of every country in which they operate.

Governance and compliance are part regulatory and part ethical concepts. Risk management and enterprise performance management go together.

Chapter 30

Performance Management Summary

We need holistic measures that look at organizations for what they are—dynamic systems capable of anticipating and embracing change instead of merely reacting to change.

Performance management does not have a universally accepted definition. A Gartner study shows that 70% of managers of 500 large corporations equate performance management with measuring individual performance. Unfortunately, this view misses the point.

The competitive environment of the 21st century has three key components: complexity, ambiguity, and rapid change. Product life cycles have shrunk dramatically. Organizational mortality is at an all-time high, with life-spans in many industries being less than five years.

While human capital is critical to business success, we need to measure much more than individual performance. We need holistic measures that look at organizations for what they are—dynamic systems capable of anticipating and embracing change instead of merely *reacting* to change.

*Only one in four American employees
say they have the freedom to improve
their performance through creativity.*

The section on performance management has introduced you to such holistic measures.

Reflective Questions

Reflection Question # 1:

What are the performance measures in your organization? Assuming resources are available, how would an ideal performance measurement look? What are the gaps between the ideal and the actual? How would you prioritize addressing the gaps? Justify your answer.

Reflection Question # 2:

Choose any organization among the top five in its industry/ category by revenues and profits. Using information available in the public domain, or collecting information from the organization, map the performance management system of the organization. What are the distinguishing features of the system? If you had the opportunity to improve the performance management system, what would you do? Why?

Case Study: Acme Industries

Harvard Business School Professor Ethan Bernstein has studied assembly-line performance for many years. Acme

Industries produces components for the automobile industry. The company is well-known for its quality and reliability, and its customers include all the major automobile manufacturers.

The company's assembly line is built so that managers can easily supervise their employees. Every process is visible, every metric is available in real-time, and employees are trained to work exactly as the process requires.

Here is the anomaly. When the managers are not watching, the employees secretly develop better ways of doing the work. When hidden from the manager's view, an assembly line's performance went up by 15%.

Most organizations tend to look at performance as a single dimension. Psychologists and behavioral scientists emphasize that there are two types of performance. Both are critical for organizational success.

The first type, called tactical performance, denotes the extent to which the organization adheres to its strategy. The driver is consistency and focus. Essential tools of this approach are checklists, standard operating procedures, and manuals for everything imaginable. This is the secret behind some fast food giants, who claim that with your eyes closed, you cannot identify whether a dish was prepared in Tokyo or New York.

The second type, called adaptive performance, denotes the extent to which the organization diverges from its strategy. The divergence manifests in the form of creativity, resilience, problem-solving, risk-taking, agility, and citizenship. Adaptive performance allows organizations to successfully navigate a world full of uncertainty, complexity, and ambiguity. When you see an employee making that extra effort to satisfy you, you are witnessing the adaptive performance.

Tactical performance is the standard for the vast majority of organizations. Adaptive performance is the operating mode of industry leaders. There is sufficient empirical evidence to suggest that a sense of purpose, fair play, and potential can increase adaptive performance.

Only one in four American employees say they have the freedom to improve their performance through creativity. Consider the following scenarios:

- I wish my people took more ownership.

- I wish we operated like a start-up.

- I wish we were more nimble than our competitors.

Do these statements resonate with your organization? If you were the CEO, what would you do to change the emphasis from tactical performance to adaptive performance?

Case Study: Customer-focused structure drives need for dynamic organization at Plymouth State University

Introduction

When Donald Birx became president of Plymouth State University (PSU) in 2015, the institution was reeling from a 16-percent drop in undergraduate enrollment in three years. The enrollment decline created a challenging situation for a new president. PSU is a tuition-dependent regional public university meaning that declines in student population translate directly into less revenue to sustain an organization with high fixed costs. Academia is frequently seen as inflexible and notoriously slow to respond to changes in the market-place. In this case, the severity of the challenge had to be met with a more responsive and dynamic model of curriculum and teaching, the key products and services of a university.

Plymouth State University's history dates back to 1808 and the Holmes Plymouth Academy, which was a pioneer institution for teacher training. In 1871, legislation authorizing teacher training schools, termed normal schools, was passed by the New Hampshire legislature. The introduction of the normal school to Plymouth was followed by a pioneering partnership with the local primary and secondary schools to provide practical training opportunities for the teacher trainees. Poet laureate Robert Frost, who lived on campus from 1911 through 1912, commented in 1946 on the success of the institution as persisting and succeeding in a world of broken pieces.

The stature of the normal school evolved through a succession of name changes and designations. In 2003 the school became Plymouth State University. The transformation from a special-purpose institution for training teachers to a regional university has occurred in many states. The broadened mission of such colleges and universities opens new challenges because the institutions must offer a more comprehensive curriculum and compete against other state universities and private colleges for students.

The challenges that PSU faced with declining enrollment was driven by a range of factors. High school graduations peaked in the U.S. in 2013 and have since shown a decline nationwide.[5] In New England, the drop in high school graduates is the most pronounced in the nation. The Northeast has seen declining birth rates since the 1990s. The decline in births has translated into falling numbers of high school graduates and lower enrollments in universities. In addition, in the Northeast, a lesser share of students enroll in public institutions than in other parts of the country. PSU is impacted directly by these trends due to the very high percentage of its students in the 18 to 22-year age range.

Using Integrated Clusters to Address Program Relevancy

A compounding factor to the decline in applications driven by lower high school graduating cohorts is that higher education has been slow to adapt and change. Academic programs often take years to change and are often seen as outdated. Over 20 years ago management guru Peter Drucker cast doubt on the relevance of university education when he said, "Such totally uncontrollable [higher education] expenditures, without any visible improvement in either the content or the quality of education, means that the system is rapidly becoming untenable. Higher education is in deep crisis."[6]

To address issues of relevancy and decline in student numbers, Brix introduced a different learning model called integrated clusters. The idea of clusters does away with traditional academic departments as the defining element of educational experience. Instead, the integrated clusters model used by PSU groups learning into seven groupings:

[5] Peace Bransberger and Demaree K. Michelau, *Knocking at the College Door. Projections of High School Graduates by State and Race/Ethnicity* (Boulder, CO: Western Interstate Commission for Higher Education, 2016).

[6] Robert Lenzner and Stephen S. Johnson, "Seeing Things as They Really Are," *Forbes* 159, no. 5 (1997).

- Arts & Technologies;

- Education, Democracy & Social Change;

- Exploration & Discovery;

- Health & Human Enrichment;

- Innovation & Entrepreneurship;

- Justice, Security, & Tourism; and

- Environment & Sustainable Development.

The Integrated Cluster concept is a radical departure from traditional academic departments, which are often focused around disciplines that bear more resemblance to history than future job markets. The clusters were chosen and developed to respond to in-demand skills in organizations in the geographic area served by PSU. Brix noted additional design considerations, "[The clusters] also recreate an integrated perspective of a liberal arts education that features engaged scholars and promotes transdisciplinary project-based learning, something I believe was lost to some extent during the last two centuries of increasing specialization and focus on discipline-based skills"[7]

Central to the model is the extensive use of experiential learning and engaged scholarship through community-focused projects. The projects are conducted with community partners and student teams under faculty oversight. Projects begin in the first year of an undergraduate journey with an interdisciplinary project and conclude in the last year with a capstone project.

---

[7] Lori L. Ferguson "Plymouth State University's Integrated Clusters Approach," *Plymouth Magazine*, December 20, 2016.

The learning model includes the concept of open laboratory learning, which allows students to assemble a learning plan and resources and work together in a collaborative space. Through the open lab model, students can also bring in external stakeholders from the region's businesses and organizations.

Faculty Organization Challenges

Once traditional academic disciplines are eliminated as the organizing concept, the traditional academic departmental organization is called into question. Prior to introduction of the integrated clusters model, PSU was organized into three colleges (Arts and Sciences, Business Administration and Education, Health and Human Services), which included a total of 24 academic departments.

The use of colleges and departments resembles a product-centric organization in corporations. The shift to the integrated clusters model required moving away from product-based units centered on historical academic disciplines, to a dynamic customer-focused model.

How to organize into a customer-centric approach with integrated clusters presents several challenges. The first challenge is that faculty, a key group of the workforce, typically undergo years of training, which focuses their perceptions and skills very tightly into historical academic disciplines. As noted by Sir Ken Robinson, academics excel at logical deduction and propositional knowledge or knowing that something is the case.[8] Teaching and learning in the integrated clusters model ultimately will require organizing to create a dynamic

[8] Ken Robinson, *Out of Our Minds. Learning to Be Creative*, 2nd ed. ed. (Chichester, UK: Capstone Publishing Ltd., 2011).

structure that can evolve with the ever-shifting nature of the clusters caused by students' and regional stakeholders' requests for projects requiring different skills and support.

By 2018 some aspects of how to organize faculty were coming into focus. The shift from colleges and departments had started by 2017 with the use of team-based management that assumed many of the roles formerly undertaken by a dean acting as a CEO of a sub-unit of a larger business. As the model of the cluster becomes clearer, it will also be clear that a different form of organization may better serve students.

Conclusion—The need for new management processes

Because clusters have a dynamic nature, imposing a new and different organizational structure would appear unwise. A key question going forward is what type of dynamic organizational model might work. Team-based leadership models often end up re-creating a hierarchy by another name. Alternative organizational models such as holacracy, sociocracy, and the teal organization, exist but are untested in higher education. The process of discerning and implementing an organizational structure and associated ways of working will be critical to the ultimate success of the integrated clusters approach as PSU.

Reflection and Discussion Questions

Consider the following when discussing this case study:

1. What are the key challenges that an organization may face when defining a market-focused approach such as the integrated clusters?

2. Do customer-focused organizational models inherently have a downside to an engaged workforce? Why or why not?

3. Does a model such as the integrated clusters support the full range of stakeholders of an institution? Why or why not?

4. Would organizational models such as holacracy, sociocracy, or the teal organization be effective for the integrated clusters?

5. Is a concept of dynamic customer-centric model such as the integrated clusters transferable to organizations providing products other than educational services?

6. Are there elements of the integrated clusters model that are transferable to your organization?

References

Bransberger, Peace, and Demaree K. Michelau. *Knocking at the College Door. Projections of High School Graduates by State and Race/Ethnicity.* Boulder, CO: Western Interstate Commission for Higher Education, 2016.

Ferguson, Lori L. "Plymouth State University's Integrated Clusters Approach." *Plymouth Magazine*, December 20, 2016.

Lenzner, Robert, and Stephen S. Johnson. "Seeing Things as They Really Are." *Forbes* 159, no. 5 (1997): 122-28.

Robinson, Ken. *Out of Our Minds. Learning to Be Creative.* 2nd ed. ed. Chichester, UK: Capstone Publishing Ltd., 2011.

Section 7
Ethics

Ethics is at the center of organizational priorities today. Ethics and governance are closely related to each other. An important distinction exists between the two concepts.

Governance is the primary responsibility of the board and senior management. Ethics permeates all levels of the organization.

Evidence suggests that ethical organizations outperform their peers on key performance metrics. Ethical organizations seem to be able to attract and retain high-quality customers, employees, suppliers, investors, and other stakeholders.

Ethics is no longer an option. Ethics is at the core of business success.

This section introduces you to several key ethical principles. After reading this section, you should be able to:

1. **Understand** the meaning of ethics and the principles governing business ethics.

2. **Appreciate** why it is important for organizations and individuals to be ethical.

3. **Apply** ethical principles to resolve dilemmas that arise in an organization.

Chapter **31**

Business Ethics

Ethics is distinct from morals and morality
to the extent that ethics provides a theoretical framework
for right action that leads to the greatest good possible,
whereas morals and morality refer to their practice.

E thics deals with issues of right and wrong. Ethical principles are rooted in philosophy, morality, anthropology,
sociology, and human behavior. Whether we like it or not,
we face ethical dilemmas both at work and outside of work.
Resolving ethical dilemmas is challenging and requires
adherence to time-tested principles. This section explores
the reality and understanding of business ethics.

What is Ethics?

The term ethics has its origins in the Greek *ethos*, meaning
custom or *habit*. Ethics, or *Moral Philosophy,* addresses questions such as how people ought to act, and the search for a
definition of right and wrong under a given situation leading
up to a call for the right action, and the pursuit of a life
worth living.

Ethics is distinct from morals and morality to the extent that
ethics provides a theoretical framework for right action
that leads to the greatest good possible, whereas morals and

morality refer to their practice. In the ultimate analysis, ethics may reflect a person's philosophy of life.

As with every other aspect of human endeavor, ethics has also branched off into several specialized domains, such as:

- **Normative or Prescriptive** Ethics *–How should people act?*

- **Descriptive Ethics** *– What do people think is right?*

- **Applied Ethics** *–How do we translate moral knowledge into action?*

- **Meta-Ethics** *– What do* right *and* wrong *even mean?*

Socrates is considered to be the father of Western Ethics. Plato has described the principles enunciated by Socrates in his dialogues. According to Socrates, people will naturally do good provided they know what is right, and evil or bad actions are simply the result of ignorance. Thus, "There is only one good, knowledge, and one evil, ignorance." Socrates' central premise is that the wise person knows what is right, does what is good, and as a consequence, is happy (since knowledge and wisdom are synonymous with self-awareness).

Aristotle goes a step further and holds that self-realization (the full development of one's innate talents) is the surest path to happiness, which is the ultimate goal. Everything else (such as wealth) is—at best—a means to an end. Aristotle encourages moderation in everything, dismissing the extremes as degrading and immoral. Thus, courage is the moderate virtue between the extremes of recklessness and cowardice.

Ancient Greek philosophers made a conscious attempt to move away from a spiritual position based on the supernatural, and toward humanistic free thought based on science and logic.

Virtue should govern life. Virtue is doing the right thing, to the right person, at the right time, to the required extent, in the correct manner. It is not difficult to see why virtue from this perspective is so rare.

At the other end of the spectrum, Diogenes advocated cynicism, extolled people to live life according to nature and not to be dictated by social convention, and argued that a simple life is a prerequisite for virtue and happiness. Consequently, Diogenes emphasized detachment from many of the things normally sought after. Pyrrho advocated skepticism, arguing that one cannot rationally decide between right-and-wrong/good-and-bad, and that self-interest drives most human actions.

The doctrine of humanism owes its origins to Thales who emphasized the dignity and worth of all people and their inherent ability to choose between right and wrong based on the principle of rationality.

To summarize, the ancient Greek philosophers made a conscious attempt to move away from a spiritual position based on the supernatural, and toward humanistic free thought based on science and logic, freed from the shackles of emotion, authority, dogma, and tradition.

Normative Ethics

Normative Ethics, or Prescriptive Ethics, attempts to develop a set of norms for action via a set of rules to govern human conduct, based on how things should be, how to evaluate them, notions of good or bad, and right or wrong. Normative ethical theories branch out into three categories: Consequentialism, Deontology, and Virtue Ethics.

- **Consequentialism,** or Teleological Ethics, posits that the morality of an action is judged by the action's outcome or result. A morally right action, therefore, leads to a good outcome or consequence. Inevitably, we face new questions such as who decides what a good outcome is; who is the primary beneficiary of an action; and what is a good outcome anyway?

- **Deontology** approaches ethics through an effort to determine the right or wrong of actions themselves, as opposed to the right or wrong (or good or bad) of the consequences of the actions. Decisions should be made based on one's duties and others' rights (*Deon* in Greek means duty or obligation).

- **Virtue Ethics** tries to examine the inherent character of a person rather than on the nature or consequences of specific actions. Virtue ethics explores virtues, extolls practical wisdom as the means to resolve conflicts, and concludes that a virtuous life leads to happiness.

Descriptive Ethics

Descriptive Ethics explores ethics by observed behavior by moral agents in practice. It doesn't provide any guidance as to what is good or bad, and right or wrong; nor does it attempt to evaluate the reasonableness of moral norms. Descriptive ethics is a popular method of investigation in evolutionary biology, sociology, psychology, anthropology, and history. However, we can use the knowledge from descriptive ethics in philosophical arguments. Descriptive ethics is also referred to as Comparative Ethics, as it involves comparisons of some kind—one culture to another, past and present, claims and actions, or words and deeds.

Applied Ethics

Applied Ethics is a branch of philosophy which explores ways to apply theoretical principles to real-life situations. Severe adherence to a set of principles may not be able to provide universally acceptable solutions. Alternately, we may end up with solutions impossible to implement.

Applied ethics melds philosophical constructs with psychological insights, sociological contexts, and knowledge gleaned from other disciplines. These constructs, contexts, and knowledge are combined, in search of solutions. Applied ethics are extensively used in public policy. Applied ethics includes Medical Ethics, Bioethics, Business Ethics, Legal Ethics, Environmental Ethics, Information Ethics, and Media Ethics.

Meta-ethics

Meta-ethics explores the meaning of ethical judgments and tries to understand the nature of ethical properties, attitudes, and statements, and how we may support or defend them. Unlike Normative Ethics, Meta-ethics does not evaluate specific choices made; instead, it tries to find the nature and meaning of the problem. Meta-ethics has two branches—

Moral Realism and Moral Anti-Realism. An alternate classification is:

- **Moral Absolutism** – the belief that absolute standards exist. Certain actions are right or wrong when judged against these standards, irrespective of the context of the action.

- **Moral Universalism** – a set of constructs that applies continually to all people, regardless of religion, race, culture, gender, nationality, or distinguishing features.

- **Moral Relativism** – ethical constructs are not universal or objective, and are relative to cultural, social, historical, and personal circumstances.

Eastern Approaches to Ethics

Taoism (China) has a history dating back over 2500 years. Taoism has some concepts that can help in resolving ethical dilemmas and encourages a simple life in tune with nature. From these concepts arise yin and yang; the harmony of opposites and relativity; reversal and cyclicity; and non-action.

Hindu (India) ethics has its foundations in philosophy and spirituality and dates back over 3000 years. The principal moral concepts relate to Dharma and Karma. Sanskrit words have multiple meanings, and context plays an important role in interpretation. Dharma means righteousness, moral obligation, and a way of life based on the natural order of things, including concepts of truth, integrity, beneficence, and non-malfeasance. Thus, dharma includes one's duty toward parents, teachers, siblings, colleagues, all forms of life, nature, society, and the environment.

Karma is the baggage of accumulated action that transcends birth and death. It is carried forward eternally, until one realizes the ultimate truth or self-realization or *mukthi* (liberation from the cycle of births and deaths). The prescription is for doing one's duty without the expectation of the fruit thereof —in other words, selflessness.

A significant part of ethics in Hinduism corresponds to Meta-ethics of the west. Hindu philosophy has three branches, or interpretations. *Dualism* proposes that the human spirit is a part of the universal spirit. *Qualified non-dualism* proposes that the universal spirit is a part of the human spirit. *Non-dualism* proposes that the human spirit and the universal spirit are the same. We do not recognize non-duality because of our ignorance. If we remove our veil of ignorance, we can realize the universal spirit or the ultimate truth.

Business Ethics Essentials

Business ethics—or ethics in business—is merely the application of everyday moral or ethical norms to business. A ready example from the Bible is the Ten Commandments. The stated injunctions to truthfulness and honesty or the prohibition against theft and envy are all directly applicable to business situations.

Aristotle has extensively discussed trade, property, exchange, acquisition, money, and wealth in his *Politics*. He has written moral judgments about greed, the unnatural use of one's potential to build wealth for its sake and condemned the lending of money for interest because this involves a profit from currency itself. He has also defined justice (giving each his due), fairness (treating equals equally), and trading (equals for equals).

In recent history, John Locke stands out for his defense of owning property as a natural right, Adam Smith, although best known for his contribution to economic thought, emphasized how economics and ethics were inseparable in his work *The Theory of Moral Sentiments*. John Stuart Mill, G.W.F. Hagel, and Immanuel Kant have written about just distribution and property rights.

The notion of ethics in business today focuses on the moral or ethical actions of individuals, groups, or entities. Much of the discussion on ethics focuses on the immoral or unethical behavior of individuals and corporations, rather than emphasizing the positive aspects of following ethical norms. It appears in recent years that we see more unethical conduct than we do of ethical conduct. Consider the fall of Enron, WorldCom, and Arthur Andersen, or the practice of using child labor in third world countries to reduce costs, or outsourcing activities to entities that are essentially sweatshops.

The three basic principles on which business ethics revolves are honesty, fairness, and integrity.

Business ethics refers to the principles and standards that guide behavior in the world of business. Various stakeholders —investors, customers, suppliers, employees, society, and government—determine whether actions are right or wrong, ethical or unethical. While these groups may not be correct in their assessment, their perception matters while determining society's acceptance/rejection of a business and its activities. Surveys indicate that public perception of corporate trust has declined in the first fifteen years of the twenty-first century. Consider this example:

Theranos is one of the firms that gained instant stardom. The company, founded by Elizabeth Holmes, claimed to have revolutionized the testing of blood samples. Early in the company's brief history, a few drops of blood being enough for conducting as many as 200 tests was the unique selling proposition on the firm's website. The company supplied test-kits to hundreds of outlets, including the Walgreens chain. Elizabeth Holmes was featured among the most celebrated women leaders and in July 2015 was considered to be a billionaire due to her share ownership in the company and the latter's notional market value. Just a year later, the Center for Medicare and Medicaid Services, the federal regulator responsible for ensuring patient care and health, concluded that Theranos' test methods produced erroneous results. The regulator barred Elizabeth Holmes from running any test centers for two years. The company had to withdraw all the test data. Not surprisingly, *Forbes*, which had placed Holmes in the billionaire category a year back, reduced her worth to zero.

One would imagine, with such an indictment by the regulatory body, the company would be circumspect in making new claims. And one would be wrong. Elizabeth Holmes managed to get a prime speaking slot at the annual meeting of the American Association for Clinical Chemistry in August 2016 and instead of sharing details of what went wrong with the *revolutionary* testing method, used the opportunity to showcase a miniature tabletop laboratory. Commentators have pointed out this is a classic case of *bait-and-switch*. It is quite amazing how someone can cast a spell on so many by unapproved methodology and without a shred of peer-reviewed evidence in a field where large corporations struggle for a decade or more before being able to market a drug. By spinning a yarn on how the mini-lab could run some tests, including one for the Zika virus, she conveniently focused on the future without explaining the company's murky past. *Forbes* magazine live-blogged during the event: "I have to say Holmes is doing an amazing job presenting this, I understand why people invested in her."

What do you think are the ethical issues involved in this contemporary case?

The current trend in ethics is to consciously move away from legal or regulatory compliance to developing an organizational culture rooted in core values. An ethical culture is a process of making decisions in organizations intended to guide managers toward ethically justifiable actions and avoid questionable actions. An ethical culture creates a set of shared values within the organization that together support ethical decisions, is driven by top management, and flows to all levels in the organization. An ethical culture fosters customer satisfaction and retention, investor loyalty and trust, employee commitment, and superior performance.

People make ethical decisions only after they realize that a particular situation or issue has an ethical dimension. Therefore, the first step in understanding business ethics is to develop awareness of ethical issues. Ethical issues arise at the intersection of an individual's values, principles, and beliefs with those of the organization and also those of society in which the organization operates.

For example, managers may try to maximize short-term performance in order to enhance their compensation in the form of bonuses and stock options. These may not be in the best long-term interests of shareholders. Similarly, the organization's desire to increase profits may conflict with customers' expectations of product or service quality, reliability, safety, and affordable price. A manager's wish to utilize favored, specific candidates may conflict with the organization's desire to employ the best possible candidates, as well as society's expectation of providing equal employment opportunities for all.

The three basic principles on which business ethics revolves are honesty, fairness, and integrity. Honesty refers to truthfulness and trustworthiness. To be honest means to tell the truth without hiding anything.

Confucius defined different levels of honesty. The shallowest is called *Li,* and it refers to one's superficial desires. The key principle is to convey one's feelings that appear to be honest but are in reality guided by self-interest. The second level is called *Yi* in which a person does what is right on the principle of reciprocity. The deepest level of honesty is called *Ren* and denotes empathy and understanding toward others. The Confucian version of the Golden Rule is to treat inferiors as you would want superiors to treat you.

The major difficulty with honesty arises when business is perceived to be a *game* and *winning is everything or even the only thing.* Those who argue along these lines compare business with sporting activities such as boxing in which one cannot win unless one is prepared to hurt the other person. In fact, the word *strategy* originates from the Greek term for the arrangement of troops in the war. If the business is akin to war, you cannot win without metaphorically killing and wounding your competitors.

Larry Ellison of Oracle has a business principle similar to medieval age conquerors: "It's not enough that we win. Everyone else must lose." An example of this mentality is his decision to sell PeopleSoft's technology and to let go of its eight thousand employees. Those affected have challenged many of his decisions. In one instance, he was asked to pay $100 million to charity and $22 million in damages for alleged stock-trading abuses.

Miller Coors has allegedly used deceptive and illegal advertising to promote alcohol consumption among young people (below 21).

Of course, the concept of business being a *game* is not logical because customers (consumers) cannot withdraw from the *game.* Therefore, business organizations must develop practices that are appropriate for the involuntary participation of consumers. It is also true that more and more businesses make headlines for dishonesty, including lying, cheating, and stealing.

Mitsubishi's *false* claim about the fuel economy of its automobiles has apparently been going on for 25 years. Investigators hired to probe the scandal have blamed the company's *corporate culture* and called the incident *a collective failure.*

Volkswagen's attempts to *falsify* emission readings under test conditions amount to *cheating* and have severely eroded the company's reputation. Besides the churning in its top management, the company faces $20 billion or more in costs and damages. The company has also agreed to rectify the mistake.

Fairness refers to the quality of being just, equitable, and impartial. Three fundamental elements appear to matter when it comes to fairness: equality, reciprocity, and optimization. Equality is about how an organization, or society, and even the world distributes its income and wealth at different levels. Reciprocity is the principle of giving and receiving in social relationships. Reciprocity is the interchange of equal value in a transaction or relationship. For example, it is important to compensate employees equal to their effort.

A common ethical dilemma occurs when it comes to CEO compensation. The ratio of the compensation of Fortune 500 CEOs to the median income in the U.S. is a staggering 331 to 1. Like all statistics, this one also depends on the CEO universe chosen for comparison. If all the 7 million CEOs (this includes small businesses with just a few employees and the owner being the CEO) are taken into account, the ratio is reduced to an egalitarian 3.9:1. Obviously, this does not represent the reality in the sense that the U.S. is far from being an egalitarian society.

Lying is any version of an event other than the truth.

Optimization is the trade-off between equity (or equality) and efficiency (maximization of productivity). Vested interests impair the idea of fairness. One or both parties in a relationship may perceive an action to be unfair or unethical because the outcome is less beneficial than expected.

Integrity refers to being whole, sound, and in an unimpaired condition. In an organization, it means uncompromising adherence to ethical values. A good reference point to judge whether an organization (or individual) has integrity is to look at the core values of the organization—what constitutes their true north? Are these core values practiced every day with every stakeholder and with the same consistency and level of excellence?

The three principles of honesty, fairness, and integrity form the bedrock of trust. Buyers should be able to trust sellers. Lenders should be able to trust borrowers. Management should be able to trust employees. Of course, these requirements flow in both directions. Together, these virtues (honesty, fairness, integrity, and trust) form the glue which can render business relationships effective, efficient, and endearing.

An ethical issue is a problem, situation, or opportunity that requires an individual, group, or organization to choose among several actions that are right or wrong, ethical or unethical.

An ethical dilemma is a problem, situation, or opportunity that requires an individual, group, or organization to choose among several wrong or unethical actions. There is not simply one right or ethical choice in a dilemma, only less unethical choices as perceived by stakeholders.

Common Ethical Issues

Abusive and/or intimidating behavior is the most common ethical problem for employees. However, the difficulty arises because of many of the characteristics under this category —physical threats, false accusations, being annoying, insults, profanity, yelling, harshness, ignoring someone, or unreasonableness—are subjective. What one person might consider yelling may constitute normal speech to another.

Bribery is the practice of offering something (money or something else of value) to gain an illicit advantage.

What sounds unreasonable to one person may appear perfectly reasonable to another. Equally important is the context within which a particular problem arises. Further, today's business environment has to deal with multiple cultures, ethnicities, languages, and demographic groups. A word or term that is acceptable in one culture may not be acceptable in another. What sounds innocuous in one language may mean something quite different in another. The key to addressing this is to understand that diversity is inevitable and diversity—if appropriately nurtured—can create exceptional value.

Intimidating behavior can even extend to organizations. Even respected companies occasionally face serious legal problems. For example, the microprocessor maker Intel has been challenged by its competitor AMD as having used strongarm tactics to ensure PC manufacturers used only Intel microprocessors. After a protracted legal battle in which Intel is reported to have spent over $100 million in legal expenses, Intel settled the issue for $1.25 billion without accepting any of the charges.

> *Conflict of interest exists when an individual must choose whether to advance her or his interests, those of the organization, or those of some other group or entity.*

Lying is any version of an event other than the truth. Business has become so complex that even this concept is sometimes viewed as one of degrees rather than being a binary choice. Thus, lying can be of a degree that causes harm, a *white lie* that does not cause any harm or damage and may be something told to benefit someone else, and statements that are obviously meant to engage or entertain with no malice intended. *Commission lying* is creating a perception or belief which intentionally deceives the receiver of the message. *Noise* is a technical explanation that the communicator knows the receiver cannot understand. *Omission lying* is intentionally not informing a channel member of any differences, problems, safety warnings or negative issues related to the product, service, or the organization.

Conflict of interest exists when an individual must choose whether to advance her or his interests, those of the organization, or those of some other group or entity. Employees must be able to separate their private interests from their business dealings to avoid conflicts of interest.

Bribery is the practice of offering something (money or something else of value) to gain an illicit advantage. *Corporate intelligence* is the collection and analysis of information on markets, technologies, customers, competitors, and on socioeconomic and political trends.

There are many tools of corporate intelligence. One tool is *hacking*. Another is *social engineering* in which someone reveals valuable corporate information through trickery. Other techniques include *dumpster diving* (collecting trash and trying to piece together valuable information from the trash), *whacking* (wireless hacking) and *phone eavesdropping*.

Another ethical/legal issue is *discrimination*. Discrimination is illegal in the U.S. and many other countries if it occurs due to race, color, religion, sexual orientation, gender, marital status, disability, nationality, or veteran status. Discrimination by political affiliation or union membership is a form of harassment. *Sexual harassment* is a form of gender discrimination. Even though organizations claim to be equal opportunity employers, the reality is that inequalities do exist in different forms that are often difficult to determine and prove.

With concerns growing as to the state of our planet, environmental issues such as air, water, and waste are becoming ethical issues in business. *Fraud* is any purposeful communication that deceives, manipulates, or conceals facts to create a false impression. There are several types of fraud: accounting, marketing, product or service related, and consumer.

When It Comes to Ethics, The Buck Stops with YOU!

Ethics is everyone's business. You are responsible. So is everyone else. Consider the 3R Framework for Ethical Conduct as shown in Figure 31.1.

Respect	Responsibility	Results
• Treat everyone with dignity and courtesy • Use organizational assets for business purposes only • Protect and enhance your work environment through compliance and thoughtful action • Embrace diversity in all forms	• Timeliness and quality • Collaboration and contribution to the overall good • Meet all performance expectations • Create value	• Remember, the means are as important as the ends • Don't take what is not yours • Reflect and improve all the time

Figure 31.1. The 3R Framework for Ethical Conduct.

Everything Counts in Ethics

As illustrated in Figure 31.2, everything truly counts in ethics.

Being ethical is a 24/7 activity!	Honor your promises and commitments	Talk WITH people – not AT them – and NEVER talk ABOUT them
Align your actions with organizational values and mission	Eliminate offensive words from your vocabulary	Recognize others' efforts and contributions
Practice mindfulness – patience, understanding, and empathy – makes you a better person		Be transparent and open
Let people know when you are bothered—and why	Walk the talk	Share your knowledge and experience

WATCH OUT FOR THE "BIG FOUR"

Greed – being selfish at someone's expense   **Laziness** – taking the path of least resistance
Speed – cutting corners to get things done   **Haziness** – acting without thinking

Figure 31.2. Everything Counts in Ethics.

A System Framework for Business Ethics

An organization implementing the model shown in Figure 31.3 is likely to see a perceptible reduction in unethical or illegal behaviors. As human beings, we are sure to make mistakes. Whenever mistakes do occur, corrective action in the form of training (where the error is considered an honest mistake)/ disciplining/firing, and preventive action to ensure that such mistakes do not recur.

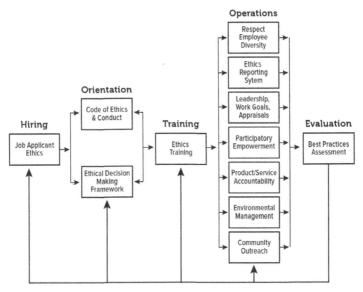

Figure 31.3. A System Framework for Business Ethics, adapted from Collins (2009).

The model is a variation of the Total Quality Management (TQM) perspective. The idea is to determine the cause of any given situation that leads to unethical behavior, and to address the cause, just as one would do in a manufacturing or service situation. In other words, a conscious effort is made to find out what happened. At a basic level, one might realize they have hired an unethical person. If not, the organization's core values or code of ethics might not have addressed the hiring issue adequately. The decision-making process of the organization might not have prepared the employee to face ethical issues. Processes for reporting unacceptable conduct can be inadequate.

If the aberration is at an intermediate level, one has to examine whether the manager is a desirable role model or not. In some situations, errors can occur if the goals set are beyond what one could expect under normal circumstances.

Sometimes, the failure of auditors and regulators can lead to a problem perpetuating itself. Perpetuating problems are common in accounting, insider trading, product safety, and reliability issues. In all these cases, an effort should be made to correct the problem, existing processes should be modified as needed to ensure similar problems would not arise in the future, and clear lines of accountability should be drawn. If pursued diligently, the effort would lead to a library of best practices acting as a guideline for managers and employees.

Recruitment and Selection: Hiring Ethical People

Just as a teaspoon of lime can spoil a gallon of milk, one employee who is bent on adopting shortcuts or who is worried only about the end and not the means can destroy an organization. If organizations wish to avoid these disasters, they need to start at the beginning—the hiring process. A five-step screening process would be useful:

1. The application process and the information gathered concerning these applicants should facilitate selecting the best possible candidate while avoiding the possibility of discrimination.

2. The information provided in the candidate's resume should be verified for accuracy and tested for integrity through reference and background checks.

3. Personality tests can help determine any undesirable traits or characteristics.

4. During the interview process, an adequate number of ethical dilemma questions should be posed to determine the extent of fit between the candidate's responses and the organization's core values and principles.

5. For jobs requiring a high state of alertness or those requiring a high degree of confidentiality, the organization should conduct other appropriate tests.

Such a process has two distinct advantages. It helps the organization to choose ethical persons. While diligent implementation requires considerable effort for the organization, the outcome would be significant and positive. The process also signals that ethics is important to current employees.

Summing Up

Ethics deals with issues of right and wrong. Ethical principles are rooted in philosophy, morality, anthropology, sociology, and human behavior. Whether we like it or not, we face ethical dilemmas, both at work and outside of work. Resolving ethical dilemmas is challenging and requires adherence to time-tested principles. This section has explored the contours of business ethics.

Chapter 32

Ethics in Practice

A code of ethics outlines the core values
of an organization and the ideal state to which
the organization aspires to evolve.

Organizations focus on codes of conduct to instill ethical behavior. Codes of conduct are useful but should not be an end in themselves. All decisions need ethical reasoning and outcome. Leaders need to set the right example through their words and actions. Ethical behavior should extend to all stakeholders.

Organizations should have supportive mechanisms in place for managing conflict. Employee empowerment is critical to success in ethical practice. This section explores the above concepts.

Code of Ethics and Code of Conduct

A *code of ethics* outlines the core values of an organization and the ideal state to which the organization aspires to evolve. A *code of conduct* outlines acceptable behavior under various circumstances and situations that the organization is likely to face as part of its business operations.

Codes of Ethics tend to emphasize Trustworthiness, Respect, Responsibility, Fairness, Caring, and Citizenship. A simple code of ethics would include:

- **Integrity** – focuses on honesty and openness; deliver on one's promises
- **Respect** – treat others as you would like to be treated by others
- **Communication** – with courtesy, listen more than talk, information is meant to move, information moves people
- **Excellence** – giving the best to everything and everyone
- **Continuous Improvement** – excellence and quality are journeys, not destinations
- **Mindfulness** – self-management, regularly taking stock, learning, enhancing one's contribution to the greater good

A code of conduct would include:

- **Fairness** – in all interactions with all stakeholders
- **Confidentiality** – of all information related to the organization's operations that might be used by competitors or others
- **Conflict of interest** – between individual and organizational goals
- **Protection** and **Use** of organizational assets
- **Compliance** with all laws and regulations

- **Whistle-blower protection** that allows reporting of any suspicious activity without the fear of retaliation

It would be useful to have an exercise at least once a year to enable employees and teams to highlight the extent to which they follow ethical principles, and—equally important —to identify areas needing improvement. The best practices, as and when identified, need to be documented and used as goals.

In today's typical organization, diversity plays a key role. People come from different backgrounds and cultural contexts. Ethics may not mean the same to everyone. A code of ethics is a baseline that people can easily connect with and practice in their daily lives. As with any other activity, ethics also needs to be constantly honed within the spirit that the largest room in the world is the room for improvement.

Ethical Decision-Making

Decision making involves arriving at a course of action from a list of possible alternatives. How does one make sure that the decision meets the ethical requirements in any given situation?

A framework that has its roots in Lawrence Kohlberg's stages of moral reasoning, as shown in Figure 32.1, may be useful.

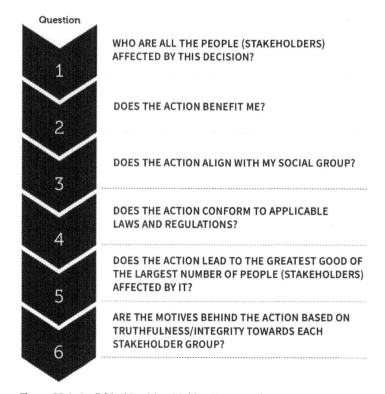

Figure 32.1. An Ethical Decision-Making Framework.

KEY:

- **Go ahead** with the action if the answer to Questions 2–6 are all YES.

- **DO NOT proceed** with the action if the answer to Questions 2–6 are all NO.

- If the answer to Questions 2–6 are a mix of yes and no:

  - Answers to **5 and 6 are YES:** This is a **Highly Ethical** action—modify as required to address Questions 2–4.

- The answers to **5 and 6 are NO:** This is a **Least Ethical** action—modify as required to address shortcomings and also to address Questions 2–4.

- The answers to **5 and 6 are different:** This is a **Moderately Ethical** action—modify as required to address shortcomings and also to address Questions 2–4.

A *yes* answer to questions 5 *and* 6 provides the maximum level of morality. However, what if the action would result in the decision-maker or the group being adversely affected? The action would need to be modified as required.

It is worth noting that the *legal* course of action might not be the ethically strongest. Laws are supposed to be made out of concern for everyone but often make compromises due to political and social considerations. Questions 2–6 have roots in five ethical theories:

1. **Egoism** – How does this action affect me? If it is beneficial to me, it is right? If it contradicts my interests, it is wrong.

2. **Social group relativism** – How does this action relate to my social group? If it conforms, it is right. If it does not conform, it is wrong.

3. **Cultural relativism** – How does this action relate to society's norms or laws? If it conforms, it is right. If it does not conform, it is wrong.

4. **Utilitarianism** – How does this action relate to all affected stakeholders? If it benefits the largest number, it is right. If it does not benefit the largest number, it is wrong.

5. **Deontology** – How does this action relate to my existential duty to become an ideal human being? Does it treat everyone as it treats me? Does it treat every stakeholder truthfully, with respect and integrity? If yes, it is right. If not, it is wrong.

Most managers are essentially social group relativists (Question 3) and concerned with the legality of their actions (Question 4). However, an action doesn't have to be ethical merely by being legal. Managers who, at one extreme, may be egoists (Question 2) would do well to look at utilitarians (Question 5) and deontologists (Question 6) while making critical decisions.

Whenever a conflict arises in an organization, the person at the higher level in the organizational structure usually gets her or his way. The underlying assumption is that the higher-ranking manager is, by default, the more ethical person.

Empirical evidence from history and the social sciences tells a different story. Simply pushing a decision down by one's position is likely to lead to a drop in employee morale, and can lead to unethical behavior at other levels in the organization, and in some cases, to expensive litigation. Organizations should try to build ethical consensus so they can avoid the pitfalls. A win-win outcome is possible if the following process is adopted:

Both parties:

Step 1: **State** their respective positions.

Step 2: **Articulate** the underlying core principles or values for their respective positions.

Step 3: **Summarize** each other's position.

Step 4: **Summarize** each other's values or principles.

Step 5: **Work** toward resolving the conflict.

Step 6: **Verify** and ensure that the solution does not contradict the values of either party.

Ethical Leadership

Managers are role models, and subordinates constantly watch them (managers) for ethical cues. Actions speak much louder than words. Thus, a manager's commitment to ethical principles, or lack thereof, trickles down to those below and other employees. Since managers are supposed to have advanced to their positions by their actions, subordinates start mimicking the actions in the hope of getting promoted. Mission-driven, empathetic, and conscientious managers who produce exceptional results are likely to attract like-minded employees.

By the same yardstick, a manager who is perceived to place themselves above service is angry at others, does not manage time effectively, and produces mediocre results is also likely to attract similar employees. The single most desired characteristic that employees look for in a manager and a leader is honesty. Honesty is the mutually reinforcing ethical bond between leaders and managers and employees. Dishonesty at any level destroys this vital bond.

The Great Place to Work® Institute provides a useful framework for creating a work culture that nurtures and facilitates superior performance. A great place to work is a place where people "trust the people they work for, have pride in what they do, and enjoy the people they work with. The five dimensions measured by the Institute to identify great places to work are:

1. Credibility

   • Communications are open and accessible

   • Competence in coordinating human and material resources

   • Integrity in carrying out the organization's vision with consistency

2. Respect

   • Support professional development and show appreciation

   • Collaborate with employees on relevant decisions

   • Care for employees as individuals with personal lives

3. Fairness

   • Equity: balanced treatment for all regarding rewards

   • Impartiality: absence of favoritism in hiring and promotions

   • Justice: lack of discrimination and process for appeals

4. Pride

   • In personal job, individual contributions

   • In work produced by one's team or workgroup

- In the organization's products and standing in the community

5. Camaraderie

   - Ability to be oneself
   - Socially friendly and welcoming atmosphere
   - The sense of *family* or *team*

Similar to research on ethical organizations, researchers report that great workplaces receive more qualified applicants, have lower levels of employee turnover, lower healthcare costs, and have higher levels of customer satisfaction, productivity, and profitability.

Virtues and Leadership Practices: The top seven leadership virtues, or foundations of ethical behavior, are:

1. Mission-driven
2. Honest
3. Fair
4. Supportive
5. Respectful
6. Quality-focused
7. Accountable

Correspondingly, successful leaders:

- Make sure people not only see the vision, but they also live and breathe it.
- Establish trust using candor, transparency, and credit.

- Constantly upgrade their team through feedback and coaching.

- Always exude enthusiasm and positive energy.

- Have the courage, after listening to others, to make unpopular decisions.

- Probe and inquire with a curiosity that borders on skepticism.

- Take risks, learn from their mistakes, and inspire others to do likewise.

- Celebrate organizational and employee accomplishments.

Work Goals

Work goals can become problematic and lead to unethical behavior. Research shows that stretch goals tend to tempt employees to *stretch* the truth. For example, a system rewarding people solely on production outcomes can lead to inadequate quality checks in a manufacturing plant. Similarly, if a financial institution rewards employees merely based on the number of loans and mortgages and not the quality of the loans, many of the loans may be unrecoverable.

Sales performance goals are a particularly troublesome area. Accounting and auditing goals have also been found to be causes of unethical behavior. The collapse of a once highly acclaimed firm, Arthur Andersen, can be attributed to the flawed practices of Sunbeam Corporation; Waste Management, Inc.; Enron; Global Crossing; WorldCom; and Qwest Communications. Therefore, it is prudent for organizations and leaders to set SMART Goals:

- **Specific** – the outcome is identifiable
- **Measurable** – the outcome can be measured
- **Aligned** – the outcome contributes to the organizational strategy
- **Reachable** – the outcome is challenging but realistically attainable
- **Time-bound** – the outcome is to be achieved by a specific point in time

It is worth noting that *doing one's best* is not an adequate employee goal. To the extent that employees are involved in the goal-setting process, an increase in commitment and accountability is a fair expectation.

Managing Stress

As noted above, SMART goals have specific timelines. Timelines can cause stress. High-stress levels, if not managed appropriately, can lead to health problems, low productivity, absenteeism, turnover, and unethical behavior (typically cutting corners to achieve the desired goal). Organizations can help employees manage stress through a variety of interventions such as:

- Wellness Programs – opportunities for improving health through a combination of diet, exercise, and mindfulness sessions
- Employee Assistance Programs – originally designed for substance abuse, now include financial planning and family care

- Delegation Training – what needs to be done by an individual and what can be delegated to others (without causing stress in the process)

- Time Management – prioritizing and use of project management software can help employees to break down large tasks into manageable modules

- Quiet Time – a specified time when the employee will not be disturbed by phone calls, e-mails, or urgent meetings

- Meditation – relaxation techniques for body and soul

Measuring the Ethical Dimension of Performance

One of the best practices is to include the ethical dimension while measuring employee performance. Organizations can foster an ethical culture by communicating a clear signal; i.e., between two employees which produced similar results, the one scoring higher on the ethical dimension receives more recognition. The measurement can be done on a Likert Scale using the following criteria:

- Demonstrates a commitment to integrity and respect

- Provides exceptional service (to internal/external customers)

- Communicates promptly with courtesy and professionalism

- Embraces the concept of continuous improvement in all activities

- Actively engages in self-management (continuous assessment of one's holistic growth)

Measuring Leadership Skills

Besides measuring performance relating to work and ethics, it would be useful to measure leadership skills where appropriate. A skill set creates an inventory of outstanding performers who can be considered for greater responsibilities as an organization grows. We can also measure leadership skills on a Likert Scale with the following criteria:

- Being positive

- Good listener

- Comfortable giving feedback

- Trusted by others

- Easily approachable

- Available to others when needed

- Seeks inputs from others

- Communicates clearly

- Appreciates others

- Patient

- Delivers on commitments

After measuring, leaders should provide appropriate feedback related to areas for improvement, and specific courses of action for the employee to score better. In practice, an even-numbered Likert Scale is better than an odd-numbered scale as this forces the leader to take a position instead of marking the midpoint that has been found to happen in a majority of such measurements.

Managing Code of Ethics and Code of Conduct Infractions

Any violation of an organization's value system needs to be dealt with promptly and fairly. Depending on the nature of the violation, corrective measures can range from counseling and coaching, oral warning, written warning, in-house or offsite training, and transfer to probation, fine, suspension, and termination. Termination should be the last resort, as it can have debilitating consequences. The main aim should be to reform and rehabilitate. Thus, forgiveness plays an important role in the process of managing violations to the organizational code.

Stakeholder Relations

Stakeholders—customers, suppliers, employees, investors, government agencies, and society at large—can shape the ethical dimension of an organization. Employees and investors can face disastrous consequences when corporations act in blatantly unethical ways.

When Enron collapsed, thousands of employees lost their jobs, retirees and those nearing retirement saw their pension funds erased, and investors lost billions as the stock plummeted. Customers and the community suffer when organizations act in an unethical manner, such as in the case of Volkswagen and its attempts to cover up unacceptable emission levels in automobiles. The Coca-Cola company has faced numerous problems and lawsuits; from the quality of water used in its beverages to contamination with pesticide residues; discrimination against African American employees; and harassment of executives for whistleblowing. Besides affecting suppliers, bottlers, employees, and consumers, the alleged practices dented the reputation of the firm and led to an erosion of investor confidence reflected in the stock price.

The current thinking on business ethics focuses on the Stakeholder Synthesis Approach because businesses do have moral responsibilities to stakeholders, but they are not part of a fiduciary obligation. Consequently, management's primary fiduciary responsibility to shareholders is kept intact, but it is expected to be within the context of ethical responsibility to other stakeholders. The ethical responsibility of a business is not to harm, coerce, lie, cheat, steal, and so on.

Any discussion of business and society must consider the role of government. Business and government invariably have opposing systems of belief, and yet their functioning interconnects in our socioeconomic system. The government exerts a host of nonregulatory influences on business. Two influences with a macro-orientation are industrial policy and privatization. A more specific influence is the fact that government is a major employer, purchaser, subsidizer, competitor, financier, and persuader. These roles permit the government to have a significant influence on business.

As far as the role of government is concerned, the controversial role of regulation needs emphasis. In recent times, we can see a tilt toward social regulation as opposed to economic regulation. As with any policy initiative, regulation has its advantages—particularly when one deals with scarce resources—and disadvantages—not the least of which is the apparent relationship between regulation and corruption. One response to the problem is the pressure for deregulation.

If the track records of industries such as utilities, communication systems, airlines, and financial services are any indication, one wonders whether deregulation can provide real benefits to end users. A judicious mix of regulation and deregulation is the obvious answer, but the degree to which these measures are required will always be debatable.

Even as we look at government's influence over business, we should remember the converse relationship. Businesses influence government policy and actions in some ways— contributions to political campaigns, lobbying, and joining with like-minded organizations to push for changes. Just as the role of government in regulation is questionable, the role of business, particularly its use and abuse of power, is just as equally questionable. It is difficult to say what this will lead to, much less when it leads to any desired outcome or to any outcome at all.

A minimum baseline of sustainability
should be the bottom line for business
as it moves into the future.

Consumers easily become the most critical stakeholders, particularly in the context of consumption-driven markets. Consumer expectations relate to the right to safety, to be informed, to have choices, and to have a voice. Product information issues compose a major area in the business-consumer stakeholder relationship. Foremost among these is advertising. One estimate suggests that an average person is exposed to some 3,000 advertisements every day. Issues which have arisen concerning advertising include ambiguity, concealing facts, exaggerations, and psychological appeals. Controversial issues include comparative advertising, advertising to children, use of sex in advertising, marketing to the poor and vulnerable sections of society, advertising of harmful substances, misleading health and environmental claims, and ad creep. Other issues are warranties, packaging, and labeling. The multinational giant Nestle recently lost about $500 million in India due to a basic error in labeling, despite having been in that market for thirty years.

The natural environment is critical to human survival, and some complex and inter-connected human activities are threatening the environment. Problems such as pollution, deforestation, and expanding populations pose a challenge to non-human species and ecosystems, and in the process, reduce the quality of human life. Individuals and organizations have to assume responsibility for this. A minimum baseline of sustainability—meeting the needs of the present without compromising the ability of future generations to meet their needs—should be the bottom line for business as it moves into the future.

Community stakeholders are very important to business organizations. Business can impact the community in which it operates in two ways: it can deploy managers and employees to projects that benefit the community (voluntarism), and it can donate to philanthropic entities. Two types of community partnerships are common: *strategic philanthropy* in which the business attempts to align its strategy and the needs of the community; and *cause-related marketing*, which enhances the relationship between a firm's profits and its contribution to worthwhile causes. Just as a business can impact the community in meaningful ways, it can also cause severe disruptions in the community.

When a business decides to close down, several stakeholder groups—employees, local government, other businesses, and ordinary citizens—may be adversely affected. Therefore, as an ethical imperative, businesses need to carry out a stakeholder impact analysis before taking drastic decisions. Training employees with alternate skills, providing opportunities for transfer and relocation, gradual tapering of operations, and efforts to attract alternate businesses can mitigate the suffering of stakeholders. Displacement due to technological and other changes is a sensitive area, one which is highly emotional, and societies and governments are constantly watching the behavior of businesses. It is in the interests of businesses that they take a measured and prudent view of this issue.

The social contract between employers and employees is undergoing significant changes. Emerging out of these changes are such aspects as the right not to be fired without sufficient cause, the right to due process and fair treatment, and the right to freedom of speech. Several judicial rulings have nullified the traditional employment-at-will doctrine. Major exceptions are the public policy exemption, the idea of an implied contract, and breach of good faith. Society's perception of what constitutes fair treatment is also constantly changing. New methods such as having an ombudsman and peer review are especially worth considering if businesses wish to avoid scandals and expensive litigation.

The Sarbanes-Oxley Act does provide some protection to whistleblowers, but whistleblowers still face many obstacles. A stakeholder approach emphasizing ethical relationships with employees can create an organizational environment where employees feel free to express their concerns openly and without the fear of retribution, lessening the need to blow a whistle. Related employee stakeholder issues are the rights to privacy, safety, and health. With technological advances, it has become increasingly easy for organizations to monitor their employees. Organizations need to weigh constant monitoring against the advantages of having a workplace based on trust and high morale. The OSHA is the federal government's major instrument for protecting employees on the job.

Several state laws have attempted to extend the protection, particularly against exposure to toxic substances. It is worth noting that current laws and regulations can only address known problems. Today, the threat of terrorism poses new challenges, both for organizations and employees. The threat of terrorism has led to increased security and surveillance systems.

With increased mobility among managers and employees, organizations must contend with new threats—for example, diseases such as Ebola and Zika—and hostilities. Wise leaders and managers plan for these eventualities, even as they grapple with meeting employee expectations. With globalization becoming a true reality, managers also need to look at best practices in diversity, even as they follow local laws about non-discrimination and equal opportunity in letter and spirit.

Empowering Ethical Employees

An ethical organization is a community of people in which every employee has a sense of organizational ownership and accountability. Such an organization empowers its people to control their immediate surroundings and provides them with the autonomy and authority to do what is required to meet the organization's goals. A majority of organizations have three types of employees as reflected in the employee's attitude toward work:

- **Go-getters**: Employees who are engaged with the work experience, enjoy work, and consistently produce desired results.

- **Fence-sitters**: Those who do enough to retain their jobs and do what they believe to be appropriate for the compensation that they receive.

- **Adversarial**: Those who do not have the temperament to work, shun authority, and are a negative influence on others.

An ethical organization committed to high integrity (resulting in superior performance) is likely to have a high percentage of go-getters. Mediocre organizations typically have a preponderance of the latter two categories.

Management's approach to the three categories can be:

1. Go-getters
   - Provide autonomy
   - Give new challenges
   - Prepare for leadership positions

Praise and offer rewards

2. Fence Sitters

- Raise minimum expectations

- Team with go-getters

- Separate from adversarial

3. Adversarial

- Confront and discipline

- Counsel and train

- Separate from fence-sitters

- Team up with go-getters and observe changes, if any

- Examine whether too much supervision could be the reason (evidence suggests that many adversarial employees can become go-getters if given the required autonomy)

Effective Teams

Members of great teams trust one another implicitly. They are not afraid to share their weaknesses and to seek help whenever necessary. They are open to each other and do not resort to filters while communicating. At the same time, members of great teams are not afraid to discuss any issue, are not afraid to disagree and to challenge a given proposal, all in the spirit of arriving at the best possible solutions. They are committed to the overarching goals of the organization and try hard to obtain buy-in on all critical decisions. Members are not afraid to be held accountable, and invariably solve all problems with peer groups instead of escalating every issue to a higher level. Thus, effective teams can be termed *self-directed*.

The following method is likely to ensure participation of all members:

1. Present the problem – ensure everyone understands the problem

2. Define individual solutions – each member writes down possible solutions

3. Present individual solutions – each member presents possible solutions

4. Clarify individual solutions – answer questions, if any

5. Discuss and prioritize solutions

6. Play devil's advocate – articulate what might be wrong with solutions

7. Decide on final solution

8. Implement and monitor

9. If results are appropriate, strive for further improvement

10. If results are not satisfactory, go back to defining the problem

Appreciative Inquiry

Appreciative Inquiry is a team-based management technique that aligns employee strengths with organizational strengths and leads to a mission-driven organization. Developed by David L. Cooperrider and Diana Whitney, the process presents opportunities for employees to:

- **Discover** (identify organizational processes that work well)

- **Dream** (envision processes that would work well in the future)

- **Design** (plan and prioritize processes that would work well)

- **Destiny** (implement the processes)

Appreciative Inquiry is conducted when teams and individuals:

- Individually reflect on superior customer service

- As a small team, determine the critical elements of superior customer service

- Develop a collective vision of what is needed to achieve superior customer service

- Create a draft of an organizational mission that emphasizes superior customer service at every level and across every interaction

- Determine the organization's current *core* that already supports superior customer service

- Make personal commitments

- Make organizational action recommendations

- Managers to follow up and provide feedback

- Repeat the process at regular intervals

Periodical (daily/weekly/monthly) performance reflections:
Set apart ten to fifteen minutes during scheduled meetings
where team members share the following information:

- A performance accomplishment or satisfaction
experienced

- A problem faced

- How they solved the problem

- A lesson learned that might benefit others

- A problem that still needs attention

**Other Mechanisms to Foster Exceptional & Ethical
Performance**

- Scanlon Plans based on savings in costs

- Open Book Management (transparency in all
activities)

- Profit Sharing

- Stock Options

- Cooperatives (producer or consumer)

Equal Exchange was founded in 1986. All members have the
right to vote (one vote per member), right to serve as a manager or board director, right to information (Open Book
Management), and right to freedom of speech within the
organization. Of the net profits, the company donates 7% to
non-profit organizations and 3% to other cooperatives.
Two-thirds of the remaining 90% are reinvested in the
organization, and one-third is divided equally among the
member-owners.

Summing Up

Organizations focus on codes of conduct to instill ethical behavior. Codes of conduct are useful but should not be an end in themselves. All decisions require an ethical reasoning and outcome. Leaders need to set the right example through their words and actions. Ethical behavior extends to all stakeholders. Successful organizations have supportive mechanisms for managing conflict. Employee empowerment is critical to success in ethical practice.

Chapter 33

Current Trends
in Ethical Practice

Ethics is difficult to practice in normal times.
During turbulent times, the difficulty increases
exponentially.

The 21st-century business landscape has three characteristics—rapid change, complexity, and ambiguity. Ethics
is difficult to practice in normal times. During turbulent times,
the difficulty increases exponentially. Successful organizations
follow some best practices:

- Corporate Citizenship
- TNS (The Natural Step) framework

Concepts with examples of corporate citizenship and the natural step framework are paramount in successful organizations
practices.

Corporate Citizenship

Environmental Management Systems: One of the greatest
ethical challenges of the 21st century relates to environmental
management. Climate change is real and has unimaginable
consequences. If left unchecked, several coastal regions of
the world are expected to disappear in the next two or three

decades. Glaciers are disappearing. Satellite imagery shows the gradual shrinking of the polar ice caps. Unpredictable weather patterns mean drought in some regions, flooding in other regions, and a declining quality of life for everyone due to increased pollution of the atmosphere, water, and the earth. Until the 1960s, the response of business was one of denial. From the 1960s to the turn of the millennium, the response was one of eco-friendliness as exemplified in such initiatives as green marketing. Today, this isn't enough. We need a responsible and responsive environment management system leading to sustainable development.

Benefits of sustainable development include:

- Production cost savings

- Lower insurance premiums

- Lower bank loan rates

- Reduced liability risks

- Rapid market expansion

- Customer attraction and retention

- Employee attraction and retention

- Reduced concept-to-market time

- Regulatory flexibility

- Industry self-regulation

- Better relations with community

- Better activist and media relations

- Pride in being part of a worthwhile movement

Elements of developing an Environment Management System (EMS) are:

- Nominate a manager to be Environmental Manager

- Provide top management support

- Build *Green Committee*

- Develop Environmental Vision and Strategy

- Train, educate, and coach employees at all levels

- Involve all employees in EMS effort

- Identify *low-hanging fruits*, and implement and obtain agreement to achieve buy-in

- Develop mechanisms for measurement and feedback

- Influence value chain partners to adopt sustainable practices

- Integrate into all business functions and activities

- Develop and implement mechanism for Environmental Risk Assessment

The Natural Step (TNS) Framework and Cost Reductions is a three-step framework toward sustainable development used to:

- Reduce dependence on fossil fuels, underground minerals, and metals

- Reduce dependence on chemicals and synthetic compounds

- Reduce encroachment on nature

Specific areas to address include:

- Energy reduction
- Waste management (recycle wherever possible)
- Paper reduction (one-ton of paper requires 16 fully grown trees)
- Product shipment reduction (aggregation and alternate packing methods)
- Toxic substances reduction
- Business travel reduction

Green Buildings and LEED Certification

Leadership in Energy and Environmental Design (LEED) rating system provides eco-friendly measurement standards for certifying building construction and remodeling. The four levels of LEED certification are Basic (26 points), Silver (32 points), Gold (39 points), and Platinum (52 points). Factors considered are sustainable sites, water efficiency, energy and atmosphere, materials and resources, indoor environmental quality, and innovation and design process.

Key Environmental Metrics

1. **Energy**
   - Energy used
   - Renewable energy used or bought

2. **Water**
   - Total water used
   - Water pollution

3. Air

- Greenhouse gas emissions
- Releases of heavy metals and toxic chemicals
- Emissions of particulates, volatile organic compounds, sulfur and nitrogen compounds

4. Waste

- Hazardous waste
- Solid waste
- Recycled materials

5. Transportation

- Company vehicle mileage
- Business travel mileage
- Freight mileage and tonnage

6. Compliance

- Notices of violations
- Fines or penalties levied

Global Reporting Initiative (GRI), an international multi-stakeholder coalition, provides guidelines for sustainability reporting and facilitates environmental performance comparisons between organizations.

Starbucks Environmental Mission Statement: "Starbucks is committed to a role of environmental leadership in all facets of our business. We will fulfill this mission by a commitment to:

1. Understanding environmental issues and sharing information with our partners.

2. Developing an eco-system that can support sustainable development.

3. Striving to buy, sell, and use environmentally friendly products.

4. Recognizing that fiscal responsibility is essential to our environmental future.

5. Instilling environmental responsibility as a corporate value.

6. Measuring and monitoring our progress for each product.

7. Encouraging all partners to share our mission."

Office Depot's Advice on How to Save Money by Going Green include

1. Energy Star-qualified office equipment saves up to 75% in electricity use.

2. Compact Fluorescent Lamps (CFL) last ten times longer than incandescent lamps and save electricity.

3. Power strips save electricity.

4. Daylighting saves electricity.

5. Remanufactured ink and toner cartridges cost an average of 15% less than national brands—many come with a 100% money-back quality guarantee.

6. Recycle empty ink and toner cartridges for discounted prices with repurchases.

7. Use digital storage solutions.

8. Donate unwanted products and furniture for tax deductions.

9. Use reusable coffee mugs instead of disposable cups.

Summing Up

The 21st-century business landscape has three characteristics: rapid change, complexity, and ambiguity. Ethics is difficult to practice in normal times. During turbulent times, the difficulty increases exponentially. Successful organizations are following some best practices of Corporate Citizenship and TNS (The Natural Step) framework.

Chapter **34**

Ethics Summary

Ethical organizations outperform
unethical organizations on all critical parameters.

Ethics or **Moral Philosophy** addresses questions such as how people should act and the search for a definition of right and wrong under a given situation. In the ultimate analysis, ethics may reflect a person's philosophy of life. Branches:

- **Normative** or **Prescriptive** – How should people act?

- **Descriptive** – What do people think is right?

- **Applied** – How do we translate moral knowledge into action?

- **Meta** – What do right and wrong even mean?

The competitive advantage of ethical organizations— empirically, ethical organizations outperform unethical organizations on all critical parameters in the long run.

- Triad of Business Ethics – Honesty, Fairness, and Integrity

- Common Ethical Issues – Intimidating Behavior, Lying, Conflict of Interest, Bribery, Discrimination, Environmental Issues, and Fraud

- Systems Framework of Ethics – Similarities to TQM Model; Corrective and Preventive Actions; Recruitment; Code of Ethics and Code of Conduct

- Ethical Decision Making – Six Step Process; Underlying Concepts: Egoism, Social Group Relativism, Cultural Relativism, Utilitarianism, and Deontology

- Ethical Hazards – Temptations to Follow the Easy Path

- Ethical Leadership – Mission-Driven, Honest, Fair, Supportive, Respectful, Quality-focused, and Accountable

- Characteristics of Great Place To Work* – Credibility, Respect, Fairness, Pride, and Camaraderie

- Managing Stress (that can lead to unethical behavior) – Wellness Programs, Employee Assistance, Training, Time Management, Quiet Time, and Meditation

- Measuring Ethical Dimensions of Performance – of Leaders and Employees

- Managing Infractions to the Code of Conduct

- Stakeholder Relations and Mechanisms to Foster Exceptional and Ethical Performance

- Corporate Citizenship and Environmental Management Systems

Reflective Questions

Reflective Question #1: Work as a Calling. When did you first feel drawn to the kind of work you are doing? How did it feel? Has this feeling increased or decreased over the years? If the feeling has decreased, how can this feeling be recaptured?

Do you experience joy in your work? When and under what circumstances? How often do you experience this? How does this joy relate to difficulties associated with your work?

Do others experience joy as a result of your work? Directly? Indirectly? How can this experience of joy be increased?

What do you learn at work? In what ways is work a learning experience for you? In what ways is work a learning experience for others around you? How is your work a blessing for future generations?

If you were to quit work today, what difference would it make to your personal or spiritual growth? The personal or spiritual growth of your colleagues? The organization?

Short Case Study

Please refer to Appendix G – *Ethical Dilemmas* for the case studies on ethics.

Section 8
Continuous Quality Improvement

Continuous improvement is the ongoing improvement of products, services, or processes through incremental and breakthrough improvements.

Continuous improvement is the ongoing improvement of products, services, or processes through incremental and breakthrough improvements. Some scholars make a distinction between *continuous* improvement and *continual* improvement.

Continual improvement refers to general processes of improvement and encompassing *discontinuous* or *non-linear* improvements—that is, many different approaches, covering different areas.

Continuous improvement is a subset of continual improvement, with a specific focus on linear, incremental improvement within an existing process. When this distinction is made, continuous improvement is closely associated with statistical quality control. For our discussion, we can use the terms interchangeably. An alternative definition of continuous improvement is the identification of opportunities for streamlining the work process.

This section introduces you to the various methods of achieving continuous improvement.

After reading and understanding this section, you will be able to:

1. **Understand** the basic concepts of Quality Management and Continuous Improvement.

2. **Use** different approaches to achieve process improvement.

3. **Develop** a problem-solving approach applicable in a variety of situations.

4. **Understand** the current approaches to quality, such as Six Sigma and Lean.

Chapter 35

Quality and
Continuous Improvement

Quality management systems can assist organizations in enhancing the customer experience.

Q uality is one of the four pillars of competitive advantage (the other three being efficiency, innovation, and customer responsiveness). Quality has a two-fold advantage:

1. Quality reduces wastage and re-work. As a result, quality reduces costs. Contrary to popular perception, the higher the level of quality, the lower the level of per-unit cost.

2. A customer-held perception of superior quality allows the firm to charge a premium (higher prices) for its products or services. The higher price results in higher profits.

Thus, quality is the only pillar of competitive advantage facilitating the simultaneous pursuit of cost leadership and differentiation.

Understanding Quality Management & Continuous Improvement

Quality management systems can assist organizations in enhancing the customer experience.

Customers require products and services with characteristics and attributes that satisfy their needs and expectations. The characteristics and attributes that customers look for in products and services can be termed **Customer Requirements**. The requirements may be explicit (as gathered through surveys and listening to the Voice of the Customer), implicit (not expressed but welcome), or created (by the organization).

Consider the MP3 player. In its original form, it was a device to store and reproduce music. The device was bulky, had too many switches, and the sound quality was not great. The development and release of the iPod revolutionized the industry. With its tracking wheel and superb sound quality in a miniature device, Apple was able to create a need to augment the then-prevailing customer experience in personal music systems. Coupled with iTunes, the company established a new standard for downloading and enjoying music on the go.

A quality management system can provide the framework for continual improvement to increase the probability of enhancing the customer experience even while meeting the expectations of other stakeholders (shareholders, employees, suppliers, and society). A well-orchestrated quality management system provides confidence to the organization and its stakeholders that it can roll out products and services that consistently meet or exceed requirements.

Quality is the inherent degree of excellence of a product or service. It is also referred to as conformance to requirements at the start of use. Reliability refers to the state of the product or service after an interval of time (will it continue to perform adequately after a week, a month, or a year?). While quality can be expressed as time zero defects, reliability needs a probability model known as the life distribution model.

Continuous improvement teams are cross-functional in composition.

One of the most widely used tools for continuous improvement is a four-step quality model—the **plan-do-check-act (PDCA)** cycle, also known as the Deming Cycle or Shewhart Cycle.

1. **Plan** – Identify an opportunity and plan for change

2. **Do** – Implement the change on a small scale (pilot, trial, experiment)

3. **Check** – Use data to analyze results and determine whether it made a difference

4. **Act** – If the change was successful, implement it on a wider scale and continuously assess results. If the change did not work, begin the cycle again.

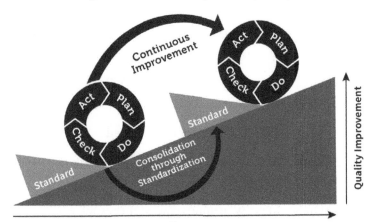

Figure 35.1. The PDCA Cycle for Continuous Quality Improvement.

Other widely used methods of continuous improvement are:

- **Six Sigma**

- **Lean**

- **Total Quality Management (TQM)**

These methods emphasize management commitment, employee involvement, teamwork, measurement, systems approach, and reduction of variation, defects, and cycle times.

Continuous Improvement Methodology

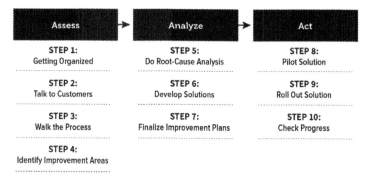

Figure 35.2. A Continuous Improvement Methodology.

- Step 1 – Who initiates? Top Management? Business Unit? Department? Team? An individual?

- Step 2 – Voice of the Customer (VOC)—can be external or internal

- Step 3 – Tentative approach to be used

- Step 4 – What do we want to achieve? Reduce costs? Increase revenue? How?

- Step 5 – Identify primary cause for present state

- Step 6 – Alternatives to improve present state; pros and cons

- Step 7 – Which plan to adopt? Why? Measurable outcomes?

- Step 8 – Implement as a pilot/trial/experiment; check outcome to expectation

- Step 9 – If outcome matches or exceeds expectation, implement in other areas/processes; else, go back to beginning

- Step 10 – Check progress at regular intervals; make changes as required

Continuous Improvement Teams

- Process Owner/Initiator
- Team Leader
- Facilitator
- Members
- Observers
- Communication Specialists
- Documentation Specialists

The continuous improvement team is actively engaged in defining and implementing projects while managing the overall process.

Team members need to be high-performers with leadership potential.

Ideally, continuous improvement teams are cross-functional in composition. There is hardly any process in an organization that does not cut across boundaries. Therefore, it is necessary to involve members of all functions which are part of a process. The team size should not be so small that sufficient alternatives cannot be considered. Similarly, it should not be so large that rational decisions are difficult. Empirical studies indicate that teams with 4–6 members deliver timely and sustained results.

Continuous improvement is also popular as Kaizen (*change for the better* in Japanese). Toyota Motor pioneered the concept, and other companies were quick to follow.

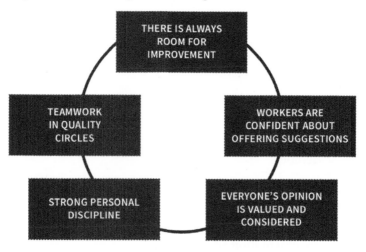

Figure 35.3. The Kaizen Continuous Improvement Model.

The Kaizen framework starts with the premise that quality is a journey—not a destination. Thus, there is always room for improvement. The people who are responsible for any process are in the best position to offer suggestions for improvement.

Quality is everyone's responsibility.

Quality becomes a bottom-up approach in which everyone participates, and everyone's views are valued. The emphasis on personal discipline places the ownership of any process on those responsible for the outcomes. Achieving quality and continuous improvement is the responsibility of cross-functional teams—the composition of a quality circle is a team drawn from different functions.

Basic Tools of Quality

Cause-and-Effect Diagram—also called the Ishikawa Diagram or Fishbone Chart – Identifies many possible causes for an effect or problem and sorts ideas into useful categories or clusters.

Check Sheet – A structured, prepared form for collecting and analyzing data; a generic tool that can be adapted to a wide variety of purposes. A check-sheet is a simple tool to analyze the frequency of certain occurrences.

Control Charts – Graphs used to study how a process changes over time. A control chart is a graph used to study how a process changes over time. Data are plotted in time order. A control chart always has a central line for the average, an upper line for the upper control limit and a lower line for the lower control limit. These lines are determined from historical data. By comparing current data to these lines, you can conclude whether the process variation is consistent (in control or within the upper/lower limits) or is unpredictable (out of control or values outside the limits).

Histogram – The most commonly used graph for showing frequency distributions, or how often each different value occurs in a set of data. A histogram allows us to discover and show the underlying frequency distribution of a set of continuous data. In turn, an inspection of the data reveals the underlying distribution—normal distribution, number of outliers, degree of skewness and whether any corrective/preventive action is necessary. The results can be compared with historical data or with data from other courses or sources. The objective is determining whether our distribution is similar to that of others, or whether it is better or worse than the others. Thereafter, we can decide whether to initiate any action to improve the situation.

Pareto Chart – Shows on a bar graph which factors are more significant than others. Based on the Pareto Principle that states that in any system or process, a few vital elements are responsible for a large percentage of outcomes, the chart is useful in identifying the few processes, problems, departments, or any other phenomena that need to be addressed first in any given situation. Resources are scarce, and prioritization is a key factor in determining opportunities for improvement. In any process, a few causes are responsible for a large number of failures or defects. Pareto first enunciated this principle to explain the distribution of wealth in society—that 80% of wealth is held by 20% of the people. Today, it is used to explain practically all phenomena—80% of defects are caused by 20% of causes; 80% of work is done by 20% of people and so on. While the 80:20 ratio may not be valid in all cases, the general principle is that of a vital few being responsible for a large percentage of outcomes. Pareto charts can help us to prioritize on particular issues instead of spreading our resources too thin.

Scatter Diagram – Plots pairs of numerical data, one variable on each axis, to look for a possible relationship. The objective of the scatter diagram (or scatter plot or X-Y graph) is to look for a relationship between two variables. For example, are health and income related? Are education and income related?

Stratification – A technique that separates data gathered from a variety of sources so that patterns can be seen (sometimes replaced with *flowchart* and *run chart*). Stratification is used in conjunction with other data analysis tools. When it is impossible to see patterns in a data set, stratification may provide some clues. Consider census data as an example. By itself, the data has little meaning. Suppose we break the data down by age, gender, income, ethnicity, occupation, geographic location and education; then we can make sense of the census data. If we find that a particular group is lacking along some variable, we can address that particular variable.

Similarly, in an organization, we generate so much data that it may not make much sense. Breaking it down into customer segments, revenue segments, product or service categories, or value creation components, we can see where we are doing well and where we are not.

Flow Chart – A visual representation of a process. Representing a process visually helps us to understand the steps easily. From the service provider's perspective, the process may help determine the number of service personnel. From the customer's perspective, the process may provide insights into the time required to complete the process.

Run Chart – A graphical display of data over time. Run charts are used to visually analyze processes according to time or sequential order. They are useful in assessing process stability, discovering patterns, and facilitating diagnosis and identification of opportunities for improvement. An organization may want to find how its sales are doing every month, or every week, or every day. A steady upward trend is desirable but may not always occur. If there are too many high and low points, we have to find the underlying cause. Is our product or service subject to seasonal changes? If yes, what can we do to smooth the changes? The answer could be to find alternate markets.

Summing Up

Quality is everyone's responsibility. Quality is not an attribute thrust from outside—rather, it is the way we think, speak, and act. The biggest room in the world is the room for improvement. Organizations need to transform from a functional orientation to a process orientation. Processes are relatively easy to manage, to improve, and even to innovate.

The basic tools of quality include:

- Cause-and-effect diagram (also called the Ishikawa diagram or fishbone chart) identifies many possible causes for an effect or problem and categorizes ideas into useful units.

- Pareto charts help us to identify the critical few from the many possible causes.

- Control charts are used to study how processes change over time.

- Histograms are used to depict frequency distributions, or how often each different value in a data set occurs.

- Scatter diagrams graph pairs of numerical data to look for a relationship.

Stratification is a technique to separate data gathered from a variety of sources so that patterns can be seen.

Processes can also be depicted as flow charts. Run charts help us to identify trends of key variables such as sales, revenues, expenses, and profits.

Chapter **36**

Problem-Solving

*Problem-solving is the act of defining a problem,
determining the cause of the problem, identifying,
prioritizing, and selecting alternatives for a solution,
and implementing a solution.*

Problems are a part of our daily lives at work and away from work. Organizations face problems from internal as well as external forces. One of the key ingredients to success in our quest for continuous improvement is the ability to look at problems objectively, minimize the effects of our biases, and come up with solutions that have a high probability of achieving the desired results.

You will learn a proven method for solving problems in any situation.

Doing Problem-Solving

Problem-solving is the act of defining a problem, determining the cause of the problem, identifying, prioritizing, and selecting alternatives for a solution, and implementing a solution. Every organization needs to articulate some standard for problem-solving so that at every level, the mechanism for identifying and resolving issues is understood and implemented. In the absence of such a standard, processes would be *ad hoc*, and results would be by chance and not by choice.

A four-step methodology for problem-solving includes:

1. **Define the problem** – often, organizations focus on the symptom and lose sight of the real problem. For example, declining sales is a symptom. The underlying problem could range from poor quality to high prices to inadequate marketing effort to doubtful positioning, among others. Helpful techniques to define the problem are flow charts to depict the process and cause-and-effect diagrams to identify the root cause.

   • Review and document current processes: who does what, when, how, and why?

   • Evaluate possible impact of new processes: look for an ideal or *what should be*.

2. **Generate alternative solutions** – postpone the selection of one solution until several alternatives have been explored and assessed. Considering multiple alternatives can significantly enhance the value of your final solution. Once the team or individual has decided the ideal model, this target standard becomes the basis for developing a road-map for investigating alternatives. Brainstorming and team problem-solving techniques are both useful tools in this stage of problem-solving. Many alternative solutions should be generated before evaluating any of them. A common mistake in problem-solving is that alternatives are evaluated as they are proposed so that the first acceptable solution is chosen, even if it is not the best fit. If we

focus on trying to get the results we want, we miss the potential for learning something new that will allow for real improvement.

3. **Evaluate and select an alternative** – Skilled problem-solvers use a series of considerations when selecting the best alternative. They consider the extent to which:

- A particular alternative will solve the problem without causing other unanticipated problems.

- All the individuals involved accept the alternative.

- Implementation of the alternative is likely.

- The alternative aligns with the organizational mission, core purpose, objectives, and constraints.

4. **Implement and follow up on the solution** – Leaders may be called upon to order the solution to be implemented by others, promote the solution to others or facilitate the implementation by involving the efforts of others. The most effective approach is to involve others in the implementation as a way of minimizing resistance to subsequent changes.

Feedback channels must be built into the implementation of the solution, to produce continuous monitoring and testing of actual events against expectations. Problem-solving and the techniques used to derive elucidation can only be effective in an organization if the solution remains in place and is updated to respond to future changes.

Return on Investment

In the realm of quality, return on investment is the ratio derived from the sum of the improvement benefits divided by the sum of the costs of the improvement. For example, a 10:1 ratio means that $10 of benefits were derived for every $1 of cost. The ROI concept can help you to justify the cost of quality improvement projects and loss prevention processes, determine the value of continuing a project already underway, and evaluate the overall organizational effectiveness of an implemented quality initiative.

Quality improvement projects are often not subjected to pre-implementation cost justification, and even fewer projects are evaluated after implementation. For most short-term quality improvement projects, ROI is an effective measure that ensures that every dollar invested in projects yields something better for the organization.

> *Without an After Action Review,*
> *you run the risk of* repeatedly
> learning your lessons the hard way.

To compute ROI, you need a baseline for comparison to measure an improvement—a dollar value for the process, operation, product, or service to be improved. These costs should include people costs, materials, supplies, and overhead. It is common practice to gather only the more substantive costs. Similarly, the possible benefits from the improvement need to be quantified.

While the ROI calculation can be extended to the life of a project, it is typical to deduct the entire implementation cost from the benefits derived in the first full year after implementation. For larger or longer duration projects, implementation costs can be amortized until the year in which payback occurs.

Remember:

1. It is easier to sell a project idea if you can propose an ROI.

2. Get stakeholder buy-in; without this, the project is likely to fail.

3. Don't exaggerate the benefits; obtain inputs from everyone involved.

After Action Reviews

Organizational learning requires that teams continuously assess their performance to identify and learn from successes and failures. The After Action Review (AAR) is a simple but powerful tool to help you do this. Conducting an AAR at the end of a project, program, or event can help you and your team learn from your efforts. Further, sharing the results from your AAR can help future teams learn your successful strategies and avoid the pitfalls you have worked to overcome. First used by the Army on combat missions, the AAR is a structured approach for reflecting on the work of a group to identify strengths, weaknesses, and areas for improvement. Without an AAR, you run the risk of *repeatedly learning your lessons the hard way.*

An AAR is centered on four questions:

1. What was expected (or supposed) to happen?

2. What actually happened?

3. What went well and why?

4. What can be improved and how?

An AAR features:

- An open and honest professional discussion

- Participation by each one of the team members

- A focus on results or outcomes of a project or an event

- Identification of ways to sustain what was done well

- Recommendations on how to overcome obstacles

- Pitfalls to be avoided

AAR requires advanced planning. A neutral facilitator, someone who is not a member of the team, can enhance the quality of the discussions. The AAR should result in a report capturing the lessons learned.

Sample ground rules for AAR include:

- Active participation: everyone needs to participate

- Everyone's views should have equal value

- Avoid blaming anyone

- Remember: it is easy to be wise in hindsight; there are no *right* and *wrong* answers

- Be open to new ideas

- Be creative in proposing solutions to barriers
- *Yes...and* rather than *either-or* thinking
- Consensus where possible, clarification and accommodation where not
- Commitment to identifying opportunities for improvement
- Report should have agreement of all participants
- Do not attribute quotes to individuals

SIX SIGMA

Six Sigma is a method that provides organizations with the tools to improve the capability of their business processes. This increase in performance and decrease in process variation lead to defect reduction and improvement in profits, employee morale, and quality of products and services. At the heart of Six Sigma is the **DMAIC** approach (**Define, Measure, Analyze, Improve, and Control**). Processes require inputs (x) and produce outputs (y). If you control the inputs, you will control the outputs. This is expressed as: $y = f(x)$.

LEAN SIX SIGMA

Lean Six Sigma is a fact-based, data-driven philosophy of improvement that values defect prevention over defect detection. It drives customer satisfaction and bottom-line results by reducing variation, waste, and cycle time while promoting the use of work standardization and flow, thereby creating a competitive advantage. It applies anywhere variation and waste exist and involves every employee. The demarcation between Six Sigma and Lean Six Sigma has blurred.

POKA-YOKE

Poka-yoke is the Japanese term for mistake-proofing. Poka-yoke is the first step in creating an error-free system. Error-proofing is a manufacturing technique of preventing errors by designing the manufacturing process, equipment, and tools so that an operation cannot be performed incorrectly.

You are surrounded by examples of the concept in your daily life.

- An electric outlet and a telephone outlet are distinctly different. You cannot insert a telephone plug into an electrical socket and vice versa.

- At the gas station, the gasoline and diesel dispensers are designed such that you cannot fill a gasoline tank with diesel.

- A wash basin has a small hole opposite the tap. The hole ensures that water cannot overflow even if you forget to turn off the tap.

If you look carefully, you can see many more examples of mistake-proofing around you. The ultimate aim of any system is to be error-free. An error-free system may be unrealistic, but it is worth aspiring towards. For example, Boeing's quality goal is to reach a level of 10 raised to the power—9 defects—as close to zero as one can get.

A Contrarian View

Some scholars tend to look at continuous improvement as an impediment to radical innovation. Innovation expert Vijay Govindarajan says: "The more you hardwire a company on total quality management, the more it is going to hurt break-through innovation. The mindset that is needed, the capabilities that are needed, the metrics that are needed, the whole culture that is needed for discontinuous innovation, are fundamentally different."

Professor Clayton Christensen of Harvard Business School has argued that the engine that propels sustaining innovations and efficiency innovations is ill-suited for disruptive innovation. While sustaining innovations are capital and labor neutral, efficiency innovations lead to job losses while releasing capital. When capital costs are zero or negligible, there is no incentive to stick one's neck out. Managers tend to focus on the short-term, effectively killing any possibility for disruptive innovation, which alone can create jobs.

The question that inevitably arises is: should we abandon continuous improvement? The answer is a resounding no. Continuous improvement is an important factor in determining competitive advantage in several industries. However, we certainly need to rethink our approach to continuous improvement. We need a nuanced approach that addresses a few important issues:

- Customization – a one-size-fits-all approach is self-defeating. What might be very appropriate in a manufacturing situation may be inappropriate in a design situation. While discipline is required in every activity, it should not be at the expense of creativity and risk-taking.

- Validation – continuous improvement projects, like any other, should be grounded in sound reasoning.

Challenging the status quo is important. Equally important is asking the vital questions regarding whether a process needs to be improved, disrupted, or eliminated.

- Cultural Impact – many improvement projects fail because they do not address the context or culture of an organization, a business unit, or even a team. For example, a purely data-driven mindset may stifle managers from thinking laterally or encourage them to ignore inconsistent data that does not fit into their pre-conceived notions.

It would be fair to say that continuous improvement and disruptive innovation are not incompatible. Unless you think of continuous improvement within the overall context of the environment in which businesses operate, you may well end up treating the two as mutually exclusive.

Summing Up

In the realm of quality management, return on investment is the ratio of the benefits expected from a project to its costs. Quantifying return on investment can help in obtaining stakeholder buy-in.

An After Action Review is a part of organizational learning. The review compares achievement to expectation, identifies strengths as well as weaknesses or opportunities for improvement. An After Action Review provides a useful framework for future teams. After Action Reviews are about issues, not about persons.

Chapter 37

Continuous Quality Improvement Summary

*The basic tools of quality are Cause and Effect Diagram,
Check Sheet, Control Charts, Histogram, Pareto Chart,
Scatter Diagram, and Stratification.*

Continuous improvement can be incremental or radical.
The Plan–Do–Check–Act (PDCA) cycle is a useful
method for continuous improvement. The continuous
improvement methodology starts with someone initiating
a process, listening to the Voice of the Customer (VOC),
identifying the root cause of a problem or issue, determining
alternatives, finalizing one for implementation, a pilot run,
adaptation as required, and full implementation.

Quality Management Systems (QMS) have the potential to
enhance the customer experience. The basic tools of quality are
Cause and Effect Diagram, Check Sheet, Control Charts,
Histogram, Pareto Chart, Scatter Diagram, and Stratification.

Problem Solving is comprised of four steps: defining the
problem, generating alternative solutions, evaluating and
selecting an alternative, implementation, and follow-up.

As applied to Quality Management Systems, Return on
Investment is the ratio of the benefits expected from a

project to its costs. Quantifying ROI can help in obtaining stakeholder buy-in.

An After Action Review (AAR) is a part of organizational learning. The review compares the achievement to the expectation, identifies strengths as well as weaknesses or opportunities for improvement, and provides a valuable framework for future teams. It is important that AARs focus on issues and not on persons.

Reflective Questions

Reflection Question #1: Identify any process in your work. List methods that have the potential to improve the process. Identify one method for pilot implementation. Implement the chosen method on a trial basis. Record the result.

- What should have happened?
- What did happen?
- Were there gaps between achievement and expectation?
- If yes, how do you propose to bridge the gap?

Justify your answer. Draw a flow chart of the process before and after the change.

Reflection Question #2: Assume you have the opportunity to bring about improvement in any area of your organization. The only criterion is that the improvement should have a measurable value. Assume that resources are not a constraint. You can choose anyone in the organization to be a part of your team.

- How will you start?

- How will you choose team members?

- How will you measure the result?

- What is the time you envisage for the improvement project?

- What methodology will you adopt?

Justify your answer.

Case Study: Motorola

Motorola was the first company to achieve the Six Sigma level in quality. At one time, Motorola dominated the Personal Digital Assistant (PDA) market with the ability to produce a device in any language within two hours. Motorola was also the first company to introduce satellite telephones—phones which could be used anywhere in the world.

In 2006, Motorola had a market capitalization of $29 billion. Today (October 2017) Motorola has a market capitalization of $13.5 billion. Once a pioneer in mobile phone technology, today Motorola is struggling to remain in the industry. The satellite phone was a disaster.

Quality is supposed to be the ultimate differentiator that also allows you to be a cost leader. Motorola's performance appears to question the premise of quality being a valuable source of competitive advantage. What went wrong? Why has Motorola not been able to leverage its early advantages?

Assume you are the CEO of Motorola. What steps would you take to re-invent the company? Justify your answer.

Section 9
Our Final Thoughts

Throughout this book, we have presented, discussed, outlined, and described many actions and skills needed to be a successful organizational leader. We thought we would leave you with a brief discussion regarding the *behaviors* of successful organizational leaders. We invite you to self-assess your strategic leadership behaviors and consider areas of possible emphasis as you continue with your senior leadership journey.

10 Behaviors of Successful Organizational Leaders

1. **Self-reflection** – Great leaders take the time to identify and articulate how they are at their best and then organize their life, so they consistently show up with those qualities. They use their understanding of how they are at their best as a reference point to regularly, often daily, stop and reflect on where they are hitting the mark, where they are not, and making one or two adjustments to get back or stay on track.

2. **Self-awareness** – Great leaders are aware and intentional. They tune into what's going on around them and notice the physical, mental,

and emotional reactions they are having to what's going on around them. Based on that awareness, they are then intentional about what they're going to do or not do next. Throughout the day, they ask themselves two guiding questions: *What am I trying to do? How do I need to show up to make that happen?*

3. **Self-care** – Great leaders understand that they perform at their best when they take care of their health and well-being. They move throughout the day. They are intentional about eating moderate amounts of healthy food. They get at least seven hours of sleep at night. By doing all of that they put themselves in position to better manage their stress and hit the sweet spot between their fight-or-flight and rest and digest responses.

4. **Continuous learning** – Great leaders never stop learning. They challenge their own assumptions by asking why, seeking fresh sources of input, asking for feedback on their performance and going out of their way to experience and understand the lives of others.

5. **Listening** – Great leaders listen. They ask open-ended questions and pay attention to the answers. They listen to gather the ideas and perspective needed to solve problems collaboratively. They do not stop there, though. They move beyond transactional listening and regularly practice transformational listening. They often listen with no other agenda than to deepen their connection with someone else.

6. **Operating Rhythm** – Great leaders know and leverage their operating rhythm. They know what times of the day and the week are the best fit for getting particular things done and then they schedule it. If they know their best thinking and creative work comes early in the day, they keep their first hour or two clear of meetings. They pay attention to when they need breaks and change things up to get them. If they know that they're energized by meeting and working with other people, they try to schedule their time so that those meetings can help them power through their day.

7. **Gear shifting** – Great leaders know how to quickly shift gears. Their calendars are usually racked and stacked with meetings and any given day can skip across dozens of topics and settings. It is wave after wave. Great leaders recognize and leverage the space between the waves to shift gears. Between one conversation and the next, they take a few moments to breathe deeply, clear their mind from the last thing, and visualize what they are trying to do next and how they need to show up to do it.

8. **Focus** – Great leaders focus on who or what is in front of them. They are aware of the things that could distract them and are intentional about removing those things from their environment. They have smartphone-free zones. They hold meetings in places that enable them and others to focus. They set themselves and others up for success by creating space to focus.

9. **Clarity of purpose** – Great leaders know what they are in it for. They have developed a clear answer to the question, *Why am I here? On this earth, in this life, for the limited amount of time that I have here, why am I here?* Their answer to that question informs what they do each day and how they do it.

10. **Gratitude** – Great leaders are grateful. They recognize and acknowledge the good things in their life. They understand that even on days when it feels like everything is going wrong, there is always something that is going right. They build on that to create positive outcomes for themselves and the people they love and lead.

Section 10
Appendices

A – Selection and Orientation for New Members to the Board of Directors

B – Responsibilities of the Board of Directors

C – Position Description for a Member of the Board of Directors

D – Committee Template of the Board of Directors

E – Key Terms and Definitions for the Board of Directors

F – Developing a Manual for the Board of Directors

G – Ethical Dilemmas

Appendix **A**

Selection and Orientation for New Members to the Board of Directors

Before Submitting the Prospective Director's Name for Election: Best Practices for the Board

- Meet with the prospective director.

- Review a copy of the position description for a board member.

- Before agreeing to be nominated, a prospective director should understand the responsibilities and expectations of the position, especially the time required for board meetings, education, and public/ community events.

- Make participation in orientation mandatory during the director's first term. Do not reappoint directors who fail to fulfill this requirement.

- Schedule an annual new member orientation session well in advance on the board's calendar, so all new members can set aside this date when they are elected.

After Election: The Initial Orientation

- **Plan an orientation session.** The duration varies with the type of organization. Large organizations may have an orientation of 1–2 days. Medium and small organizations can usually complete in 3–4 hours. The orientation should enable the new member to answer the following questions:

  - What are the board's fiduciary duties, roles, and responsibilities?

  - How is the board organized to do its work? How are major decisions made?

  - What is the role of the new board member?

  - What information does the member have access to in the firm?

  - How can the member suggest agenda items for board and committee meetings?

  - What is the mission of the organization?

  - What is the vision of the organization?

  - What are the values of the organization?

  - When, how, and why was the organization founded? What are the major milestones of the organization's history, and how do they relate to today's priorities?

  - What are the major industry trends of which a board member should be aware?

  - What are the organization's major offerings and services?

- What is the organizational structure? Has it been changed recently? How does the structure align with the organization's strategy?

- What is the organization's current financial position? Include a review of the financial statements, trends, and key performance indicators.

- What is the organization's strategic direction? Include a review of the strategic plan, long-term financial plan, and facilities plan.

- How does the organization achieve and maintain superior quality and performance? Include a review of continuous improvement mechanisms.

- How does the organization measure and improve customer satisfaction?

- How does the organization measure and improve stakeholder satisfaction?

- If a group of new members is joining the board, schedule the orientation session as a seminar or workshop. If there are just one or two new members, the session can be informal, but it should still cover the same content.

- Ensure that the material is at the governance level. Emphasize high-level issues and concerns, the big picture, the mission, vision, and strategy. DO NOT include operational matters.

- Tap several individuals, not just the CEO, to deliver the orientation:

  - Chairperson of the Board – Describes the board's role and responsibilities of individual members.

  - Legal Counsel – Outlines fiduciary duties, conflict of interest procedures, and current legal issues, if any.

  - CEO – provides an overview of the organization's strategic direction, its major offerings and services, and industry trends.

  - CFO – explains the financial statements and key performance indicators.

  - CMO – explains markets and geographies covered, opportunities and challenges.

  - CTO – explains technology backbone, currency, and preparedness for the future.

  - COO – explains operations and alignment to strategic direction, as well as efforts to achieve superior quality.

  - CPO – explains human capital and practices to retain talent.

- **Avoid lectures** – after all, you are dealing with accomplished people. Turn the orientation into discussions. Include case studies from the organization to stimulate thinking and facilitate understanding.

- Include a tour of major facilities. Ask staff to lead the tour in their areas.

- Provide each new member with an Orientation Manual.

- Send new members to external orientation programs, such as The Governance Institute's seminars.

After the Initial Orientation: The First Year

- Ask new members to write and share a *Personal Learning Plan* that describes additional areas where they would like inputs, people they would like to meet, and resources they wish to review.

- Based on the Personal Learning Plans, conduct *drill-down* sessions on pertinent subject areas of interest. Examples might include:

  - A new member of the Finance Committee meets with CFO to review capital budgeting, financing, and dividend decisions.

  - A new member of the Quality Committee meets with COO to gain a deeper understanding of operational excellence and quality initiatives.

- In large corporations with multiple divisions and business units, it may be useful to assign a buddy or mentor to each new member.

- At the end of the year, ask new members to evaluate the orientation process, and use the feedback to improve continuously.

Board Member Orientation Checklist

1. General Information

- Bylaws
- Vision and Mission
- Board Structure and Composition
- Organizational Chart with notes on Responsibilities
- History of the Organization
- Strategic Plan – Strategic Priorities, Goals, and Objectives
- Summary of Offerings (Products, Services, and Geographies)
- List of board members with their affiliation(s)

2. Roles and Responsibilities

- Board Member Position Description
- Roles of Executive Officers
- Chief Executive roles and responsibilities
- Key staff position roles
- Committees and their role
- New board member expectations
- List of events that board members are expected to attend

3. Policies and Procedures

- Board policies and procedures
- Board culture – overview of how the board works

4. Other Information

- Minutes of board meetings
- Tour of facilities and offices
- Brochures and PR materials
- Board agreement to sign
- Confidentiality, and Conflict of Interest clauses to sign
- Member fees and reimbursement of expenses

Appendix B

Responsibilities of the Board of Directors

The board is responsible in five key areas:

1. **Establish the organization's mission, vision, and strategic direction**

   - Mission

   - Vision

   - Goals and Objectives

   - Overarching Values

   - Strategic Plan

   - Offerings (products, services, and geographies)

   - Evaluation of key results (strategic, financial, market, operational, people, innovation and technology)

2. **Ensure the financial health of the organization**

   - Ensure resource availability

   - Long-term financial goals and objectives

   - Short-term financial goals and objectives

   - Alignment of short-term goals with long-term goals

   - Portfolio management

3. Ensure currency, adequacy, and performance of human capital

- Organizational Culture

- Working Conditions

- Hiring and Retention Strategies

- Compensation Strategies

- Capability, Suitability, and Vitality of human capital

- Nominating Committee Composition and Procedures

4. Provide Broad Direction for Operations

- Compliance with legal and regulatory requirements

- Corporate Citizenship

- Structure and Agency administration

- Ethical conduct and behavior

5. Effective Community Relations

- Corporate Social Responsibility (CSR)

- Environment Protection and Sustainability (Triple Bottom Line Approach—Profit, People, and Planet)

- Meet community expectations and needs

- Public Relations

- Disaster Management

Appendix C

Position Description for a Member of the Board of Directors

Position: What is the position title?

Authority: What authority does the position have? Discretionary? Delegated by the Board?

Responsibility: To whom is the position accountable? What are the broad areas of responsibility?

Term: How are board members elected and for how long? How do board members leave the board?

General Duties: What are the typical duties that board members are expected to perform? To the organization? To the community? To society at large?

Qualifications: What specialized or practical skills are needed to do the job? What are the human relations skills required?

Benefits: What benefits can a board member expect (besides intangibles such as making a difference, opportunity to work with individuals of diverse backgrounds, enhanced understanding of group dynamics and relationships, and improved decision-making)?

Travel: How much travel does the position entail? Within the home country? Outside?

Time Requirements: What is a realistic estimate of time and effort required to be an effective board member?

Evaluation: How will the effectiveness of board members be measured? When? By whom?

Review: When will the position description be reviewed?

Approval: When was this position description last approved? By whom?

Appendix D

Committee Template of the Board of Directors

Committee Name: Gives an identity and thereby conveys the committee's general objectives.

Type: Standing, advisory, *ad hoc*.

Chairperson: Must be skilled at conducting meetings, need not be a subject matter expert.

Responsible To: The board, unless this is a sub-committee.

Purpose: Outline the reason for the committee's existence.

Authority: Limited or complete, agent or advisor.

Timeframes: Duration of committee, frequency of meetings, completion date.

Reports: Interim, final, milestones.

Composition: Total number, board members, customer representatives, community representatives, staff, outside experts, officers of government/regulatory body, financial institution representatives, collaborators/junior partners/ alliance partners.

Staff Support: Position and type, duration.

Resources: Facilities, technology, files from previous committees, office space, budget.

Communication with Board: Usually through the chairperson of the committee.

Specific Areas of Responsibility: Define what the expectations are.

Approval Date: Date on which the board approves these terms.

Review: Date on which a review of the work will be conducted; by whom.

Appendix **E**

Key Terms and Definitions for the Board of Directors

Assets: Anything of value that is owned by the business. Assets include money that others owe.

Audit: An examination of financial accounts or records to verify their authenticity and accuracy.

Balance Sheet: A balance sheet is a statement of the financial worth of a business or organization at a given point in time. It has three parts: Assets, Liabilities, and Equity.

Board of Directors: A group of individuals elected by the shareholders of a corporation to manage the corporation's business and appoint its officers.

Budget: An itemized summary of estimated or intended expenditures for a given period along with proposals to finance the same (revenues).

Committee: A formal working group within a large organization. Formed either by election or selection. The committee has authority and legitimacy of some specific kind (audit, compensation, regulatory compliance). A committee is usually small enough to facilitate informal discussion, exchange of ideas, and rational decision making.

Equity: An amount that a business is worth beyond what it owes. Equity is the net worth of business. It represents the original investment plus the retained earnings since its inception. Equity = Assets – Liabilities.

Executives/Officers: Key personnel (CXOs) appointed by the board of directors and responsible for the day-to-day operations of the corporation. The titles and duties of such officers are usually a part of the corporation's bylaws. Common titles are president, chief executive officer, vice president(s), secretary, and treasurer.

Fiduciary: A person who or organization that holds, manages, and has discretionary authority and control over money belonging to another person or organization.

Financial Statements: A report providing financial statistics relative to a given part of an organization's operations or status. The two most common financial statements are the income statement and the balance sheet.

Income Statement: A financial statement that lists revenues, expenses, and income for a given period.

Liabilities: Anything of value owed to another, payable now or in the future, or an obligation to remit money or render services at a future date.

Operational Planning: The process of determining short-term (one year or less), functional (marketing, financial, operations, human resources, technology) goals and mechanisms for achieving the goals. Operational plans should align with the strategic plan.

Policy: A guiding principle designed to influence actions and decisions. Typically, a policy designates a process or procedure within an organization. They can be rules of practice and procedure which supplement the constitution and bylaws.

Strategic Planning: The process of determining an organization's long-term goals and identifying the best approach for achieving the goals.

Appendix F

Developing a Manual for the Board of Directors

The manual should be concise and easy to read. The following is a model template:

Quick Reference or FAQ section:

- Include short and crisp explanations of key topics or answers to frequently asked questions.

General Information

- Copy of the organization's constitution and bylaws
- Terms of reference of all board committees
- Organization's most recent strategic and operational plans—key points only
- List of board members and their contact information
- Key Staff listing with contact information
- Position descriptions (key positions)

Policies and Procedures

- Codes of Conduct
- Confidentiality clause/oath
- Abuse and harassment policy

- Conflict of interest guidelines

- Travel and related remuneration procedures

- Nomination procedure for new Board members

- Financial structure and policies

- Insurance (Directors' liability information)

- Risk management strategy

- Media/Public Relations strategy

Financial Management

- Most recent audited/unaudited financial statements

- Key Performance Indicators (current and trend)

- Copy of current budget

Other Information

- Goals for the ensuing year

- Copy of board meeting(s) minutes

- Meeting procedure overview (proposing, seconding, discussion, dissent, recording, adjournment)

Appendix **G**

Ethical Dilemmas

Ethical Dilemma #1: "Taxing" Questions.

While in college, I worked part-time for a reputed tax preparation service. I prepared customers' taxes along with about twenty other employees at different offices. Bill had been working with the service for three seasons, but this was my first tax season. Bill was very good at tax preparation and had earned a reputation for dependable service. He was respected by management and seemed to do what he was asked to do.

On a few occasions, I had customers come in and want to see Bill. When I explained that Bill was not in the office that day and asked if I could assist them with any questions, they would want to wait for Bill before continuing any further. The customer's wish to wait struck me as odd because all of the files are located in the office as well as on the hard drives of the firm's computers. As per company policy, any employee can assist any customer, no matter who did the actual return.

When I later asked Bill about these customers, he told me that he did a few on his own time for people who couldn't afford the company's fees. Bill's response was bothersome to me because there was no telling how many times Bill had done this and how many customers he took away from the business.

    1. Who are the stakeholders in this case and what are their stakes?

2. Was it unethical for Bill to be doing these taxes on his own time and meeting his customers at our office?

3. If you were in my position, what would you do?

Ethical Dilemma #2: Ethics in the Mailroom.

To make some money to take care of my expenses during college, I got a part-time job in a mailroom at a rather large business. The business would send out hundreds of pieces of mail each day, all going through the mailroom. Our job as the staff in the mailroom was to package this mail to be shipped, put the proper amount of postage on it, and then take it to the post office. To put the postage on the items, we used a postage meter that was in the mailroom. The postage meter would weigh the mail and then stamp it with the current amount of postage; my employers would pay the postage costs in lump sums periodically throughout the year.

Occasionally, my boss would run some of his mail along with the business mail. When I asked him if sending personal mail through the meter was stealing money from the company, he justified it by saying that he only used the meter to mail his bills, and he would never use it for anything that cost more than sixty cents. He also said that he had been working there for 13 years, the pay was not great, and sending out an occasional letter or bill would not hurt the company.

1. Was my boss's practice ethical? Does working for a company for 13 years justify sending out personal mail on the company's account?

2. What should I do? My salary is important to me. If I report the incident, I might lose the part-time job.

Ethical Dilemma #3: What they don't know won't hurt them.

During my last two years in college, I worked at an animal hospital in my hometown. In my time there, many animals passed away in their sleep or for unknown reasons. It was not uncommon. In these situations, our facility would offer the owners the service of a necropsy. A necropsy is a procedure in which the doctor would surgically open the animal to check for any signs of what might have caused the animal's death.

Mrs. Johnson, a client of ours, brought in her dog that had unfortunately passed away while she was at work. Her dog was only five years old, and the owner was not aware of any health problems. No one, including the doctor, could figure out what had caused the death of Mrs. Johnson's dog. The hospital asked Mrs. Johnson if she would give her consent for the doctor to perform a necropsy on her dog so they might be able to answer the many questions surrounding his death.

Mrs. Johnson did not want the necropsy. She just wanted the facility to take care of the dog's remains. The office manager at the animal hospital told the doctor that she would let the vet students, who were doing their rotations at our hospital, go ahead and perform a necropsy as a learning experiment. The office manager mentioned that the owner would never know because we were in charge of the disposal so that it wouldn't be a problem.

1. Is it ethical for the doctor to allow the vet students to perform the necropsy?

2. Should the fact that the owner would never know about the necropsy affect the doctor's decision?

3. What would you do in this situation? Why?

4. Would your answer be different if instead of an animal hospital, we were discussing a hospital for humans, and the decision related to a loved one? On the one hand, students will never learn unless they perform autopsies and understand the complexities of the human system. On the other, it is not common for people to allow autopsies on their loved ones who have passed away. How can such dilemmas be resolved?

Ethical Dilemma #4: Flowers Vs. Eyes: When Would You Have Paid?

It is human nature to think that ethical behavior is more likely when we observe a person. But, what if the eyes doing the observing are not real? In an interesting experiment, some fascinating results followed. Apparently, a psychology department of a university in the United Kingdom, less than three hours from London, was experiencing a problem. Like most departments, there was a coffee station where faculty and staff could help themselves to coffee and then leave their money in the tray (approximately $1). However, it was obvious that some people were helping themselves to coffee and not paying.

One of the professors came up with an idea. He initiated an experiment. For ten weeks, he his assistants alternately taped two poster signs above the coffee station. One week, the poster displayed a picture of flowers. Another week, the poster displayed a picture of *staring eyes*. They wondered whether the different posters or pictures would evoke different responses regarding whether people honestly paid for their coffee.

After the ten weeks, the researchers noted an interesting pattern. When the *eyes* poster was at the coffee station, the coffee and tea drinkers contributed 2.76 times more money than when the *flower* poster was displayed. The researchers surmised that the sensation of *being watched*, though the eyes were not real, motivated people to be more honest about paying for their coffee or tea. The originator of the idea admitted that the results were more dramatic than what he had expected.

Later, officers in a police department in Birmingham, England, read a paper about this experiment and were impressed. They decided to slap posters of staring eyes all around the city. They named their venture "We've Got Our Eyes on Criminals." The officers hoped that vandalism and other crimes would come down.

1. Was it ethical for the professor to conduct such an experiment on his colleagues without announcing it?

2. Are you surprised at the results? Why or why not?

3. Do you think the police department scheme will work? Why or why not?

Ethical Dilemma #5: Higher Goals, More Pressure, Lower Ethics?

Recently, I held a position as a sales representative for a multi-national Fortune 500 phone company. My job was to place unsolicited phone calls to people and convince them to switch their local and long-distance calling carrier to my company. As I went through training, I was taught to *sell, sell, sell!* Once we got a customer on the line, we were not to hang up unless we sold her or him a phone package.

There was also a big emphasis on meeting daily sales goals that were set by the company. As soon as I got out of training and on the phone lines, I began to encounter older adults who had no use for the product. One day, my supervisor noticed that I was not selling the product to everyone that I talked to, and she thought this was the reason I was not meeting my sales goal.

She soon asked why I did not *push* the product more. I told her that the people I was letting off the hook were too old to need anything that the company offered and that they did not even understand half of what I was talking about. She told me that I should just sell them the product and that the customer service representative would fix it later.

I asked my mentor what he did in these situations, and he said that he just tells the older people that they are getting a smaller package and then *adds on* other features without them noticing. The next time I got an older adult on the phone, I just told her to have a nice day, and then I hung up.

1. What are the ethical issues facing the company and me?

2. Does this illustrate personal, organizational, or industry-level ethical issues?

3. Should I succumb to the pressure to meet company goals?

4. Is it an ethical practice for my company to raise goals continually and expect that people in my position will just *sell* and let customer service *fix* the problems?

Ethical Dilemma #6: The Anonymous CEO: Strong or Weak Ethical Leader?

John Mackey is the founder and co-CEO of Whole Foods, one of the largest natural and organic grocery store chains. The company has been ranked No. 181 in the Fortune Global 500 list for 2016. It reported revenues of over $15 billion and had over 76,000 employees.

A few years ago, it came to light that John Mackey had written more than 1,300 anonymous postings on a web-based Yahoo! Finance stock forum. His messages on the discussion forum bashed competitors and praised his own company.

Mackey took on the pseudonym "Rahodeb" (an anagram of his wife's name Deborah) and bashed Wild Oats for lack of vision while noting that it wasn't a profitable company. He questioned the leadership of Wild Oats about competence and integrity. Interestingly, the FTC exposed Mackey's alter ego, and filed a complaint with the SEC and a lawsuit seeking to block Whole Foods' planned purchase of Wild Oats, its main competitor, on antitrust grounds.

Mackey apologized to the Whole Foods' board for his actions. In a public statement, he claimed that his anonymous postings did not reflect his or his company's policies and that some of the views of Rahodeb did not even match his own beliefs. He explained that he made the online comments anonymously because he had fun doing it.

After months of delay, Whole Foods did acquire Wild Oats. The board of Whole Foods announced an internal investigation at the time. However, John Mackey continues as CEO to this day.

1. Were Mackey's actions more representative of a strong, moral leader or a weak, uncertain leader? Is it ethical for a CEO to engage in such deceptions?

2. Do you see Mackey's actions as positive, negative, or indifferent regarding setting a strong ethical culture for his company?

3. Were Mackey's deceptions just a harmless or fun activity? Do you see them having harmful implications for the company in the future?

Ethical Dilemma #7: Yahoo in China

Yahoo has come under criticism by human rights groups who allege that the company has helped the Chinese government identify four people. Shi Tao, a journalist and editor of a Chinese newspaper, claims that Yahoo helped the Chinese government by providing information about his e-mail account, his Internet Protocol (IP) address, log-on history, and the contents of his e-mail, leading to a jail term of ten years.

Another Chinese political prisoner, Wang Xiaoning, and his wife filed suit against Yahoo under the Alien Tort Claims Act and the Torture Victims Protection Act, claiming the company helped turn him in and that it led to physical beatings and a 10-year prison sentence.

Yahoo, along with other companies, argues that issues of human rights and censorship in China are too great for them to handle alone, and they have appealed to the U.S. government to take a leadership role in this issue.

1. Has Yahoo violated the privacy rights of the Chinese dissidents? What e-mail privacy protection could they reasonably expect from Yahoo!?

2. Does Yahoo have a responsibility in global markets to go extra lengths to protect e-mail privacy?

3. Should the U.S. government, or any government, take a leadership role in cases like this? If so, what should they do?

Ethical Dilemma #8: An Innocent Revelation?

For a couple of years, Jane worked as an assistant manager at a gas station in Denmark. The location of the station was perfect, and this was proven every day by long lines and big sales. The way the job was scheduled was that the person on duty would always manage the station single-handedly, standing behind the desk, running the cash register. Every day, the person on duty placed several thousand dollars in the station's safe. Six people worked the gas station—all in the age group 18–20.

The key to the station's safe was in the back, and only the employees and the manager knew the hiding place. The manager would take the money stored in the safe and deposit it at the local bank every third day, but one week this action was postponed a couple of days because of a holiday. Therefore, a large sum of money was accumulating at the station. One employee revealed it to her friends. At the same time, she agreed to tell about the hiding place for the key, and within a few days her friends broke into the station and stole close to $19,000.

The employee and her friends had figured that the insurance company would pay for the manager's loss and all parties would be satisfied, except for the insurance company, who, they thought, would not be affected by the loss. They claimed, "Everybody knows how rich these insurance companies are." The insurance company did not pay because the key was hidden in the same room the safe was kept and this apparently voided the insurance.

1. What are the ethical problems in this case? Is it a situation unique to business in Denmark?

2. If the employee's decision to tell about the hidden key had never been discovered, could her action somehow be justified as an innocent revelation? Why or why not? What are the ethical principles involved?

3. Imagine that the employee's revelation is never discovered. Would you have chosen to do as she did if we assume that the manager got reimbursed? Many of us pay a lot of money in insurance premiums, so why not get a little back?

Ethical Dilemma #9: FDA's Incompatible Goals.

When it comes to life-saving drugs, we want both safety and speed. We want safety because a drug that cures one illness should not cause another. We want speed because the longer it takes for a life-saving drug to hit the market, the more people will die because it was not available in time to save their lives.

In the 1980s, there was a public outcry because the FDA took nearly three years to approve most drugs; with the AIDS epidemic in full swing, that meant that many people died before the drugs that would save them became available. With the help of Congress, the FDA and the drug industry eventually worked out an arrangement in which companies would pay millions of dollars in fees in return for an FDA guarantee to complete drug reviews within a year or within six months for a medicine that would save lives.

The arrangement effectively addressed the problem of the time required for FDA approval. However, a new problem arose. Drug companies would not let their money pay for drug safety monitoring after the drug was on the market. As federal funding slowed, and the FDA became increasingly dependent on industry funds, the safety program diminished and speed became the watchword. The deal required that the FDA submit annual reports on time spent reviewing but not on the safety of drugs already on the market.

We judge managers by the speed with which they make decisions. Questions about safety are simply slowing down the decision process. FDA employees who speak out about safety report that they are often ostracized and penalized.

1. What are the ethical issues involved? Who are the stakeholders and what are their stakes?

2. When dealing with life-saving drugs, how do you decide between speed and safety, when enhancing one diminishes the other? On what basis are you making your decision?

3. If you were responsible for regulating drugs, what changes would you make to alleviate the situation? What trade-offs would you make? Please be specific.

Ethical Dilemma #10:
Influencing Local Government.

Jack runs a small Atlanta chemical company that produces alum. Alum has many uses, including water purification, and the company had a contract with Fulton County for this use for many years. In all the years they had this contract, they received it through open bidding. Open bidding was the norm every renewal year until this year when the company was again the lowest bidder. A larger company based in the north with a division in Georgia was awarded the contract, even though its bid was about 3% higher. The contract to the Georgia firm would have been acceptable if there had been a quality or delivery problem in the past, but this had never been the case.

Jack met with a former county commissioner to seek advice about, and reasons for, this situation. The commissioner believed that there was an under-the-table agreement and advised Jack to sue the county and its purchasing manager. The problem is that the contract is relatively small, and the lawsuit would almost certainly cost more than the contract.

1. Is filing a lawsuit the best way for this chemical company to influence the county commission? What options does the company have?

2. Do companies have to lobby local or other governments to get business? Do they need to make PAC contributions? Bribes or kickbacks?

3. What action should Jack take?

Ethical Dilemma #11: A Moral Dilemma: Head vs. Heart.

A 42-year-old male suddenly and unexpectedly died of a brain tumor, leaving behind a wife and small child. During a review of employee benefits, it came to light that although he was eligible for an additional company-sponsored life insurance plan used for plant-decommissioning purposes, the insurance rolls did not have his name.

It was determined that when the employee was promoted to supervisor three years before his death, his paperwork had been submitted to the corporate office for inclusion in the program. Coincidentally, the program was under review at the time, and the employee was not entered into the program due to an administrative oversight.

A legal department review determined that the program was offered to certain supervisory employees at the discretion of the company. Therefore, there was no legal obligation to pay.

The death benefit was twice the employee's salary. Because the employee was not enrolled in the life insurance program, if the company were to pay any benefit, it would have to come from the general fund (paid from the business unit's annual operating budget).

The company could argue that it must start acting like a business and use its head, not its heart. Existing company programs adequately compensate the individual's family; no additional dollars should be paid. On the other hand, it was an administrative oversight that failed to enter the employee into the program. What would you want the company to do for your family if you were the one who suddenly died?

1. What are the ethical issues involved in this case?

2. Since there is no legal obligation to pay, would you be perceived as a weak manager if you decided to pay?

3. As a steward of company funds, how would you justify your decision to pay or not to pay?

Ethical Dilemma #12: To hire or not to hire.

As a manager of human resources, part of my job is to guide the process by which my company selects new employees. Recently we selected an applicant to fill a computer analyst position. The supervising manager and a selection panel selected this applicant over others based on her superior qualifications and personal interview.

However, a routine background check indicated that the applicant had been convicted 18 years earlier for false check-writing. The application form has a section where a question relates to any conviction of the applicant other than a traffic violation. In response to that question, the applicant wrote "no." When informed of this, the supervising manager stated that she would still like to hire the applicant but asked me for my recommendation. The job does not involve money handling.

1. Should the fact that the applicant did not tell the truth on one part of the application automatically disqualify her from further consideration?

2. Should the supervising manager be allowed to hire the applicant despite the fact that the applicant lied on her application, provided the manager is

willing to take the risk and assume responsibility for the applicant?

3. If the applicant freely admitted the conviction, should she still be considered for the position? Should a minor offense committed 18 years ago, when the applicant was in her early twenties, disqualify her when she is overall the most qualified applicant? What type of convictions, and how recent, should disqualify potential new hires?

If the applicant mistakenly thought that her record had been cleared over time and therefore did not lie intentionally, would that make any difference?

Brief Biographies of the Authors

Olin O. Oedekoven, PhD

 Dr. Olin Oedekoven has an extensive background in leadership, organizational development, higher education, strategic planning, and institutional evaluation. His undergraduate degree is in Wildlife and Fisheries Management (South Dakota State University), and his first master's degree is in Wildlife Ecology (University of Wyoming). Olin then worked in state government as a natural resource specialist for twenty years.

Olin continued his formal education at Northcentral University, earning an MBA and a doctorate in Business Administration with concentrations in Management and Public Administration. He later earned a post-doctoral certification in Human Resource Management. Dr. Oedekoven taught doctoral-level students for ten years, including chairing approximately forty doctorate committees.

Concurrently, General Oedekoven served for nearly thirty-three years in the U.S. Army Reserves and U.S. Army National Guard. He retired in 2011 as the Deputy Adjutant General of the Wyoming National Guard, leading an organization that included nearly 3,500 members (civilian and uniformed employees). Brig. Gen. Oedekoven has a master's degree in Strategic Planning from the U.S. Army War College. He also served on several U.S. government councils and committees during his tenure as a general officer.

Olin Oedekoven founded Peregrine Leadership Institute in 2003 and Peregrine Academic Services in 2009. The Leadership Institute provides leadership development training, organizational assessment, strategic planning assistance, and executive leadership seminars. Highlights associated with the leadership development services include management training throughout the U.S. with government and private sector organizations, and ongoing leadership training throughout the world.

Peregrine Academic Services provides online assessment and educational services to institutions of higher education throughout the world. Services include program-level assessments in disciplines such as business, criminal justice, public administration, and accounting/finance. Peregrine has consulted with both governmental and academic institutions and organizations concerning higher education needs, compliance, academic accreditation, assurance of learning, quality, and reform.

Krishnamurthy B. Venkateshiah, PhD

Krishna has over twenty years of experience in the corporate sector, including five years as the CEO of a conglomerate, and eighteen years of experience as an academic leader and distinguished professor of strategy and international business.

Krishna has a bachelor's degree in Engineering, a master's degree in Systems, a master's degree in Business Administration, and two doctoral degrees – one in Project Management and the second in Strategy.

Starting his career with a conglomerate with thirty-two business units, Krishna has successfully delivered exemplary results in marketing, quality, and strategy. He has been trained in Japan on quality methods, in Germany on manufacturing technologies, and in the U.S. on strategy. He has led two business units to the Deming Award in quality, and the company which he led as CEO to the No. 1 position in its category.

Krishna was deputed in 1998 to lead a start-up business school. Within 10 years he led the school to the 6th position among B-Schools in India and the first international accreditation. The International Assembly for Collegiate Business Education (IACBE), USA has honored him with the *Education Leader of the Year* and the Accreditation Council for Business Schools and Programs (ACBSP) in the U.S. has honored him with the *Teaching Excellence Award*. The American Society for Quality (ASQ), USA has awarded Krishna a gold award, a star award and two awards of distinction.

Krishna has undergone advanced training in Business Intelligence, Analytics, and Knowledge Management at SAS Institute, USA. He has conducted over fifty executive training programs for CXOs, including ten for Fortune 100 Companies.

Douglas J. Gilbert, DBA, JD, MBA

Doug Gilbert has held a range of leadership positions in the private sector, in academia, and in federal and local government. Over the past fifteen years Doug has served as a Business Department Chair supervising over 90 faculty for the University of Phoenix—Colorado Campus, Dean of the School of Organizational Leadership at the University of the Rockies, and as a faculty at the University of Colorado, School of Public Affairs. Doug holds a Juris Doctorate from the University of Iowa, an MBA from IMD in Switzerland, and a Doctor of Business Administration from the University of Phoenix.

Prior to joining academia, he worked in the legal profession, in industry, and management consulting. Positions held included several international leadership roles at Novartis AG, in Basel, Switzerland. His work included serving as a strategy and transformation consultant for Ernst & Young and Gemini Consulting in life sciences and biotech. He was also an attorney law clerk for the Honorable Warren K. Urbom, Chief Judge of the U.S. District Court in Nebraska.

Doug was instrumental in the incorporation of Colorado's newest city, the City of Castle Pines, Colorado, where he was one of the original founding members of the new city in 2008 and later served four years on the city council. He has served as a Senior Examiner on the Board of Examiners of the Baldrige Performance Excellence Program and for the regional affiliate, Rocky Mountain Performance Excellence, for which he is also chairman of the board of directors.

Deborah K. Robbins, MPA, SPHR

Deborah has over thirty years of experience in the public sector, private sector, and non-profit organizations at all organizational levels from line employee to senior leadership. With fourteen years in the public sector, Deborah has a good understanding of the challenges faced by state and local governments. Deborah has worked in the mining industry in both the site and corporate environments.

Debbie holds a bachelor of science degree in Personnel Management and Industrial Relations and a master's degree in Public Administration from the University of Wyoming. She is a graduate of the CDR Associates as a Mediator and holds the SHRM designation of Senior Professional in Human Resources (SPHR).

Her background covers a wide spectrum of disciplines including benefits design and administration, compensation administration, succession planning, leadership development, EEO and Affirmative Action plan development, organizational development, individual development, conflict resolution, change management, handbook design, recruiting and retention, internal investigations and safety.

PEREGRINE
Leadership Institute • Academic Services

Working with the Peregrine Leadership Institute

Peregrine Pathways is the publishing subsidiary of Peregrine Global, which is headquartered in Gillette, Wyoming. *Peregrine Pathways* is dedicated to lifelong leadership development, recognizing that leadership is a journey, not a destination.

Peregrine Global includes two interrelated companies – Peregrine Academic Services and Peregrine Leadership Institute – along with our strategic partners and associates. Together, we make a difference in leadership and higher education by leveraging a diversity of talents across a broad spectrum of disciplines, backgrounds, experiences, and cultures. Through our individual and collective efforts, we enrich, enlighten, and invigorate not only our clients and customers, but ourselves as well.

Our distinction lies within the areas of leadership and higher education. We provide excellence in customer service and professionalism. We apply thought-partner approaches to problem-solving and organizational strategic development.

Our strategy is to learn and understand your needs first, then provide specific services in leadership development and higher education support that are aligned with your goals and objectives. Together, we will make a difference in our world.

Peregrine Leadership Institute was formed in 2004 as a Limited Liability Company registered in Wyoming, USA. and subsequently as an S-Corp in 2006. The Institute employs experienced leadership consultants who provide consulting services, training workshops, and leadership seminars. The Institute's clients include both private and public-sector organizations. Our focus is on values-based leadership, workplace application, and quality. Client organizations include publicly-owned companies, small businesses, non-profit organizations, and government agencies (federal, state, and local).

The Peregrine Leadership Institute includes professionals with practical, real-world experience. Leadership facilitators have the right combination of professional training, practical experience, and the values-based competency needed to facilitate impactful workshops and seminars, and conduct human resource management consulting.

Leadership seminars and team development workshops focus on application and topical areas include strategic planning, executive leadership, coaching and mentoring, character leadership, workplace compliance, performance management, team development, governance, overcoming conflict, and leading change. The online 360° Leadership Assessment service helps participants assess their leadership strengths and opportunities for further development. Our Executive Leadership Program is based on the Baldrige Excellence Framework, designed to develop senior leaders who can lead change, grow organizational capacity, evaluate performance, and respond effectively to the uncertain strategic environment.

Peregrine's Online Leadership Courses for business leadership include courses focused on business writing fundamentals, leadership communications, leadership essentials, leading teams, dealing with workplace conflict, leading change, and leading the leaders. Each course is organized into eight modules with instructional content and post-course assessment. The courses are often used to supplement an academic specialization in leadership.

For more information about our leadership seminars, workshops, and online leadership courses, please contact us at:
Info@PeregrineLeadership.com
800 260-1555
www.PeregrineLeadership.com.

For more information about our online and consulting services for higher education, please contact us at:
Info@PeregrineAcademics.com
800 260-1555
www.Peregrine Academics.com

Coming Soon from Peregrine Pathways

Retention: Developing and Retaining Employee Talent

Is your backdoor open? You got them in the front door by hiring the best available talent, but are they leaving through the backdoor? Consider that the total cost of turnover, including all direct and indirect costs, is about three times the annual salary of the position. *Retention* will help you close that backdoor so that the talent you hire today will truly be with you tomorrow.

Index